THE
CAPITALIST
READER

THE CAPITALIST READER

Edited with an Introduction by
Lawrence S. Stepelevich

ARLINGTON HOUSE·PUBLISHERS
NEW ROCHELLE, NEW YORK

Library of Congress Cataloging in Publication Data

Main entry under title:

The Capitalist reader.

  Bibliography: pp. 271–272

   1. Capitalism—Addresses, essays, lectures.

I. Stepelevich, Lawrence S., 1930-

HB501.C24275   330.12′2   77-6261

ISBN 0-87000-379-8

Manufactured in the United States of America

CONTENTS

PART II: CAPITALISM AND JUSTICE

PART III: CAPITALISM AND FREEDOM

ACKNOWLEDGMENTS

The selections from Frederic Bastiat's *The Law* are reprinted by permission of the Foundation for Economic Education, Irvington-on-Hudson, New York. Copyright 1950 by the Foundation for Economic Education.

The selection from Wilhelm Roepke's *International Economic Disintegration* is reprinted by permission of William Hodge and Co., Glasgow. Copyright 1942 by William Hodge and Co.

The selections from Ludwig von Mises' *The Anti-Capitalist Mentality* are reprinted by permission of the Libertarian Press, South Holland, Illinois. Copyright 1956 by D. Van Nostrand Co.

The essays "What is Capitalism," copyright 1965 by the Objectivist Newsletter, Inc., and "The Roots of War," copyright 1966 by The Objectivist, Inc., published in *Capitalism: The Unknown Ideal*, copyright 1966 by New American Library, Inc., are reprinted by permission of the author and New American Library, Inc.

The selection from John Chamberlain's *The Roots of Capitalism* is reprinted by permission of the author. Copyright 1959 by D. Van Nostrand Co. A new edition is scheduled for publication in

INTRODUCTION

It is the intention of this limited collection of readings to introduce the student to the theory and general practice of capitalism as expressed by its foremost advocates.

Unquestionably, the term "capitalism" has acquired a morally dubious connotation among many of the citizens who actually live within a capitalist society, and for those who live without, capitalism simply designates an economics of greed and exploitation. A number of capitalist adherents have sought to employ terms less provocative, such as "free enterprise," "the free market," or others less likely to evoke images of an economic monster that, as Marx asserts, "lives off the lifeblood of the workers." Still, the term capitalism is not ready to be relegated to a footnote, not only because its opponents delight in its note of impersonality, but also because some of its defenders would consider the abandonment of the term an unnecessary concession implying the validity of the critique.

Whatever the economic attitude held by the reader of these selections, he cannot but feel some small admiration for these capitalist advocates, for they have turned to the study and defense of an economic system that may not be a "system" at all, according to the common understanding of the word, and have manifested an unpopular impiety by attempting to justify reasoned self-interest and competition rather than collective and cooperative economic activity.

If capitalism is to be considered an economic system, then it is a system that operates without conscious direction from an external lawgiver; it resists all attempts to predict its future course and it governs itself through a myriad of personal choices that are often no more than whims. Unplanned and consequently a mystery to the rationalist, capitalism as "ordered anarchy" resists simple explanation as well as attempted direction. Its proponents are faced with not only its apparently anarchic character but its reliance upon individual self-interest as its primary mover. Hence, confusion and selfishness characterize capitalism to its critics, freedom and individualism to its advocates.

Taking an existential stance that accepts man as a morally indesignate individual, prone to good or evil and subject to boredom in any utopia as well as satisfaction in any present, the capitalist offends both utopian and therapist.

Among a number of visions that guide the practice of the utopian-therapist, perhaps the best offering is that of Engels:

> The seizure of the means of production of society puts an end to commodity production, and therewith to the domination of the product over the producer. Anarchy in social production is replaced by conscious organization on a planned basis. . . . And at this point, in a certain sense, man finally cuts himself off from the animal world, leaves the conditions of animal existence behind him and enters conditions which are really human. . . . It is only from this point that men, with full consciousness, will fashion their own history. . . . It is humanity's leap from the realm of necessity into the realm of freedom.
>
> *Anti-Dühring* (1878)

This is the enthusiastic vision of an economic prophet who seeks to elevate mankind into a "really human" existence by replacing productive anarchy with planned productivity. It is the apparently cynical task of the capitalist economist to reject such inspirations, difficult because the majority of men seek authoritative guidance to ultimate goals and relish historical missions as relief from the mundane present.

10

The two views represent more than a debate over which economics is the more efficient and productive; they reflect opposing views of man. To the capitalist, his is an economics of reality as given:

> We would uphold this economic order even if it imposed upon nations some material sacrifice while socialism held out the certain promise of enhanced well-being.

But Wilhelm Roepke goes on to add that capitalism is still the more productive system, and in this view he finds total agreement among his fellows.

The attack launched against capitalism, though, was never grounded in the issue of productivity but rather in the issue of its morality. Does a system based upon competition, self-interest, and monetary profit befit the true nature of man? Are freedom and justice possible within such an economic matrix, or must the economics be changed to insure that these values prevail? It is to these issues that the capitalist apologist must address himself, and it is hoped that the brief selections included within this text will indicate how these issues are confronted by a number of major free-market economists.

Adam Smith considered himself to be a philosopher, but insofar as he directed his attention to the operations and principles of the market, he became the first to be termed an "economist." As an economist, Smith confined himself principally to describing rather than criticizing market activity. Later, with Malthus and Ricardo, the untrammeled operations of the market were alleged to produce major social evils. Capitalism, now on the defensive, found an early advocate in the lively person of Frederic Bastiat. In a number of treatises he turned the arguments of the protectionists against them, overthrowing their premise that a regulated economy is the best economy. But both Smith and Bastiat, although they did lay down the guiding principles of attack and defense for all future capitalist champions, are still of another age and perhaps of interest only to the more intense student, capitalist or not.

Many excellent modern representatives of the theory have been left out of these selections, some by reason of the high technical level of their writings, others by reason of the limited area developed within their studies. As for those included, it is hoped that all can be considered "major" representatives, and that their studies cover enough economic ground to provide the reader with an accurate, although perhaps circumscribed, view of capitalism. In short, the editor of this collection of readings did not envisage any further role for the book than simply to introduce the interested student to the vast and growing literature of the free economy and free society.

THE
CAPITALIST
READER

PART I: THE THEORY

"This is not mere self-love: for it is natural to man, as to other creatures, to do everything for his own sake . . . in general Zeus has so created the nature of the rational animal, that he can attain nothing good for himself, unless he contributes some service to the community. So it turns out that to do everything for his own sake is not unsocial."

EPICTETUS
Discourses I, 19

THE INVISIBLE HAND

Adam Smith

from THE WEALTH OF NATIONS (1776)

By restraining, either by high duties, or by absolute prohibitions, the importation of such goods from foreign countries as can be produced at home, the monopoly of the home market is more or less secured to the domestic industry employed in producing them. Thus the prohibition of importing either live cattle or salt provisions from foreign countries secures to the graziers of Great Britain the monopoly of the home market for butcher's meat. The high duties upon the importation of corn, which in times of moderate plenty amount to a prohibition, give a like advantage to the growers of that commodity. The prohibition of the importation of foreign woollens is equally favourable to the woollen manufacturers. The silk manufacture, though altogether employed upon foreign materials, has lately obtained the same advantage. The linen manufacture has not yet obtained it, but is making great strides towards it. Many other sorts of manufacturers have, in the same manner, obtained in Great Britain, either altogether, or very nearly a monopoly against their countrymen. The variety of goods of which the importation into Great Britain is prohibited, either absolutely, or under certain circumstances, greatly exceeds what can easily be suspected by those who are not well acquainted with the laws of the customs.

That this monopoly of the home-market frequently gives great encouragement to that particular species of industry which enjoys

17

it, and frequently turns towards that employment a greater share of both the labour and stock of the society than would otherwise have gone to it, cannot be doubted. But whether it tends either to increase the general industry of the society, or to give it the most advantageous direction, is not, perhaps, altogether so evident.

The general industry of the society never can exceed what the capital of the society can employ. As the number of workmen that can be kept in employment by any particular person must bear a certain proportion to his capital, so the number of those that can be continually employed by all the members of a great society, must bear a certain proportion to the whole capital of that society, and never can exceed that proportion. No regulation of commerce can increase the quantity of industry in any society beyond what its capital can maintain. It can only divert a part of it into a direction into which it might not otherwise have gone; and it is by no means certain that this artificial direction is likely to be more advantageous to the society than that into which it would have gone of its own accord.

Every individual is continually exerting himself to find out the most advantageous employment for whatever capital he can command. It is his own advantage, indeed, and not that of the society, which he has in view. But the study of his own advantage naturally, or rather necessarily, leads him to prefer that employment which is most advantageous to the society.

First, every individual endeavours to employ his capital as near home as he can, and consequently as much as he can in the support of domestic industry; provided always that he can thereby obtain the ordinary, or not a great deal less than the ordinary profits of stock.

Thus, upon equal or nearly equal profits, every wholesale merchant naturally prefers the home-trade to the foreign trade of consumption, and the foreign trade of consumption to the carrying trade. In the home-trade his capital is never so long out of his sight as it frequently is in the foreign trade of consumption. He can know better the character and situation of the persons whom he trusts, and if he should happen to be deceived, he knows better the laws of the country from which he must seek redress. In the carrying trade, the capital of the merchant is, as it were, divided between two foreign countries, and no part of it is ever necessarily brought home, or placed under his own immediate view and command. The capital which an Amsterdam merchant employs in carrying corn from Konnigsberg to Lisbon, and fruit and wine

18

from Lisbon to Konnigsberg, must generally be the one-half of it at Konnigsberg and the other half at Lisbon. No part of it need ever come to Amsterdam. The natural residence of such a merchant should either be at Konnigsberg or Lisbon, and it can only be some very particular circumstances which can make him prefer the residence of Amsterdam. The uneasiness, however, which he feels at being separated so far from his capital, generally determines him to bring part both of the Konnigsberg goods which he destines for the market of Lisbon, and of the Lisbon goods which he destines for that of Konnigsberg, to Amsterdam: and though this necessarily subjects him to a double charge of loading and unloading, as well as to the payment of some duties and customs, yet for the sake of having some part of his capital always under his own view and command, he willingly submits to this extraordinary charge; and it is in this manner that every country which has any considerable share of the carrying trade, becomes always the emporium, or general market, for the goods of all the different countries whose trade it carries on. The merchant, in order to save a second loading and unloading, endeavours always to sell in the home-market as much of the goods of all those different countries as he can, and thus, so far as he can, to convert his carrying trade into a foreign trade of consumption. A merchant, in the same manner, who is engaged in the foreign trade of consumption, when he collects goods for foreign markets, will always be glad, upon equal or nearly equal profits, to sell as great a part of them at home as he can. He saves himself the risk and trouble of exportation, when, so far as he can, he thus converts his foreign trade of consumption into a home-trade. Home is in this manner the center, if I may say so, round which the capitals of the inhabitants of every country are continually circulating, and towards which they are always tending, though by particular causes they may sometimes be driven off and repelled from it towards more distant employments. But a capital employed in the home-trade, it has already been shown, necessarily puts into motion a greater quantity of domestic industry, and gives revenue and employment to a greater number of the inhabitants of the country, than an equal capital employed in the foreign trade of consumption: and one employed in the foreign trade of consumption has the same advantage over an equal capital employed in the carrying trade. Upon equal, or only nearly equal profits, therefore, every individual naturally inclines to employ his capital in the manner in which it is likely to afford the greatest support to domestic industry, and to give revenue and employment to the greatest number of people of his own country.

Secondly, every individual who employs his capital in the support of domestic industry, necessarily endeavours so to direct that industry, that its produce may be of the greatest possible value.

The produce of industry is what it adds to the subject or materials upon which it is employed. In proportion as the value of this produce is great or small, so will likewise be the profits of the employer. But it is only for the sake of profit that any man employs a capital in the support of industry; and he will always, therefore, endeavour to employ it in the support of that industry of which the produce is likely to be of the greatest value, or to exchange for the greatest quantity either of money or of other goods.

But the annual revenue of every society is always precisely equal to the exchangeable value of the whole annual produce of its industry, or rather is precisely the same thing with that exchangeable value. As every individual, therefore, endeavours as much as he can both to employ his capital in the support of domestic industry, and so to direct that industry that its produce may be of the greatest value; every individual necessarily labours to render the annual revenue of the society as great as he can. He generally, indeed, neither intends to promote the public interest, nor knows how much he is promoting it. By preferring the support of domestic to that of foreign industry, he intends only his own security; and by directing that industry in such a manner as its produce may be of the greatest value, he intends only his own gain, and he is in this, as in many other cases, led by an invisible hand to promote an end which was no part of his intention. Nor is it always the worse for the society that it was no part of it. By pursuing his own interest he frequently promotes that of the society more effectually than when he really intends to promote it. I have never known much good done by those who affected to trade for the public good. It is an affectation, indeed, not very common among merchants, and very few words need be employed in dissuading them from it.

What is the species of domestic industry which his capital can employ, and of which the produce is likely to be of the greatest value, every individual, it is evident, can, in his local situation, judge much better than any statesman or lawgiver can do for him. The statesman, who should attempt to direct private people in what manner they ought to employ their capitals, would not only load himself with a most unnecessary attention, but assume an authority which could safely be trusted, not only to no single person, but to no council or senate whatever, and which would nowhere be so dangerous as in the hands of a man who had folly and presumption enough to fancy himself fit to exercise it.

To give the monopoly of the home-market to the produce of domestic industry, in any particular art or manufacture, is in some measure to direct private people in what manner they ought to employ their capitals, and must, in almost all cases, be either a useless or a hurtful regulation. If the produce of domestic can be brought there as cheap as that of foreign industry, the regulation is evidently useless. If it cannot, it must generally be hurtful. It is the maxim of every prudent master of a family, never to attempt to make at home what it will cost him more to make than to buy. The taylor does not attempt to make his own shoes, but buys them of the shoemaker. The shoemaker does not attempt to make his own clothes, but employs a taylor. The farmer attempts to make neither the one nor the other, but employs those different artificers. All of them find it for their interest to employ their whole industry in a way in which they have some advantage over their neighbours, and to purchase with a part of its produce, or what is the same thing, with the price of a part of it, whatever else they have occasion for.

What is prudence in the conduct of every private family, can scarce be folly in that of a great kingdom. If a foreign country can supply us with a commodity cheaper than we ourselves can make it, better buy it of them with some part of the produce of our own industry, employed in a way in which we have some advantage. The general industry of the country, being always in proportion to the capital which employs it, will not thereby be diminished, no more than that of the above-mentioned artificers; but only left to find out the way in which it can be employed with the greatest advantage. It is certainly not employed to the greatest advantage, when it is thus directed towards an object which it can buy cheaper than it can make. The value of its annual produce is certainly more or less diminished, when it is thus turned away from producing commodities evidently of more value than the commodity which it is directed to produce. According to the supposition, that commodity could be purchased from foreign countries cheaper than it can be made at home. It could, therefore, have been purchased with a part only of the commodities, or, what is the same thing, with a part only of the price of the commodities, which the industry employed by an equal capital would have produced at home, had it been left to follow its natural course. The industry of the country, therefore, is thus turned away from a more, to a less advantageous employment, and the exchangeable value of its annual produce, instead of being increased, according to the intention of the lawgiver, must necessarily be diminished by every such regulation.

LET US NOW TRY LIBERTY

Frederic Bastiat

from THE LAW (1848)

This must be said: There are too many "great" men in the world —legislators, organizers, do-gooders, leaders of the people, fathers of nations, and so on, and so on. Too many persons place themselves above mankind; they make a career of organizing it, patronizing it, and ruling it.

Now someone will say: "You yourself are doing this very thing."

True. But it must be admitted that I act in an entirely different sense; if I have joined the ranks of the reformers, it is solely for the purpose of persuading them to leave people alone. I do not look upon people as Vancauson looked upon his automaton. Rather, just as the physiologist accepts the human body as it is, so do I accept people as they are. I desire only to study and admire.

My attitude toward all other persons is well illustrated by this story from a celebrated traveler: He arrived one day in the midst of a tribe of savages, where a child had just been born. A crowd of soothsayers, magicians, and quacks—armed with rings, hooks, and cords—surrounded it. One said: "This child will never smell the perfume of a peace-pipe unless I stretch his nostrils." Another said: "He will never be able to hear unless I draw his ear-lobes down to his shoulders." A third said: "He will never see the sunshine unless I slant his eyes." Another said: "He will never stand upright unless I bend his legs." A fifth said: "He will never learn to think unless I flatten his skull."

"Stop," cried the traveler. "What God does is well done. Do not claim to know more than He. God has given organs to this frail creature; let them develop and grow strong by exercise, use, experience, and liberty."

*   *   *

God has given to men all that is necessary for them to accomplish their destinies. He has provided a social form as well as a human form. And these social organs of persons are so constituted that they will develop themselves harmoniously in the clean air of liberty. Away, then, with quacks and organizers! Away with their rings, chains, hooks, and pincers! Away with their artificial systems! Away with the whims of governmental administrators, their socialized projects, their centralization, their tariffs, their government schools, their state religions, their free credit, their bank monopolies, their regulations, their restrictions, their equalization by taxation, and their pious moralizations!

And now that the legislators and do-gooders have so futilely inflicted so many systems upon society, may they finally end where they should have begun: May they reject all systems, and try liberty; for liberty is an acknowledgment of faith in God and His works.

CAPITALIST PRODUCTION

Eugen von Boehm-Bawerk

from THE POSITIVE THEORY OF CAPITAL (1884)

The end and aim of all production is the making of things with which to satisfy our wants; that is to say, the making of goods for immediate consumption, or consumption goods. We combine our own natural powers and natural powers of the external world in such a way that, under natural law, the desired material good must come into existence. But this is a very general description indeed of the matter, and looking at it closer there comes in sight an important distinction which we have not as yet considered. It has reference to the distance which lies between the expenditure of human labor in the combined production and the appearance of the desired good. We either put forth our labor just before the goal is reached, or we, intentionally, take a roundabout way. That is to say, we may put forth our labor in such a way that it at once completes the circle of conditions necessary for the emergence of the desired good, and thus the existence of the good *immediately* follows the expenditure of the labor; or we may associate our labor first with the more remote causes of the good, with the object of obtaining, not the desired good itself, but a proximate cause of the good; which cause, again, must be associated with other suitable materials and powers, till, finally—perhaps through a considerable number of intermediate members—the finished good, the instrument of human satisfaction, is obtained.

The nature and importance of this distinction will be best seen from a few examples. A peasant requires drinking water. The spring is some distance from his house. There are various ways in which he may supply his daily wants. First, he may go to the spring each time he is thirsty, and drink out of his hollowed hand. This is the most direct way; satisfaction follows immediately on exertion. But it is an inconvenient way, for our peasant has to take his way to the well as often as he is thirsty. And it is an insufficient way for he can never collect and store any great quantity such as he requires for various other purposes. Second, he may take a log of wood, hollow it out into a kind of pail, and carry his day's supply from the spring to his cottage. The advantage is obvious, but it necessitates a roundabout way of considerable length. The man must spend, perhaps, a day in cutting out the pail; before doing so he must have felled a tree in the forest; to do this, again, he must have made an axe, and so on. But there is still a third way; instead of felling one tree he fells a number of trees, splits and hollows them, lays them end to end, and so constructs a runnel or rhone which brings a full head of water to his cottage. Here, obviously, between the expenditure of the labor and the obtaining of the water we have a very roundabout way, but, then, the result is ever so much greater. Our peasant need no longer take his weary way from house to well with the heavy pail on his shoulder, and yet he has a constant and full supply of the freshest water at his very door.

Another example. I require stone for building a house. There is a rich vein of excellent sandstone in a neighboring hill. How is it to be got out? First, I may work the loose stones back and forward with my bare fingers, and break off what can be broken off. This is the most direct, but also the least productive way. Second, I may take a piece of iron, make a hammer and chisel out of it, and use them on the hard stone—a roundabout way, which, of course, leads to a very much better result than the former. Third method—Having a hammer and chisel I use them to drill a hole in the rock; next I turn my attention to procuring charcoal, sulphur, and nitre, and mixing them in a powder, then I pour the powder into the hole, and the explosion that follows splits the stone into convenient pieces—still more of a roundabout way, but one which, as experience shows, is as much superior to the second way in result as the second was to the first.

The lesson to be drawn from these examples is obvious. It is—that a greater result is obtained by producing goods in roundabout ways than by producing them directly. Where a good can be produced in either way, we have the fact that, by the indirect way, a greater product can be got with equal labor, or the same product with less labor. But, beyond this, the superiority of the indirect way manifests itself in being the only way in which certain goods can be obtained.

That roundabout methods lead to greater results than direct methods is one of the most important and fundamental propositions in the whole theory of production. It must be emphatically stated that the only basis of this proposition is the experience of practical life. Economic theory does not and cannot show *a priori* that it must be so; but the unanimous experience of all the technique of production says that it is so. And this is sufficient; all the more that the facts of experience which tell us this are commonplace and familiar to everybody. But *why* is it so?

In the last resort all our productive efforts amount to shiftings and combinations of matter. We must know how to bring together the right forms of matter at the right moment, in order that from those associated forces the desired result, the product wanted, may follow. But, as we saw, the natural forms of matter are often so infinitely large, often so infinitely fine, that human hands are too weak or too coarse to control them. We are as powerless to overcome the cohesion of the wall of rock when we want building stone as we are to put together a single grain of wheat from carbon, nitrogen, hydrogen, oxygen, phosphorus, potash, etc. But there are other powers which can easily do what is denied to us, and these are the powers of nature. There are natural powers which far exceed the possibilities of human power in greatness, and there are other natural powers in the microscopic world which can make combinations that put our clumsy fingers to shame. If we can succeed in making those forces our allies in the work of production, the limits of human possibility will be infinitely extended. And this we have done.

The condition of our success is that we are able to control the materials on which the power that helps us depends, more easily than the materials which are to be transformed into the desired good. Happily this condition can be very easily complied with. Our weak yielding hand cannot overcome the cohesion of the rock, but the hard wedge of iron can; the wedge and the hammer to drive at we can happily master with little trouble. We cannot gather the atoms of phosphorus and potash out of the ground, and the atoms of carbon and oxygen out of the atmospheric air, and put them together in the shape of the corn or wheat, but the

27

organic chemical powers of the seed can put this magical process in motion, while we on our part can very easily bury the seed in the place of its secret working, the bosom of the earth. Often, of course, we are not able directly to master the form of matter on which the friendly power depends, but in the same way as we would like it to help us, do we help ourselves against it; we try to secure the alliance of a second natural power which brings the form of matter that bears the first power under our control. We wish to bring the well water into the house. Wooden rhones would force it to obey our will, and take the path we prescribe, but our hands have not the power to make the forest trees into rhones. We have not far to look, however, for an expedient. We ask the help of a second ally in the axe and the gouge; their assistance gives us the rhones; then the rhones bring us the water. And what in this illustration is done through the mediation of two or three members may be done, with equal or greater result, through five, ten, or twenty members. Just as we control and guide the immediate matter of which the good is composed by one friendly power, and that power by a second, so can we control and guide the second by a third, the third by a fourth, this, again, by a fifth, and so on—always going back to more remote causes of the final result—till in the series we come at last to one cause which we can control conveniently by our own natural powers. This is the true importance which attaches to our entering on roundabout ways of production: every roundabout way means the enlisting in our service of a power which is stronger or more cunning than the human hand; every extension of the roundabout way means an addition to the powers which enter into the service of man, and the shifting of some portion of the burden of production from the scarce and costly labor of human beings to the prodigal powers of nature.

The kind of production which works in these wise circuitous methods is nothing else than what economists call capitalist production as opposed to that production which goes directly at its object. And capital is nothing but the complex of intermediate products which appear on the several stages of the roundabout journey.

ORDERED ANARCHY

Wilhelm Roepke

from ECONOMICS OF THE FREE SOCIETY (1963)

Grasp the exhaustless life that all men live! Each shares therein, though few may comprehend: Where'er you touch, there's interest without end.

GOETHE
Faust (Prelude on the Stage)

On the threshold of every scientific speculation about the universe (as the Greek philosophers taught us long ago) is inscribed the word "wonder." Before explaining anything, we must first feel that it needs explanation; before answering questions, we must first learn how to ask them. Science cannot progress where men take the world, their own existence, for granted. If our knowledge of these phenomena is to increase, we must see them naively, with the eyes of children. Unfortunately, if understandably, the more the familiar and commonplace is a given fact, the less does it excite the sensation of "wonder." Is there anything, for instance, more familiar or more humdrum than economic life? What is so usual, even banal, as the housewife's daily marketing, the farmer's sale of a calf, the workingman's weekly pay check, the sale of a share on the stock exchange? Still, it needs but a moment's reflection to discover behind these banal occurrences something unexplained, even mysterious. Once we have made this discovery, we have already taken the first steps onto the terrain of economics.

Despite the power of the human imagination, it can only feebly picture the economic life of our age in all its variety and complexity. If only we might at this moment have the gift of omnipresence, what an unimaginable number of activities, mutually interacting with and determining each other, we would behold. We would see millions of factories in which thousands of different products are being manufactured; people sowing somewhere, somewhere reaping; a thousand boats and trains hauling to the four corners of the earth cargoes of fantastic variety; shepherds tending flocks in Australia and New Zealand; miners digging copper ore in the Congo or in the American far West and starting it on its way throughout the whole world: the Japanese spinning silk, the Javanese gathering tea—all swelling an unbroken stream of goods flooding across the land into warehouses and factories and from thence into millions of shops. We would see a still finer network of little streams going from the shops into countless households, rivulets of food and clothing and all the other things required by an army of billions: laborers, office workers, clerks, businessmen, farmers—the very ones whose work has created the mighty river of goods. Simultaneously, we would see another current of goods (machines, tools, cement, and similar products not intended for direct consumption) supplying the factories in city and country—the auxiliary goods needed to keep the first stream of consumption goods flowing. And still the panorama would not be complete, for in every direction we would see a host of services being performed: a surgeon beginning an operation, a lawyer making a plea, an economist endeavoring to explain the economic system to a circle of unknown readers. And more than this: we would behold the bewildering moment-to-moment fluctuations of the money market and the securities market—phenomena which we sense are contributing in a mysterious fashion to the movement and progress of our economic system. Finally, our attention would be drawn to small and large ducts labeled "taxes" and "excises" debouching at all stages of the economic process and serving to divert part of the flow of goods to the state for the maintenance of the army, the administrative agencies of the government, the schools, and the courts.

Today, we are witnessing a rapid decline in the number of individuals who satisfy their wants independently of the outside world. The modern farmer manages to retain in a greater degree than any other class the independence of the self-sufficient man, although even he satisfies a growing share of his needs by selling his surplus produce in exchange for the things he does not raise. The rest of mankind, however, is almost completely dependent upon this indirect method of want satisfaction. Indirect production, in turn, is based upon the principle, familiar to everyone, of the *division of labor,* but it presupposes, nonetheless, a harmonious coordination of the divided elements of the economic process. Who in the countries of the free world is charged with this coordination? What would happen if no one were in charge?

Consider, for a moment, the problem of the daily provisioning of a great city. Its millions of inhabitants must be provided with the basic necessities, to say nothing of the "luxuries" which cheer and brighten existence: so many tons of flour, butter, meat, so many miles of cloth, so many millions of cigars and cigarettes, so many reams of paper, so many books, cups, plates, nails, and a thousand other things must be daily produced in such wise that a surplus or deficiency of any particular good is avoided. The goods must be available hourly, monthly, or annually (according to the kind of good in question) in exactly the quantities and qualities demanded by a population of several millions. But the people's demand for goods is necessarily dependent upon their purchasing power (money). The existence of purchasing power presupposes, in turn, that the millions who appear in the market as consumers have previously as "producers" (whether employees or independent proprietors) so adjusted their output, both in quantity and quality, to the general demand for goods that they were able to dispose of their stock without loss. Now the highly differentiated modern economic system encompasses not alone a single city, however great, not alone a country however vast, but, in a way to which we shall give our particular attention later, the whole terrestrial globe. The craftsman in an optical instrument factory makes lenses for export to the most distant countries, which in turn supply him with cocoa, coffee, tobacco, and wool. While he is polishing lenses he is also producing, indirectly, all these things more abundantly and more cheaply than if he produced them directly. This immensely extended and intricate mechanism can function only if all its parts are in such constant and perfect synchronization that noticeable disorder is avoided. Were this not the case, the provisioning of millions would be immediately imperiled.

Who is charged with seeing to it that the economic gears of society mesh properly? Nobody. No dictator rules the economy, deciding who shall perform the needed work and prescribing what goods and how much of each shall be produced and brought to market. Admittedly, people today must perforce accept a great

31

deal more dictation from authorities of all kinds than a few decades ago. Yet by and large the world outside of the Communist bloc—the "capitalist" world, to use a popular if vague expression —still adheres to the principle that decisions about production, consumption, saving, buying and selling, are best left to the people themselves. *Thus, the modern economic system, an extraordinarily complex mechanism, functions without conscious central control by any agency whatever.* It is a mechanism which owes its continued functioning really to a kind of anarchy. And yet capitalism's severest critics must admit that all of its parts synchronize with amazing precision. Political anarchy leads invariably to chaos. But anarchy in economics, strangely, produces an opposite result: an orderly cosmos. Our economic system may be anarchic, but it is not chaotic. He who does not find this a wondrous phenomenon and thereby deserving of the most patient study cannot be expected to take much of an interest in economics.

The order which is immanent in our economic system compels recognition even by those who are far from finding it perfect. Indeed, even those who radically disapprove of this kind and degree of order and who wish to replace it with a system of conscious and centralized control (socialism) cannot deny that it exists. Order there is in our economic system; we have a centuries-long proof of it; it is a fact which is beyond debate but which is at the same time compatible with every political faith. Honesty compels the admission that the existence of ordered anarchy is cause for astonishment, that it is something which urgently requires explanation. Further reflection, moreover, must occasion serious doubt as to whether an enormously complicated and differentiated process such as is represented in the economic systems of the advanced industrial nations could be "commanded" in all its details from on high, after the fashion of an army or a factory, without the direst consequences. The existence of order in spite of anarchy—"spontaneous order" if we wish—is not alone an astounding phenomenon in itself. The processes peculiar to economic life in a free society make evident the fundamental superiority of the *spontaneous order* over the *commanded order*. Spontaneous order is not just another variety of order, albeit one with the surprising ability to function, if need be, even without command from on high. For if the organization of the economic system of a free society can be shown to differ fundamentally from the organization of an army, there is reason for believing that a spontaneous economic order is the only possible one. Notwith-

32

standing, our enthusiasm for spontaneous order will be tempered by the realization that as measured against any given ideal, it may leave much to be desired.

from A HUMANE ECONOMY (1960)

The questionable things of this world come to grief on their nature, the good ones on their own excesses. Conservative respect for the past and its preservation are indispensable conditions of a sound society, but to cling exclusively to tradition, history, and established customs is an exaggeration leading to intolerable rigidity. The liberal predilection for movement and progress is an equally indispensable counterweight, but if it sets no limits and recognizes nothing as lasting and worth preserving, it ends in disintegration and destruction. The rights of the community are no less imperative than those of the individual, but exaggeration of the rights of the community in the form of collectivism is just as dangerous as exaggerated individualism and its extreme form, anarchism. Ownership ends up in plutocracy, authority in bondage and despotism, democracy in arbitrariness and demagogy. Whatever political tendencies or currents we choose as examples, it will be found that they always sow the seed of their own destruction when they lose their sense of proportion and overstep their limits. In this field, suicide is the normal cause of death.

The market economy is no exception to the rule. Indeed, its advocates, in so far as they are at all intellectually fastidious, have always recognized that the sphere of the market, of competition, of the system where supply and demand move prices and thereby govern production, may be regarded and defended only as part of a wider general order encompassing ethics, law, the natural conditions of life and happiness, the state, politics, and power. Society as a whole cannot be ruled by the laws of supply and demand, and the state is more than a sort of business company, as has been the conviction of the best conservative opinion since the time of Burke. Individuals who compete on the market and there pursue their own advantage stand all the more in need of the social and moral bonds of community, without which competition degenerates most grievously. As we have said before, the market economy is not everything. It must find its place in a higher order of things

33

which is not ruled by supply and demand, free prices, and competition. It must be firmly contained within an all-embracing order of society in which the imperfections and harshness of economic freedom are corrected by law and in which man is not denied conditions of life appropriate to his nature. Man can wholly fulfill his nature only by freely becoming part of a community and having a sense of solidarity with it. Otherwise he leads a miserable existence and he knows it.

SOCIAL RATIONALISM

The truth is that a society may have a market economy and, at one and the same time, perilously unsound foundations and conditions, for which the market economy is not responsible but which its advocates have every reason to improve or wish to see improved so that the market economy will remain politicially and socially feasible in the long run. There is no other way of fulfilling our wish to possess both a market economy and a sound society and a nation where people are, for the most part, happy.

Economists have their typical *déformation professionelle*, their own occupational disease of the mind. Each of us speaks from personal experience when he admits that he does not find it easy to look beyond the circumscribed field of his own discipline and to acknowledge humbly that the sphere of the market, which it is his profession to explore, neither exhausts nor determines society as a whole. The market is only one section of society. It is a very important section, it is true, but still one whose existence is justifiable and possible only because it is part of a larger whole which concerns not economics but philosophy, history, and theology. We may be forgiven for misquoting Lichtenberg and saying: To know economics only is to know not even that. Man, in the words of the Gospel, does not live by bread alone. Let us beware of that caricature of an economist who, watching people cheerfully disporting themselves in their suburban allotments, thinks he has said everything there is to say when he observes that this is not a rational way of producing vegetables—forgetting that it may be an eminently rational way of producing happiness, which alone matters in the last resort. Adam Smith, whose fame rests not only on his *Wealth of Nations* but also on his *Theory of Moral Sentiments*, would have known better.

All of this has always been clear to us, and this is why we have never felt quite comfortable in the company of "liberals," even when styled "neo-liberals." But for everything there is season. We have been through years of untold misery and disorders which so many Western countries, including, in particular, Germany, brought upon themselves by their disregard of the most elementary principles of economic order. During these years there was a compelling need to put the accent on the "bread" of which the Gospel speaks and on the reestablishment of an economic order based on the market economy. To do this was imperative. Today, when the market economy has been revived up to a point and when even its partial reestablishment more than fulfills our expectations, it is equally imperative to think of the other and higher things here under discussion. That the hour is ripe for this is appreciated by all who are wise enough to sense the danger of stopping short at "bread." It is a sign of the times that those who experience and voice these misgivings have become surprisingly numerous everywhere. They include a growing number of economists in several countries who, independently of each other, are stepping out of the ivory tower of their science to explore the open country "beyond supply and demand." [1] As far as this author is concerned, he is doing no more than returning to scientific work of a kind which he has considered paramount ever since he wrote his book on *The Social Crisis of Our Time.*

To the economist, the market economy, as seen from the restricting viewpoint of his own discipline, appears to be no more than one particular type of economic order, a kind of "economic technique" opposed to the socialist one. It is significant of this approach that the very name of the structural principle of this economic order has been borrowed from the language of technology: we speak of the "price mechanism." We move in a world of prices, markets, competition, wage rates, rates of interest, exchange rates, and other economic magnitudes. All of this is per-

[1] Among contemporary economists who have turned their attention to the ethical framework of the economy, we may mention J.M. Clark, *The Ethical Basis of Economic Freedom* (The Kazanjian Foundation Lectures, 1955) and David McCord Wright, *Democracy and Progress* (New York, 1948). It is also pertinent to recall the following passages from J. C. L. Simonde de Sismondi's *Nouveaux principes d'économie politique* (2nd ed.; Paris, 1827): "The mass of the people, and the philosophers, too, seem to forget that the increase of wealth is not the purpose of political economy but the means at its disposal for insuring the happiness of all" (p. iv). "When England forgets people for thinking of things, is she not sacrificing the aim to the means?" (p. ix). "A nation where no one suffers want, but where no one has enough leisure or enough well-being to give full scope to his feelings and thought, is only half civilized, even if its lower classes have a fair chance of happiness" (p. 2). Indeed, the entire first chapter of this book is well worth reading.

fectly legitimate and fruitful as long as we keep in mind that we have narrowed our angle of vision and do not forget that the market economy is the economic order proper to a definite social structure and to a definite spiritual and moral setting. If we were to neglect the market economy's characteristic of being merely a part of a spiritual and social total order, we would become guilty of an aberration which may be described as social rationalism.

Social rationalism misleads us into imagining that the market economy is no more than an "economic technique" that is applicable in any kind of society and in any kind of spiritual and social climate. Thus the undeniable success of the revival of the market economy in many countries gave quite a few socialists the idea that the price mechanism was a device which an otherwise socialist economy could well use to its own benefit. In this concept of a "socialist market economy," which Tito seems to want to translate into practice, the market economy is thought of as part of a social system that is best described as an enormous apparatus of administration. In this sense, even the Communist economic system of Soviet Russia has always had a "market sector," although it is undoubtedly no more than a technical device and contrivance and not a living organism. How could a genuine market, an area of freedom, spontaneity, and unregimented order, thrive in a social system which is the exact opposite in all respects?

The same social rationalism is evident in the attitude of certain contemporary economists who, while not open partisans of socialism and sometimes speaking in the name of the market economy, work out the most elaborate projects for regulating the movements of the circular flow of the economy. They seem to be prepared to transform the economy into an enormous pumping engine with all sorts of ducts and valves and thermostats, and they not only seem confident that it will function according to the instructions for use but they also seem to be unaware of the question of whether such a machine is compatible with the atmosphere of the market, to which freedom is essential.

All of these protagonists of social rationalism—socialists and circular-flow technicians alike—have a common tendency to become so bemused by aggregate money and income flows that they overlook the fundamental significance of ownership. The market economy rests not on one pillar but on two. It presupposes not only the principle of free prices and competition but also the institution of private ownership, in the true sense of legally safeguarded freedom to dispose of one's own property, including freedom of testation.

To grasp the full significance of ownership to a free society, we must understand that ownership has a dual function. Ownership means, as in civil law, the delimitation of the individual sphere of decision and responsibility against that of other individuals. But ownership also means protection of the individual sphere from political power. It traces limits on the horizontal plane, and also vertically, and only this dual function can fully explain the significance of ownership as an indispensable condition of liberty. All earlier generations of social philosophers agreed on this point.

But ownership is not only a condition of the market economy, it is of the essence. This becomes evident from the following considerations. We start out from competition. We all realize its central importance for a free economy, but the concept is obscured by a confusing ambiguity. Communist governments, too, claim that they are using competition extensively and successfully. We have no reason to doubt that in the factories of Soviet Russia, the managers, and even the workers and employees, have ample opportunity for competitive performance. And in Yugoslavia, Tito made a whole system of the "decentralization" of public enterprises whereby the latter were divided up into independent and mutually competing units; he seems to regard this system, with some pride, as a sort of "socialist market economy." There can be no doubt that such an introduction of competition into a collectivist economic system may raise productivity. Is this not the same virtue which we have in mind when we ascribe the rapid recovery of the German economy chiefly to the reestablishment of competition?

There is obviously some confusion here, which calls for clarification. The confusion is due to neglect of the dual nature of competition and to the lumping together of things which should be kept strictly separate. Competition may have two meanings: it may be an institution for stimulating effort, or it may be a device for regulating and ordering the economic process. In the market economy, competition is both, and it constitutes, therefore, an unrivaled solution of the two cardinal problems of any economic system: the problem of continual inducement to maximum performance and the problem of a continual harmonious ordering and guidance of the economic process. The role of competition in the market economy is to be mainspring and regulator at one and the same time, and it is this dual function which is the secret of the competitive market economy and its inimitable performance.

If we now return to the question of whether a collectivist economic order can take advantage of competition and thus appropriate the secret of the market economy's success without impairing the collectivist nature of the economic order, we know that the answer depends upon which aspect of competition is meant. Competition as a stimulant is simply a psychological technique that is as applicable in a collectivist economy as in a market economy or, indeed, in any group, be it a school or a regiment or any other. We may even note that as far as the effects of competition on human destinies are concerned, it may, in collectivist systems, be hardened in a way that is unknown and impossible in the market economy. But the other function of competition, which is at least equally important for its economic effectiveness, the function of selection in the area of material means of production, meets with the greatest obstacles in collectivist systems. In relation to people, the carrot and the stick are ruthlessly applied, but it is quite another question whether collectivist systems competition can accomplish so uncompromising, undeviating, and continual a selection of products and firms as takes place in the market economy.

Even on the unwarrantedly charitable assumption that collectivist public authorities resist the temptation to hush up investment errors and have the honest intention to carry out such a continual selection in accordance with the dictates of competition, they would lack the indispensable criterion. This brings us to the other function of competition: to serve as an instrument of the economic order as a whole and as a regulator of the economic process. Unlike the market economy, the collectivist economy is necessarily debarred from such use of competition because no collectivist system can create the necessary precondition without losing its own identity. This precondition is genuine economic independence of firms. Only on this condition is the formation of genuine scarcity prices for capital and consumer goods conceivable, but there can be no independence of firms without private ownership and related freedom of action.

Thus everything is interlocked: competition as a regulator of the economy presupposes free market prices; free market prices are impossible without genuine independence of economic units, and their independence stands and falls by private ownership and freedom of decision, unimpaired and undisturbed by government planning. No collectivist economy can possibly satisfy the last of these conditions without ceasing to be collectivist, and therefore it cannot enjoy the advantages of the regulatory and guiding functions of competition. To try to arrange such competition artificially would be as absurd for a collectivist system as it would be for me to want to play bridge with myself. It follows that "socialist competition" can, at best, stimulate (economically not necessarily rational) performance but cannot rule and guide the economic process. It is only half of what competition is in the market economy, and we may well ask whether this bisection does not reduce the effectiveness of even that half of competition which alone is accessible to collectivism, namely, the stimulating effect. Be that as it may, it remains a serious weakness in any collectivist economy that competition can, at best, fulfill only one of its functions, and even that less than optimally. And it is the incomparable strength of the market economy that it alone can take advantage of the dual nature of competition, which is genuine and fully effective only when it is whole. Just as unavoidable limitation to one aspect of competition gravely handicaps collectivism, so does the combination of both aspects of competition give the market economy a start which cannot be overtaken. This is the prerogative of the market economy, but this prerogative stands and falls by private ownership of the means of production.

The economic function of private ownership tends to be obstinately underestimated, and even more so is its moral and sociological significance for a free society. The reason is, no doubt, that the ethical universe in which ownership has its place is hard for social rationalism even to understand, let alone to find congenial. And since social rationalism is in ascendancy everywhere, it is not surprising that the institution of ownership has been badly shaken. Even discussions on questions concerning the management of firms are often conducted in terms which suggest that the owner has followed the consumer and the taxpayer into the limbo of "forgotten men." The true role of ownership can be appreciated only if we look upon it as representative of something far beyond what is visible and measurable. Ownership illustrates the fact that the market economy is a form of economic order belonging to a particular philosophy of life and to a particular social and moral universe. This we now have to define, and in so doing the word "bourgeois"[2] imposes itself, however much mass public opinion (especially of the intellectual masses) may, after a century of deformation by Marxist propaganda, dislike this designation or find it ridiculous.

In all honesty, we have to admit that the market economy has a bourgeois foundation. This needs to be stressed all the more be-

[2] The word "bourgeois" is here used to correspond to the German word *bürgerlich*, in a completely nonpejorative and nonpolitical sense. As will be seen from the context, the word is used to designate a particular way of life and set of values.

cause the romantic and socialist reaction against everything bourgeois has, for generations past, been astonishingly successful in turning this concept into a parody of itself from which it is very difficult to get away. The market economy, and with it social and political freedom, can thrive only as a part and under the protection of a bourgeois system. This implies the existence of a society in which certain fundamentals are respected and color the whole network of social reationships: individual effort and responsibility, absolute norms and values, independence based on ownership, prudence and daring, calculating and saving, responsibility for planning one's own life, proper coherence with the community, family feeling, a sense of tradition and the succession of generations combined with an open-minded view of the present and the future, proper tension between individual and community, firm moral discipline, respect for the value of money, the courage to grapple on one's own with life and its uncertainties, a sense of the natural order of things, and a firm scale of values. Whoever turns up his nose at these things or suspects them of being "reactionary" may in all seriousness be asked what scale of values and what ideals he intends to defend against Communism without having to borrow from it.

To say that the market economy belongs to a basically bourgeois total order implies that it presupposes a society which is the opposite of proletarianized society, in the wide and pregnant sense which it is my continual endeavor to explain, and also the opposite of mass society as discussed in the preceding chapter. Independence, ownership, individual reserves, saving, the sense of responsibility, rational planning of one's own life—all that is alien, if not repulsive, to proletarianized mass society. Yet precisely that is the condition of a society which cherishes its liberty. We have arrived at a point where we are simply forced to recognize that here is the true watershed between social philosophies and that every one of us must choose for himself, knowing that the choice is between irreconcilable alternatives and that the destiny of our society is at stake.

Once we have recognized this necessity of a fundamental choice, we must apply it in practice and draw the conclusions in all fields. It may come as a shock to many of us to realize how much we have already submitted to the habits of thought of an essentially unbourgeois world. This is true, not least, of economists, who like to think in terms of money flows and income flows and who are so fascinated by the mathematical elegance of fashionable macroeconomic models, by the problems of moving aggregates, by the seductions of grandiose projects for balanced growth, by the dynamizing effects of advertising or consumer credit, by the merits of "functional" public finance, or by the glamor of progress surrounding giant concerns—who are so fascinated by all this, I repeat—that they forget to consider the implications for the values and institutions of the bourgeois world, for or against which we have to decide. It is no accident that Keynes—and nobody is more responsible for this tendency among economists than he—has reaped fame and admiration for his equally banal and cynical observation that "in the long run, we are all dead." And yet it should have been obvious that this remark is of the same decidedly unbourgeois spirit as the motto of the *ancien régime: Après nous le déluge.* It reveals an utterly unbourgeois unconcern for the future, which has become the mark of a certain style of modern economic policy and inveigles us into regarding it as a virtue to contract debts and as foolishness to save.

A most instructive example is the modern attitude toward an institution whose extraordinary development has caused it to become a much-discussed problem. I have in mind installment buying, or consumer credit. In its present form as a mass habit and in its extreme extent, it is certainly a conspicuous expression of an "unbourgeois" way of life. It is significant, however, that this view and the misgivings deriving from it are hardly listened to nowadays, let alone accepted. It is not, as we are often told, mere "bourgeois" prejudice but the lesson of millennial experience and consonant with man's nature and dignity and with the conditions of a sound society to regard it as an essential part of a reasonable and responsible way of life not to live from hand to mouth, to restrain impatience, self-indulgence, and improvidence alike, to think of the morrow, not to live beyond one's means, to provide for the vicissitudes of life, to try to balance income and expenditure, and to live one's life as a consistent and coherent whole extending beyond death to one's descendants rather than a series of brief moments of enjoyment followed by the headaches of the morning after. To depart conspicuously from these precepts has always and everywhere been censured by sound societies as shiftless, spendthrift, and disreputable and has carried the odium of living as a parasite, of being incompetent and irresponsible. Even so happy-go-lucky a man as Horace was of one mind on this subject with Dickens' Mr. Micawber: "Annual income twenty pounds, annual expenditure nineteen nineteen and six, result happiness. Annual income twenty pounds, annual expenditure twenty pounds ought and six, result misery."

Installment buying as a mass habit practiced with increasing carelessness is contrary to the standards of the bourgeois world in which the market economy must be rooted, and jeopardizes it. It is, at the same time, an indicator of how much of the humus of the bourgeois existence and way of life has already been washed away by social erosion, as well as an infallible measure of proletarianization, not in the sense of the material standard of living but of a style of life and moral attitude. The representatives of this style of life and moral attitude have lost their roots and steadfastness; they no longer rest secure within themselves; they have, as it were, been removed from the social fabric of family and the succession of generations. They suffer, unconsciously, from inner nonfulfillment, their life as a whole is stunted, they lack the genuine and essentially nonmaterial conditions of simple human happiness. Their existence is empty, and they try to fill this emptiness somehow. One way to escape this tantalizing emptiness is, as we have seen, intoxication with political and social ideologies, passions, and myths, and this is where Communism still finds its greatest opportunity. Another way is to chase after material gratifications, and the place of ideologies is then taken by motor scooters, television sets, by quickly acquired but unpaid-for dresses—in other words, by the flight into unabashed, immediate, and unrestrained enjoyment. To the extent that such enjoyment is balanced not only by corresponding work but also by a reasonable plan of life, saving and provision for the future, and by the nonmaterial values of habits and attitudes transcending the moment's enjoyment, to that extent the emptiness, and with it the "unbourgeois" distress, is, in fact, overcome. But unless this is the case, enjoyment remains a deceptive method of filling the void and is no cure.[3]

The incomprehension, and even hostility, with which such reflections are usually met nowadays is one more proof of the predominance of social rationalism, with all its variants and offshoots, and of the implied threat to the foundations of the market economy. One of these offshoots is the ideal of earning a maximum amount of money in a minimum of working time and then finding an outlet in maximum consumption, facilitated by installment buying, of the standardized merchandise of modern mass production. *Homo sapiens consumens* loses sight of everything that goes to make up human happiness apart from money income and its transformation into goods. Two of the important factors

[3] Cf. my two treatises, *Borgkauf im Lichte sozialethischer Kritik* (Köln and Berlin, 1954) and *Vorgegessen Brot* (Köln and Berlin, 1955).

that count in this context are how people work and how they spend their life outside work. Do people regard the whole of the working part of their life as a liability, or can they extract some satisfaction from it? And how do they live outside work, what do they do, what do they think, what part have they in natural, human existence? It is a false anthropology, one that lacks wisdom, misunderstands man, and distorts the concept of man, if it blinds us to the danger that material prosperity may cause the level of simple happiness not to rise but to fall because the two above-mentioned vital factors are in an unsatisfactory condition. Such anthropology also prevents us from recognizing the true nature of proletarianism and the true task of social policy.

It is, for instance, a superficial and purely materialist view of proletarianism to believe complacently that in the industrialized countries of the West the proletarians are becoming extinct like the dodo simply because of a shorter working week and higher wages, wider consumption, more effective legal protection of labor and more generous social services, and because of other achievements of current social policy. It is true that the proletariat, as understood by this kind of social rationalism, is receding. But there remains the question of whether, concurrently with this satisfactory development and perhaps because of it, even wider classes are not engulfed in proletarianism as understood in a much more subtle sense, in the sense, that is, of a social humanism using other criteria which are really decisive for the happiness of man and the health of society. The criteria I have in mind are those which we know well already, the criteria beyond the market, beyond money incomes and their consumption. Only in the light of those criteria can we assess the tasks of genuine social policy, which I advocated fifteen years ago in my book on *The Social Crisis of Our Time* and for which Alexander Rüstow has recently coined the felicitous term of "vital policy."

The circle of our argument closes. It is, again, private ownership which principally distinguishes a nonproletarian form of life from a proletarian one. Once this is recognized, the social rationalism of our time has really been left behind.

THE SPIRITUAL AND MORAL SETTING

One of the oversimplifications by which social rationalism distorts the truth is that Communism is a weed particular to the

marshes of poverty and capable of being eradicated by an improvement in the standard of living. This is a fatal misconception.
Surely everyone must realize by now that the world war against
Communism cannot be won with radio sets, refrigerators, and
widescreen films. It is not a contest for a better supply of goods—
unfortunately for the free world, whose record in this field cannot
be beaten. The truth is that it is a profound, all-encompassing
conflict of two ethical systems in the widest sense, a struggle for
the very conditions of man's spiritual and moral existence. Not for
one moment may the free world waver in its conviction that the
real danger of Communism, more terrible than the hydrogen
bomb, is its threat to wipe these conditions from the face of the
earth. Anyone who rejects this ultimate, apocalyptic perspective
must be very careful, lest, sooner or later, and perhaps for no
worse reason than weakness or ignorance, he betray the greatest
and highest values which mankind has ever had to defend. In
comparison with this, everything else counts as nothing.

If we want to be steadfast in this struggle, it is high time to
bethink ourselves of the ethical foundations of our own economic
system. To this end, we need a combination of supreme moral
sensitivity and economic knowledge. Economically ignorant moralism is as objectionable as morally callous economism. Ethics
and economics are two equally difficult subjects, and while the
former needs discerning and expert reason, the latter cannot do
without humane values.[4]

Let us begin with a few questions which we, as economists, may
well put to ourselves. Are we always certain of our calling? Are
we never beset by the sneaking doubt that although the sphere of
human thought and action with which we deal is one of primary
necessity, it may, for that very reason, be of a somewhat inferior
nature? *Primum vivere, deinde philosophari*—certainly. But does
this dictum not reflect an order of precedence? And when the
Gospel says that man does not live by bread alone, does this not
imply an admonition that once his prayer for his daily bread is
fulfilled, man should direct his thoughts to higher things? Should

[4] From the characteristically plentiful recent literature, we may mention, apart
from the works cited in note 1 above: F. H. Knight, *The Ethics of Competition*
(London, 1935); K. E. Boulding, *The Organizational Revolution* (New York, 1953;)
Daniel Villey, "The Market Economy and Roman Catholic Thought," *International
Economic Papers* (No. 9, 1959); G. Del Vecchio, *Diritto ed Economia* (2nd ed.;
Rome, 1954); W. Weddigen, *Wirtschaftsethik* (Berlin-Munich, 1951); A. Dudley
Ward (ed.), *The Goals of Economic Life* (New York, 1953); and D. L. Munby,
Christianity and Economic Problems (London, 1956).

44

we be free of such scruples and doubts—and this is not a matter for pride—others will assuredly bring them to our attention.

I myself had a characteristic experience in this respect. Some years before his death, I had the privilege of a discussion with Benedetto Croce, one of the greatest minds of our age. I had put forward the proposition that any society, in all its aspects, is always a unit in which the separate parts are interdependent and make up a whole which cannot be put together by arbitrary choice. I had maintained that this proposition, which is now widely known and hardly challenged, applied also to the economic order, which must be understood as part of the total order of society and must correspond to the political and spiritual order. We are not free, I argued, to combine just any kind of economic order, say, a collectivist one, with any kind of political and spiritual order, in this case the liberal. Since liberty was indivisible, we could not have political and spiritual liberty without also choosing liberty in the economic field and rejecting the necessarily unfree collectivist economic order; conversely, we had to be clear in our minds that a collectivist economic order meant the destruction of political and spiritual liberty. Therefore, the economy was the front line of the defense of liberty and of all its consequences for the moral and humane pattern of our civilization. My conclusion was that to economists, above all, fell the task, both arduous and honorable, of fighting for freedom, personality, the rule of law, and the ethics of liberty at the most vulnerable part of the front. Economists, I said, had to direct their best efforts to the thorny problem of how, in the aggravating circumstances of modern industrial society, an essentially free economic order can nevertheless survive and how it can constantly be protected against the incursions or infiltrations of collectivism.

This was my part of the argument on that occasion, during the last war. Croce's astonishing reply was that there was no necessary connection between political and spiritual freedom on the one hand and economic freedom on the other. Only the first mattered; economic freedom belonged to a lower and independent sphere where we could decide at will. In the economic sphere, the only question was one of expediency in the manner of organizing our economic life, and this question was not to be related with the decisive and incomparably higher question of political and spiritual freedom. The economic question was of no concern to the philosopher, who could be liberal in the spiritual and political field and yet collectivist in the economic. The important move-

45

ment for the defense of spiritual and political freedom was *libera-lismo*, as Croce called it, to distinguish it from *liberismo*, by which slightening term he designated the defense of economic freedom.[5]

Croce's view hardly needs to be refuted today, and even his followers will not be inclined to defend it. But Croce's error has had a fatal influence on the development of Italian intellectuals and has smoothed the way to Communism for many of them. The mere fact that so eminent a thinker could be so utterly wrong about the place of economic matters in society proves how necessary it is to thresh this question out over and over again.

Naturally nobody would dream of denying that the aspect of society with which the economist deals belongs to the world of means, as opposed to ends, and that its motives and purposes therefore belong to a level which is bound to be low, if only because it is basic and at the foundation of the whole structure. This much we must grant a man like Croce. To take a drastic example, what interests economics is not the noble beauty of a medieval cathedral and the religious idea it embodies, but the worldly and matter-of-fact question of what place these monuments of religion and beauty occupied in the overall economy of their age. It is the complex of questions which, for instance, Pierre du Colombier has discussed in his charming book *Les chantiers des cathédrales*. We are fully aware that what concerns us as economists is, as it were, the prosaic and bare reverse side of the *décor*. When the materialistic interpretation of history regards the spiritual and political life of nations as a mere ideological superstructure on the material conditions of production, we are, as economists, very sensitive to the damning revelations of a philosophy of history that reduces higher to lower—a feeling which proves our unerring sense of the genuine scale of values.

All of this is so obvious that we need not waste another word on it. But equally obvious is the argument with which we must safeguard a proper place in the spiritual and moral world for the economy, which is our sphere of knowledge. What overweening arrogance there is in the disparagement of things economic, what ignorant neglect of the sum of work, sacrifice, devotion, pioneering spirit, common decency, and conscientiousness upon which depends the bare life of the world's enormous and ever growing population! The sum of all these humble things supports the whole edifice of our civilization, and without them there

[5] The relevant discussion has been fully reported by Carlo Antoni in A. Hunold (ed.), *Die freie Welt im kalten Krieg* (Erlenbach-Zürich, 1955).

could be neither freedom nor justice, the masses would not have a life fit for human beings, and no helping hand would be extended to anyone. We are tempted to say what Hans Sachs angrily calls out to Walter von Stolzing in the last act of *Die Meistersinger*: "Do not despise the masters!"

We are all the more entitled to do so if, steering the proper middle course, we guard against exaggeration in the opposite direction. Romanticizing and moralistic contempt of the economy, including contempt of the impulses which move the market economy and the institutions which support it, must be as far from our minds as economism, materialism, and utilitarianism.

When we say *economism,* we mean one of the forms of social rationalism, which we have already met. We mean the incorrigible mania of making the means the end, of thinking only of bread and never of those other things of which the Gospel speaks. It is economism to succumb to those aberrations of social rationalism of which we have spoken and to all the implied distortions of perspective. It is economism to dismiss, as Schumpeter does, the problem of giant industrial concerns and monopoly with the highly questionable argument that mass production, the promotion of research, and the investment of monopoly profits raise the supply of goods, and to neglect to include in the calculation of these potential gains in the supply of material goods the possible losses of a nonmaterial kind, in the form of impairment of the higher purposes of life and society. It is economism to allow material gain to obscure the danger that we may forfeit liberty, variety, and justice and that the concentration of power may grow, and it is also economism to forget that people do not live by cheaper vacuum cleaners alone but by other and higher things which may wither in the shadow of giant industries and monopolies. To take one example among many, nowhere are the economies of scale larger than in the newspaper industry, and if only a few press lords survive, they can certainly sell a maximum of printed paper at a minimum of pennies or cents; but surely the question arises of what there is to read in these papers and what such an accumulation of power signifies for freedom and culture. It is economism, we continue, to oppose local government, federalism, or decentralization of broadcasting with the argument that concentration is cheaper. It is economism, again, to measure the peasant's life exclusively by his money income without asking what else determines his existence beyond supply and demand, beyond the prices of hogs and the length of his working day; and the worst economism is the peasant's own. It is, finally, that selfsame economism which misleads us into regarding the problem of economic stability merely as one of full employment, to be safeguarded by credit and fiscal policy, forgetting that besides equilibrium of national aggregates, equal importance should be attached to the greatest possible stability of the individual's existence—just as the springs of a car are as important for smooth driving as the condition of the road.[6]

When we say *materialism,* we mean an attitude which misleads us into directing the full weight of our thought, endeavor, and action towards the satisfaction of sensual wants. Almost indissolubly linked therewith is *utilitarianism,* which, ever since the heyday of that philosophy, has been vitiating our standards in a fatal manner and still regrettably distorts the true scale of values. One of the more likable of the high priests of that cult, Macaulay, wrote in his famous essay on Francis Bacon, the ancestor of utilitarianism and pragmatism, that the production of shoes was more useful than a philosophical treatise by Seneca; but once more we must ask the familiar question of whether shoes—not to mention the latest products of progress—are likely to be of much help to a man who, in the midst of a world devoted to that cult, has lost the moral bearings of his existence and who therefore, though he may not know why, is unhappy and frustrated. It is indeed our misfortune that mankind has, but for a small remnant, dissipated and scattered the combined spiritual patrimony of Christendom and antiquity, to which Seneca contributed a more than negligible portion. This is what our reaction should be today to a passage in another and no less famous of Macaulay's essays, bursting with derision and indignation about Southey, who, at the dawn of British industry, had had the temerity to say that a cottage with rosebushes beside the door was more beautiful than the bleak workers' houses which were sprouting all over the place—"naked, and in a row."[7]

* * *

[6] The idea here expressed is treated more fully in my book *The Social Crisis of Our Time,* pp. 225-27.

[7] The economist who rejects utilitarianism finds himself in the distinguished company of J. M. Keynes, who has this to say about the Benthamite tradition: "But I do now regard that as the worm which has been gnawing at the insides of modern civilisation and is responsible for its present moral decay" (J. M. Keynes, *Two Memoirs* [London, 1949], p. 96). In connection with the passage from Macaulay's *Essays* mentioned in the text, we recall Bentham's remark: "While Xenophon was writing his history and Euclid teaching geometry, Socrates and Plato were talking nonsense under pretence of talking wisdom and morality" (quoted from *Time and Tide,* May 19, 1956.) There is a clearly visible road from this kind of Philistine utilitarianism to positivism and the philosophy of logical analysis.

Let us return to our main theme. Whatever may be the proper place of the economy in the universal order, what is the ethical place of the specific economic order proper to the free world? This economic order is the market economy, and it is with its relationships that economics as a science is largely concerned. What, then, are the ethical foundations of the market economy?

"Supply and demand," "profit," "competition," "interest," "free play of forces," or whatever other words we may choose to characterize the free economic system prevailing, even if in imperfect form, outside the Communist world—do they not, to say the least, belong to an ethically questionable or even reprehensible sphere? Or to put it more bluntly, are we not living in an economic world or, as R. H. Tawney says, in an "acquisitive society" which unleashes naked greed, fosters Machiavellian business methods and, indeed, allows them to become the rule, drowns all higher motives in the "icy water of egotistical calculation" (to borrow from the *Communist Manifesto*), and lets people gain the world but lose their souls? Is there any more certain way of desiccating the soul of man than the habit of constantly thinking about money and what it can buy? Is there a more potent poison than our economic system's all-pervasive commercialism? Or can we still subscribe to that astonishing eighteenth-century optimism which made Samuel Johnson say: "There are few ways in which man can be more innocently employed than in getting money"?

Economists and businessmen who have a distaste for such questions or who would, at any rate, prefer to hand them over, with a touch of irony, to theologians and philosophers are ill advised. We cannot take these questions too seriously, nor must we close our eyes to the fact that it is not necessarily the most stupid or the worst who are driven into the camp of collectivist radicalism for lack of a satisfactory answer to these questions. Among these men are many who have a right to call themselves convinced Christians.

There is another and no less important reason why we should examine the ethical content of everyday economic life. This reason is that the question concerns us most intimately because it reaches down to the levels from which our roots draw their life-giving sap. *Navigare necesse est, vivere non est necesse,* says an inscription on an old sailor's house in Bremen; we may generalize this into saying: Life is not worth living if we exercise our profession only for the sake of material success and do not find in our calling an inner necessity and a meaning which transcends the

49

mere earning of money, a meaning which gives our life dignity and strength. Whatever we do and whatever our work, we must know what place we occupy in the great edifice of society and what meaning our activity has beyond the immediate purpose of promoting material existence. We must answer to ourselves for the social functions for which society rewards us with our income. It is a petty and miserable existence that does not know this, that regards the hours devoted to work as a mere means of earning money, as a liability to be balanced only by the satisfactions which the money counterpart of work procures.[8]

This feeling for the meaning and dignity of one's profession and for the place of work in society, whatever work it be, is today lost to a shockingly large number of people. To revive this feeling is one of the most pressing tasks of our times, but it is a task whose solution requires an apt combination of economic analysis and philosophical subtlety. This is, perhaps, truer of commerce than of other callings because the merchant's functions are more difficult to place in society than others. An activity which, at first sight, seems to consist of an endless series of purchases and sales does not display its social significance and professional dignity as readily as do the peasant's or the sailor's pursuits. The merchant himself is not easily aware of them, nor are others, who all too often treat him as a mere parasite of society, an ultimately redundant intermediary whose "trading margins" are resented as an irksome levy and whom one would like to eliminate wherever possible. How infinitely more difficult must it be, then, to explain to a layman the functions of stock-exchange speculation and to defeat the almost ineradicable prejudices which fasten onto this favorite subject for anti-capitalist critics?

This is the place, too, to note that the hard-boiled business world, which ignores such questions or leaves them, with contempt, to the "unbusinesslike" intellectuals, and these same intellectuals' distrust of the business world match and mutually exacerbate each other. If the business world loses its contact with culture and the intellectuals resentfully keep their distance from economic matters, then the two spheres become irretrievably alienated from each other. We can observe this in America in the anti-intellectualism of wide circles of businessmen and the anti-

[8] Admirably apposite is Theodor Mommsen's summing up of the staleness of ancient Rome, which formed the background for a personage like Catiline: "When a man no longer enjoys his work but works merely in order to procure himself enjoyments as quickly as possible, then it is only an accident if he does not become a criminal" (quoted from Otto Seel, *Cicero* [Stuttgart, 1953], p. 66).

capitalism of equally wide circles of intellectuals. It is true that intellectuals have infinitely less social prestige in America than in Europe and that they are much less integrated in the network of society and occupy a much more peripheral place than their brothers in Europe. They retaliate for this seating plan at the nation's table with their anti-capitalism, and the businessmen and entrepreneurs repay the intellectuals' hostility by despising them as "eggheads."

In so dynamic a competitive economy, the American intellectuals have to admit that the gulf between education and wealth, which is derided in Europe in the person of the *nouveau riche*, is the rule rather than the exception, as it should be; on the other hand, American businessmen easily fall into the habit of treating the intellectual as a pompous and would-be-clever know-all who lacks both common sense and a sound scale of values. Since in both cases the caricature is often not very far from the truth, the result is a vicious circle of mutually intensifying resentment which threatens to end up in catastrophe. One has to break out of this vicious circle by making the world of the mind as respectable to the business world as, conversely, the business world to the world of the mind.

Naturally, there is no question of taking sides with American intellectuals when they rebel against a predominantly commercial society with which they have little in common. But it must be conceded that it will not be easy to hold down this rebellion as long as the tension between business and culture is not considerably diminished. This tension is particularly obvious in the United States and in all the overseas territories of European expansion. It would be unfair to expect the diminution to come from only one side, and the task would become harder if we were simply to blame the American anti-capitalist intellectuals and not try also to understand their point of view. The chain reaction between the business world's distrust of intellectuals and the intellectuals' retaliating resentment should be broken by both sides: the intellectuals should abandon untenable ideologies and theories, and the "capitalists" should adopt a philosophy which, while rendering unto the market the things that belong to the market, also renders unto the spirit what belongs to it. Both movements together should merge into a new humanism in which the market and the spirit are reconciled in common service to the highest values. It need hardly be mentioned that we Europeans have no reason to strike any holier-than-thou attitudes about these problems. If things are, on the whole, still a little better in Europe,

51

this is due to no merit of ours but to an historical heritage which beneficially slows down a development we share with "Europe overseas."[9]

What, then, is our answer to the great question we asked at the beginning? At what ethical level, in general, must we situate the economic life of a society which puts its trust in the market economy?

It is rather like the ethical level of average man, of whom Pascal says: *"L'homme n'est ni ange ni bête, et le malheur veut que qui veut faire l'ange fait la bête."* To put it briefly, we move on an intermediate plane. It is not the summit of heroes and saints, of simon-pure altruism, selfless dedication, and contemplative calm, but neither is it the lowlands of open or concealed struggle in which force and cunning determine the victor and the vanquished.

The language of our science constantly borrows from these two contiguous spheres to describe modern economic processes, and it is characteristic of our uncertainty that we usually reach either too high or too low. When we speak of "service" to the consumer, we obviously have in mind not St. Elizabeth but the assistant who wipes the windshield of our car at the filling station, and the "conquest" of a market brings to mind the traveling salesman, tempting prospectuses, and rattling cranes rather than thundering tanks or booming naval guns.[10] It is true that in our middle plateau of everyday economic life there is, fortunately, as much room for elevations into the higher sphere of true devotion as there is for depressions of violence and fraud; nevertheless, it will generally be granted that the world in which we do business, bargain, calculate, speculate, compare bids, and explore markets ethically corresponds by and large to that middle level at which the whole of everyday life goes on. Reliance on one's own efforts, initiative under the impulse of the profit motive, the best possible satisfac-

[9] Wilhelm Roepke, "A European Looks at American Intellectuals," *National Review*, November 10, 1956. The literature on this important subject reflects the facts, for it is divided into the two extremes of anti-capitalist intellectuals on the one hand and anti-intellectual capitalists on the other. This means that the problem as such is lost to view. This weakness is also apparent in F. A. Hayek (ed.), *Capitalism and the Historians* (Chicago, 1954), however valuable this book is in other respects as a corrective of our ideas about economic history. Cf. my review ("Der 'Kapitalismus' und die Wirtschaftshistoriker") in *Neue Zürcher Zeitung*, March 16, 1954.

[10] On the ethical "middle level" of the market economy, see M. Pantaleoni, *Du caractère logique des différences d'opinions qui séparent les économistes* (Geneva, 1897); Wilhelm Roepke, *Die Lehre von der Wirtschaft* (8th ed.; Erlenbach-Zürich, 1958), pp. 41-46 and 116-35.

tion of consumer demand in order to avoid losses, safeguarding one's own interests in constant balance with the interests of others, collaboration in the guise of rivalry, solidarity, constant assessment of the weight of one's own performance on the incorruptible scales of the market, constant struggle to improve one's own real performance in order to win the prize of a better position in society—these and many other formulations are used to characterize the ethical climate of our economic world. They are imperfect, groping, and provisional, perhaps also euphemistic, but they do express what needs to be said at this point in our reflections.

This ethical climate, we must add at once, is lukewarm, without passions, without enthusiasm, but also, in the language of one of Heine's poems, without "prodigious sins" and without "crimes of blood"; it is a climate which, while not particularly nourishing for the soul, at least does not necessarily poison it. On the other hand, it is a favorable climate for a certain atmosphere of minimal consideration and for the elementary justice of a certain correspondence of give and take and most favorable, whatever one may say, for the development of productive energy. That this energy is applied not to the construction of pyramids and sumptuous palaces but to the continual improvement of the well-being of the masses and that this happens because of the effect of all-powerful forces proper to the structure and ethical character of our free economic order is perhaps the greatest of the assets in its overall balance sheet.

This view of the ethical climate of the market has distinguished ancestors. In 1748, Montesquieu wrote in his book *L'esprit des lois* of the spirit of our market economy (which he calls *esprit de commerce*): "It creates in man a certain sense of justice, as opposed, on the one hand, to sheer robbery, but on the other also to those moral virtues which cause us not always to defend our advantage to the last and to subordinate our interest to those of others" (Book XX, Chapter 2). We may add that our era's market-economy society may claim to be less subject to compulsion and power than any other society in history, though it is perhaps for that very reason all the more prone to deception as a means of persuasion. We shall have more to say about this later.

The poem by Heine to which we alluded is "Anno 1829," and the lines we referred to are these:

> Prodigious sins I'd rather see
> And crimes of blood, enormous, grand,
> Than virtue, self-content and fat,
> Morality with cash in hand.

Who does not know such moments of despair in the face of Philistine self-satisfaction and ungenerousness? But this should not cause us to forget the real issue here, namely, the eternal romantic's contempt of the economy, a contempt shared often enough by reactionaries and revolutionaries, as well as by aloof aesthetes. Nevertheless, there remains the question of whether we really prefer to do away with "virtue" and go hungry, to give up "morality" and go bankrupt.

As a matter of fact, a certain opprobrium was attached for many centuries to that middle level of ethics which is' proper to any essentially free economy. It is the merit of eighteenth-century social and moral philosophy, which is the source of our own discipline of political economy, to have liberated the crafts and commercial activities—the banausic (the Greek βάναυσος means "the man at the stove") as they were contemptuously called in the slave economy of Athens—from the stigma of the feudal era and to have obtained for them the ethical position to which they are entitled and which we now take for granted.

It was a "bourgeois" philosophy in the true sense of the word, and one might also legitimately call it "liberal." It taught us that there is nothing shameful in the self-reliance and self-assertion of the individual taking care of himself and his family, and it led us to assign their due place to the corresponding virtues of diligence, alertness, thrift, sense of duty, reliability, punctuality, and reasonableness. We have learned to regard the individual, with his family, relying on his own efforts and making his own way, as a source of vital impulses, as a life-giving creative force without which our modern world and our whole civilization are unthinkable.

In order to appreciate just how important this "bourgeois" spirit is for our world, let us consider the difficulty of implanting modern economic forms in the underdeveloped countries, which often lack the spiritual and moral conditions here under discussion. We in the West take them for granted and are therefore hardly aware of them, but the spokesmen of the underdeveloped countries frequently see only the outward economic success of Western nations and not the spiritual and moral foundations upon which it rests. A sort of human humus must be there, or at least be expected to form, if Western industry is to be successfully transplanted. Its ultimate conditions remain accuracy, reliability, a sense of time and duty, application, and that general sense of good workmanship which is obviously at home in only a few countries. With some slight exaggeration, one might put it this way: modern economic activity can thrive only where whoever says "tomorrow" means tomorrow and not some undefined time in the future.[11]

In the Western world, "interested" activity has, without doubt, a positive value as the mainspring of society, civilization, and culture. Some may still protest in the name of Christian teaching, but in so doing, they merely reveal that they have, for their part, not yet overcome the eschatological communism of the Acts of the Apostles.[12] After all, "the doctrine of self-reliance and self-denial, which is the foundation of political economy, was written as legibly in the New Testament as in the *Wealth of Nations*," and Lord Acton, the distinguished English historian to whom we owe this bold statement, rightly adds that this was not realized until our age.[13] The history of literature is very revealing: for Molière, the bourgeois was still a comic figure, and when for once Shakespeare introduces a merchant as such, it is Shylock. It is a long way to Goethe's *Wilhelm Meister*, where we move in the bourgeois trading world and where even double-entry bookkeeping is transfigured by philosophy and poetry.

To make this even clearer, let us turn the tables and see what happens when we give free rein to those who condemn the market, competition, profit, and self-interest in the name of a "higher" morality and who deplore the absence of the odor of sanctity in individual self-assertion. They clearly do violence to one side of human nature, a side which is essential to life and which balances the other, nobler side of selfless dedication. This kind of moralism asks too much of ordinary people and expects them constantly to deny their own interests. The first result is that the powerful mo-

---

[11] Cf. my essay "Unentwickelte Länder," *ORDO, Jahrbuch für die Ordnung von Wirtschaft und Gesellschaft* (1953).

[12] How Christianity overcame this phase in the course of its development as a dogma and a church and how it came once more to acknowledge the cultural value of "loving oneself" is very evident from Augustine's example. Cf. Hans von Soden, *Urchristentum und Geschichte* (Tübingen, 1951), pp. 56-89.

[13] Lord Acton, *The History of Freedom and Other Essays* (London, 1907), p. 28.
Lord Acton was a Catholic and might well have invoked St. Thomas Aquinas: "Ordinatius res humanæ tractantur, si singulis immineat propria cura alicuius rei procurandæ; esset autem confusio, si quilibet indistincte quælibet procuraret" (*Summa Theologiae*, II, II, 66, 2. Quoted from Joseph Höffner, "Die Funktionen des Privateigentums in der freien Welt," in E. von Beckerath, F. W. Meyer, and A. Müller-Armack (eds.), *Wirtschaftsfragen der freien Welt* [Erhard-Festschrift, Frankfurt am Main, 1957], p. 122).
We might also recall the Pilgrim Fathers, the first English colonizers of New England, who, devout Calvinists as they were, thought they could set up a purely communist system of agriculture; but a few years later, they were forced by the catastrophic decline in yields to change over to a market system and private ownership.

tive forces of self-interest are lost to society. Secondly, the purposes of this "higher" economic morality can be made to prevail only by doing something eminently immoral, namely, by compelling people—by force or cunning and deception—to act against their own nature. In all countries in which a collectivist system has been set up, in the name of many high-sounding purposes and not least of an allegedly "higher" morality, police and penalties enforce compliance with economic commands, or else people are kept in a state of permanent intoxication by emotional ideologies and rousing propaganda—as far and as long as it may be possible.

This, as we all know, regularly happens whenever the market is replaced by a collectivist economy. The market economy has the ability to use the motive power of individual self-interest for turning the turbines of production; but if the collectivist economy is to function it needs heroes or saints, and since there are none, it leads straight to the police state. Any attempt to base an economic order on morality considerably higher than the common man's must end up in compulsion and the organized intoxication of the masses through propaganda. To cite Pascal again, *". . . et qui veut faire l'ange fait la bête."* This is one of the principal reasons for the fact, with which we are already familiar, that a free state and society presuppose a free economy. Collectivist economy, on the other hand, leads to impoverishment and tyranny, and this consequence is obviously the very opposite of "moral." Nothing could more strikingly demonstrate the positive value of self-interested action than that its denial destroys civilization and enslaves men. In "capitalism" we have a freedom of moral choice, and no one is *forced* to be a scoundrel. But this is precisely what we are forced to be in a collectivist social and economic system. It is tragically paradoxical that this should be so, but it is, because the satanic rationale of the system presses us into the service of the state machine and forces us to act against our consciences.

However, to reduce the motives of economic action solely to the desire to obtain material advantage and avoid material loss would result in too dark a picture of the ethical basis of our free economic system. The ordinary man is not such a *homo œconomicus*, just as he is neither hero nor saint. The motives which drive people toward economic success are as varied as the human soul itself. Profit and power do move people, but so do the satisfactions of professional accomplishment, the wish for recognition, the urge to improve one's performance, the dream of excavating Troy (as in the famous example of Schliemann), the impulse to

56

help and to give, the passion of the art or book collector, and many other things.[14] But even if we discover nothing better than the motive of bare material advantage, we should never forget that the man who decently provides for himself and his family by his own effort and on his own responsibility is doing no small or mean thing. It should be stated emphatically that he is more deserving of respect than those who, in the name of a supposedly higher social morality, would leave such provision to others. This applies also to that further category of people who pride themselves on their generosity at others' expense and shed tears of emotion about themselves when their advocacy of a well-oiled welfare state earns them a place in the hearts of the unsuspecting public—and, at the same time, on some political party's list of candidates.

Anyone who knows anything about economics will realize at once that these considerations suggest a familiar answer to an obvious question. What will happen when these individualist motives induce people to do things which are manifestly harmful to others?

Again we turn to the social philosophy of the eighteenth century and its lessons. An economy resting on division of labor, exchange, and competition is an institution which, in spite of its occasionally highly provocative imperfections, does tend, more than any other economic system, to adjust the activities governed by individual interests to the interests of the whole community. We know the mechanism of this adjustment. The individual is forced by competition to seek his own success in serving the mar-

[14] The part played by the art collector's passion in the lives of American multimillionaires of the past generation is described in an entertaining biography of the art dealer who supplied them: S. N. Behrman, *Duveen* (London, 1952). Their names are immortalized in the art galleries they created, which include the National Gallery in Washington, the Frick Gallery, and special collections at the Metropolitan Museum in New York. It seems as if this back door to immortality was one of Duveen's most effective selling points.

On the other hand, even supreme intellectual achievements are not always free from the profit motive, as Goethe's example shows. It seems that it was an attractive offer by his publisher, Cotta, which finally led Goethe to complete his *Faust*. Schiller had solicited this offer behind Goethe's back; we have his letter to Cotta of March 24, 1800: "I am afraid Goethe will completely neglect his Faust, into which so much work has already gone, unless some stimulus from outside in the form of an attractive offer stirs him to take up this great work once more and finish it. . . . However, he expects a large profit, for he knows that this work is awaited with suspense in Germany. I am convinced that you can get him, by means of a brilliant offer, to complete this work in the coming summer." Goethe's prompt reaction can be seen in his letter to Schiller of April 11, 1800. But who would therefore deprecate the profit motive?

ket, that is, the consumer. Obedience to the market ruled by free prices is rewarded by profit, just as disobedience is punished by loss and eventual bankruptcy. The profits and losses of economic activity, calculated as precisely and correctly as possible by the methods of business economics, are thus at the same time the indispensable guide to a rational economy as a whole. Collectivist economies, of whatever degree of collectivism, try in vain to replace this guidance by planning.

These simplified formulations are, of course, highly inadequate, although the truth they contain is undeniable. We need not waste many words over this or over the large and perhaps increasing number of cases where even the market and competition fail to discharge the enormous task of adjusting individual economic action to the common interest. It hardly needs to be stressed, either, how difficult it is to keep competition as such free and satisfactory. Any more or less well-informed person knows that these unsolved tasks and difficulties constitute the thorny problems of an active economic and social policy and that they cannot be taken too seriously.

However, this is not the place to discuss them. There is something else, though, which does need stressing in this context. Have we said all there is to say when we have underlined the importance of competition, and of the price mechanism moved by competition, in regulating an economic system whose principle it is to leave individual forces free? Is it enough to appeal to people's "enlightened self-interest" to make them realize that they serve their own best advantage by submitting to the discipline of the market and of competition?

The answer is decidedly in the negative. And at this point we emphatically draw a dividing line between ourselves and the nineteenth-century liberal utilitarianism and immanentism, whose traces are still with us. Indeed, there is a school which we can hardly call by any other name but liberal anarchism, if we reflect that its adherents seem to think that market, competition, and economic rationality provide a sufficient answer to the question of the ethical foundations of our economic system.

What is the truth? The truth is that what we have said about the forces tending to establish a middle level of ethics in our economic system applies only on the tacit assumption of a modicum of primary ethical behavior. We have made it abundantly clear that we will have no truck with a sort of economically ignorant moralism which, like Mephistopheles in reverse, always wills the

58

good and works the bad. But we must add that we equally repudiate morally callous economism, which is insensitive to the conditions and limits that must qualify our trust in the intrinsic morality of the market economy. Once again, we must state that the market economy is not enough.

In other words, economic life naturally does not go on in a moral vacuum. It is constantly in danger of straying from the ethical middle level unless it is buttressed by strong moral supports. These must simply be there and, what is more, must constantly be impregnated against rot. Otherwise our free economic system and, with it, any free state and society must ultimately collapse.

This also applies in the narrower sense of competition alone. Competition is essential in restraining and channeling self-interest, but it must constantly be protected against anything tending to vitiate it, restrict it, and cause its degeneration. This cannot be done unless everybody not only accepts the concept of free and fair competition but in practice lives up to his faith. All individuals and groups, not excluding trade unions (as must be stressed in view of a widespread social priggishness), who take part in economic life must make a constant moral effort of self-discipline, leaving as little as possible to an otherwise indispensable government-imposed compulsory discipline. It is by no means enough to invoke the laws of the market in appealing to people's enlightened self-interest and their economic reason, for within certain limits, cartels, labor unions, pressure groups, and trade associations serve their members' interests very well indeed when they exercise monopoly power or pressure on the government's economic policy in an attempt to get more than genuine and fair competition would give them. There must be higher ethical values which we can invoke successfully: justice, public spirit, kindness, and good will.[15]

[15] "The Benthamite delusion that politics and economics could be managed on considerations purely material has exposed us to a desolate individualism in which every man and every class looks upon all other men and classes as dangerous competitors, when in reality no man and no class can continue long in safety and prosperity without the bond of sympathy and the reign of justice" (Russell Kirk, "Social Justice and Mass Culture," The Review of Politics, October 1954, p. 447). If we want to understand fully this error of liberal immanentism, which we first meet in such disarming purity in Say's youthful work Olbie, then in the writings of Bentham and his school, and which had a last bright flicker in Herbert Spencer's work, we must remember that at that time the liberation from really constrictive bonds was an absorbing task, while the moral reserves were still intact
continued on page 60

So we see that even the prosaic world of business draws on ethical reserves by which it stands and falls and which are more important than economic laws and principles. Extraeconomic, moral, and social integration is always a prerequisite of economic integration, on the national as on the international plane. As regards the latter, it should be especially emphasized that the true and ultimate foundation of international trade, a foundation of which our textbooks have little to say, is that unwritten code of normal ethical behavior which is epitomized in the words *pacta sunt servanda*.[16]

The market, competition, and the play of supply and demand do not create these ethical reserves; they presuppose them and consume them. These reserves have to come from outside the market, and no textbook on economics can replace them. J. B. Say was mistaken in his youthful work *Olbie ou Essai sur les moyens de réformer les moeurs d'une nation*, a liberal utopian fantasy published in 1800, when he naïvely proposed to hand the citizens of his paradise "un bon traité d'économie politique" as a "premier livre de morale." That valiant utilitarian Cobden also seems to have thought in all seriousness that free-trade theory was the best way to peace.

Self-discipline, a sense of justice, honesty, fairness, chivalry, moderation, public spirit, respect for human dignity, firm ethical norms—all of these are things which people must possess before they go to market and compete with each other. These are the indispensable supports which preserve both market and competition from degeneration. Family, church, genuine communities, and tradition are their sources. It is also necessary that people should grow up in conditions which favor such moral convictions, conditions of a natural order, conditions promoting coopera-

---

enough to be taken for granted. A similar situation existed in Germany after 1945, when it was necessary to give priority to the need of overcoming intolerable poverty by releasing the economic forces weakened by repressed inflation. The one-sidedness of nineteenth-century individualism was paralleled by the equally conspicuous one-sidedness of political individualism, whose fatal ideal of unitarian democracy can be understood as a reaction to the pluralistic petrification of the *ancien régime*.

The roots of the moral blindness of individualism and utilitarianism naturally reach far back into the eighteenth century, to Helvétius, Holbach, Lamettrie, and D'Alembert, just as its ramifications ultimately reach forward to Marx and Engels.

[16] Cf. my book *International Economic Disintegration* (3rd ed.; London, 1950), p. 67 ff., and my course of lectures on "Economic Order and International Law" at The Hague Academy of International Law (*Recueil des Cours 1954* [Leiden, 1955]).

tion, respecting tradition, and giving moral support to the individual. Ownership and reserves, and a feeling for both, are essential parts of such an order. We have, a little earlier, characterized such an order as "bourgeois" in the broadest sense, and it is the foundation upon which the ethics of the market economy must rest. It is an order which fosters individual independence and responsibility as much as the public spirit which connects the individual with the community and limits his greed.

The market economy is a constantly renewed texture of more or less short-lived contractual relations. It can, therefore, have no permanence unless the confidence which any contract presupposes rests on a broad and solid ethical base in all market parties. It depends upon a satisfactory average degree of personal integrity and, at the margin, upon a system of law which counteracts the natural tendency to slip back into less-than-average integrity. Within that legal framework, the market's own sanctions undeniably foster the habit of observing certain minimum rules of behavior and thereby also integrity. Whoever always lies and deceives and breaks contracts will sooner or later be taught that honesty is the best policy. For all its resting on utilitarian calculation, this pattern of behavior is valuable and reliable, as we can see in the extreme example of Soviet Russia, which, in its relations with the outside world of the market, has tried systematically and successfully to acquire the reputation for prompt payment while adhering, in other respects, to the ethical code of gangsters. Even if we conscientiously credit the market with certain educational influences, we are, therefore, led back to our main contention that the ultimate moral support of the market economy lies outside the market. Market and competition are far from generating their moral prerequisites autonomously. This is the error of liberal immanentism. These prerequisites must be furnished from outside, and it is, on the contrary, the market and competition which constantly strain them, draw upon them, and consume them.

We would, of course, again err on the side of unrealistic and unhistorical moralism if we were to apply to modern economic behavior moral standards which would have been enough to condemn mankind at any time because men can never live up to them. Such moralism is least tolerable when it self-righteously pretends that the moralist is a better man for the mere reason that his standards are so strict. This should always be remembered whenever the talk turns to the questionable aspects of competition. Ruthless rivalry has never and in no circumstances been banned from human society. The young Torrigiani, spurred by jealousy and professional rivalry, smashed Michelangelo's nasal bone and thereby disfigured him for life; in our days, a leading German trade-union intellectual, no doubt a valiant detractor of the "capitalist jungle," tried to get rid of a rival by means of forged letters—it is always the same thing and always equally unedifying. But we get nowhere by raising our eyebrows because the market economy does not always display the sporting spirit of a tennis tournament; we would do better to reflect that no small advantage of the market economy is that it channels men's natural rivalry into forms which, by and large, are preferable to broken noses and forged letters—and also to mass executions, as in Communist countries.

But we cannot, in good conscience, let the matter rest there. It cannot be denied that the market places the constant competitive struggle for self-assertion and self-advancement in the center of the stage. Nor can it be denied that such all-pervasive competition has a disturbing tendency to lead to consequences to which we cannot remain indifferent, especially from the moral point of view. Those who are in the rough-and-tumble of the competition of modern economic life, with its nerve-racking claims on time, effort, and susceptibility, and who are worn down by this endless struggle are more sensitive than most to the questions raised thereby, and it would be both unjust and uncivil therefore to treat them as monopoly-mongers.

We all acknowledge the validity and justice of such questions when we accept as a model of a higher form of rivalry the way in which certain professions, above all the medical, submit to strict rules of competition to the point of including them among the standards of professional behavior. Unfortunately, this example of the medical profession's deontology cannot be applied to industry and trade. But it shows what a blessing for all it would be if a definite code of competitive behavior, resting on professional standards, binding for all and violable only at the price of outlawry, were to dampen competition everywhere and withdraw it from the laws of "marginal ethics,"[17] without appeal to the state but in full appreciation of the positive potentialities of professional solidarity.

In acknowledging these potentialities, we express the idea that we should aim at compensating the socially disintegrating effects

[17] Cf. Goetz Briefs, "Grenzmoral in der pluralistischen Gesellschaft," in *Wirtschaftsfragen der freien Welt.*

of competition by the integrating forces outside the market and outside competition. There is, however, the danger of abuse. On no account must competition be corrupted by its economically most questionable and morally most reprehensible perversion, namely, monopoly in any shape or form. Monopoly is precisely the worst form of that commercialism which we want to combat by trying to mitigate competition by integrating counterforces.

The truth is that competition, which we need as a regulator in a free economy, comes up on all sides against limits which we would not wish it to transgress. It remains morally and socially dangerous and can be defended only up to a point and with qualifications and modifications of all kinds. A spirit of ever alert and suspicious rivalry, not too particular in the choice of its means, must not be allowed to predominate and to sway society in all its spheres, or it will poison men's souls, destroy civilization, and ultimately disintegrate the economy.

To assert oneself at the time by ubiquitous advertising, day and night, in town and country, on the air and on every free square foot of wall space, in prose and in verse, in word and picture, by open assault or by the subtler means of "public relations," until every gesture of courtesy, kindness, and neighborliness is degraded into a move behind which we suspect ulterior motives; to fashion all imaginable relations and performances on the principle of supply and demand and so to commercialize them, not excluding art and science and religion; forever to compare one's own position with that of others; always to try out something new, to shift from one profession and from one place to the next; to look with constant jealousy and envy upon others—such extreme commercialization, restlessness, and rivalry are an infallible way of destroying the free economy by morally blind exaggeration of its principle. This is bound to end up in an unhealthy state of which the worst must be feared.

The curse of commercialization is that it results in the standards of the market spreading into regions which should remain beyond supply and demand. This vitiates the true purposes, dignity, and savor of life and thereby makes it unbearably ugly, undignified, and dull. We have had occasion earlier to note this. Think of Mother's Day, a day set aside to honor mothers and motherhood; the most tender and sacred human relationship is turned into a means of sales promotion by advertising experts and made to turn the wheels of business. Father's Day soon followed, and if we did not fortunately know better, the latest forms of Christmas might

63

make us suspect that this whip which makes the top of business spin is also a creation of modern advertising techniques. Not long ago it happened that an automobile race, which, to the horror of the spectators, led to a fatal accident, was nevertheless continued because of its commercial and technical purposes, so that even death had to defer to business and technology.

All of this cannot be castigated too severely—with the intention, not of condemning the market economy, but of stressing the need to circumscribe and moderate it and of showing once more its dependence upon moral reserves. This circumscription and moderation can take many forms. One of them is that we do not allow competition to become the dominating principle and that we keep an eye on all the circumstances which tend to mitigate it. Let me illustrate my point. Has any sociologist ever bothered to discover why there is usually fierce rivalry among actors and singers, while circus folk tend to live in an atmosphere of kindly good-fellowship? Would it not be a rewarding task to examine the whole texture of modern society for such differences in competition and their presumable causes?[18]

Nobilitas Naturalis

It cannot be said often enough that in the last resort competition has to be circumscribed and mitigated by moral forces within the market parties. These constitute the true "countervailing power" of which the American economist J. K. Galbraith speaks in his book of the same title, and not the mechanics of organized buying power, to which he mistakenly looks for the containment of competition and its monopolistic perversions. Without a fund of effective convictions regarding the moral limits of competition, the problem cannot find a genuine solution.

In a sound society, leadership, responsibility, and exemplary defense of the society's guiding norms and values must be the

---

[18] The problems of competition and the dilemma it so often involves can be studied very well in the example of universities. If one knows the system of those countries where the lecturer draws attendance fees and therefore has a financial interest in the outward success of his lectures, one realizes how poisonous an atmosphere of rivalry can thus be created and how the teacher is tempted to court outward success more than is right and proper. On the other hand, this system provides a good stimulant for weaker characters who are not sufficiently conscious of the obligations of their office.

exalted duty and unchallengeable right of a minority that forms and is willingly and respectfully recognized as the apex of a social pyramid hierarchically structured by performance. Mass society, such as we have described it earlier, must be counteracted by individual leadership—not on the part of original geniuses or eccentrics or will-o'-the-wisp intellectuals, but, on the contrary, on the part of people with courage to reject eccentric novelty for the sake of the "old truths" which Goethe admonishes us to hold on to and for the sake of historically proved, indestructible, and simple human values. In other words, we need the leadership of genuine *clercs* or of men such as those whom the distinguished psychiatrist Joachim Bodamer recently described as "ascetics of civilization," secularized saints as it were, who in our age occupy a place which must not for long remain vacant at any time and in any society. That is what those have in mind who say that the "revolt of the masses" must be countered by another revolt, the "revolt of the elite."

The conviction is rightly gaining ground that the important thing is that every society should have a small but influential group of leaders who feel themselves to be the whole community's guardians of inviolable norms and values and who strictly live up to this guardianship. What we need is true *nobilitas naturalis*. No era can do without it, least of all ours, when so much is shaking and crumbling away. We need a natural nobility whose authority is, fortunately, readily accepted by all men, an elite deriving its title solely from supreme performance and peerless moral example and invested with the moral dignity of such a life. Only a few from every stratum of society can ascend into this thin layer of natural nobility. The way to it is an exemplary and slowly maturing life of dedicated endeavor on behalf of all, unimpeachable integrity, constant restraint of our common greed, proved soundness of judgment, a spotless private life, indomitable courage in standing up for truth and law, and generally the highest example. This is how the few, carried upward by the trust of the people, gradually attain to a position above the classes, interests, passions, wickedness, and foolishness of men and finally become the nation's conscience. To belong to this group of moral aristocrats should be the highest and most desirable aim, next to which all the other triumphs of life are pale and insipid.

No free society, least of all ours, which threatens to degenerate into mass society, can subsist without such a class of censors. The continued existence of our free world will ultimately depend on whether our age can produce a sufficient number of such aristocrats of public spirit, aristocrats of a kind which was by no means rare in the feudal age. We need businessmen, farmers, and bankers who view the great questions of economic policy unprejudiced by their own immediate and short-run economic interests; trade-union leaders who realize that they share with the president of the national bank the responsibility for the country's currency; journalists who resist the temptation to flatter mass tastes or to succumb to political passions and court cheap success and instead guide public opinion with moderation, sound judgment, and a high sense of responsibility. In turn, it will be of crucial importance for the ultimate fate of the market economy whether this aristocracy includes, above all, people who, by position and conviction, have close ties with the market economy and who feel responsible for it in the moral sphere here under discussion.[19]

Evidently, many and sometimes difficult conditions must be fulfilled if such a natural aristocracy is to develop and endure and if it is to discharge its tasks. It must grow and mature, and the slowness of its ripening is matched by the swiftness of its possible destruction. Wealth gained and lost overnight is a stony ground on which it cannot prosper but on which thrive plutocracy and newly rich parvenus—the very opposite of what is desirable. Yet without wealth and its inheritance, whereby a spiritual and moral tradition is handed down together with its material foundation, a natural aristocracy is equally impossible, and it would be short-sighted egalitarian radicalism to overlook this.[20] One generation is often, indeed usually, not sufficient to produce the flower and fruit of aristocratic public spirit and leadership, and this is why the almost confiscatory limitation of the testator's rights, which today is the rule in some major Western countries, is one of the

[19] The idea of *nobilitas naturalis* is, of course, so old that it is difficult to trace its spiritual genealogy. It may be worth noting, though, that the idea was quite familiar to a democrat like Thomas Jefferson, who is above any suspicion of reactionary opinions. On October 28, 1813, Jefferson wrote to John Adams, who was a conservative: "I agree with you that there is a natural aristocracy among men. The grounds of this are virtue and talents. . . . The natural aristocracy I consider as the most precious gift of nature, for the instruction, the trusts and government of society. And indeed it would have been inconsistent in creation to have formed man for the social state, and not to have provided virtue and wisdom enough to manage the concerns of society" (A. Koch and W. Peden, *The Life and Selected Writings of Thomas Jefferson* [Modern Library, New York], pp. 632-33). The application to the particular case of the market economy can be found in my book *The Social Crisis of Our Time*, p. 134ff. See also Wright, *op. cit.*, p. 25ff.

most harmful measures imaginable and contrary to the spirit of sound policy.

But *richesse oblige.* Any privilege, be it a privilege of birth, mind, honor and respect, or of wealth, confers rights only in exactly the same measure in which it is accepted as an obligation. It will not do to hide one's talent in the earth; each must remain conscious of the responsibilities which his privileged position entails. If ever the much-abused words "social justice" are appropriate, it is here.

One of the obligations of wealth, which need not be enumerated, is to contribute to the filling of the gaps left by the market because they are in the realm of goods outside the play of supply and demand, but which gaps must not be left for the state to fill if we want to preserve a free society. I have in mind the patronage of art in the widest sense, generous grants for theatre, opera, music, the visual arts, and science—briefly, for everything whose existence and development would be jeopardized if it had to "pay." We would be hard put to name a single supreme work of art in any period of history which did not owe its origin to patronage, and it is even more difficult to think of a theatre, opera house, or orchestra which bowed to the laws of supply and demand without damage to its quality or which, therefore, could have maintained its quality without patronage. The tragedies of Aeschylus, Sophocles, and Euripides are as unthinkable without the public donations of the rich Athenians as are the plays of Shakespeare without his patrons. Conversely, in so far as in our age the laws of supply and demand determine the level of artistic performance—in extreme form, in the film industry—the devastating effects are plain for all to see.

This function is to be fulfilled by the rich in the same spirit in which in the old days the Hanseatic burghers of Bremen used to pay property taxes: in honest self-assessment of one's ability to pay and in voluntary fulfillment of an honorary duty.[21] Here it is ap-

[20] We again quote an author beyond suspicion: "[The legislator] has not fulfilled his task if, in his desire to insure equal satisfaction of all needs, he renders impossible the full development of outstanding individuals, if he prevents anyone from rising above his fellows, if he cannot produce anyone as an example to the human race, as a leader in discoveries which will benefit all" (Simonde de Sismondi, *op. cit.,* II, 2). The same idea is forcefully expressed by Alexis de Tocqueville in his *Democracy in America.* See also L. Baudin, "Die Theorie der Eliten," in *Masse und Demokratie,* pp. 39-54.

[21] H. K. Röthel, *Die Hansestädte* (Munich, 1955), p. 91.

propriate to emphasize that this spirit is smothered by the modern welfare state and its fiscal socialism. It may also be pointed out that the rich cannot exercise their function of patronage of the arts unless they are at home in the realm of the spirit and of beauty as much as in the world of business—which brings us back to what we said earlier in this chapter.

The task of leadership falls to the natural aristocracy by virtue of an unwritten but therefore no less valid right which is indistinguishable from duty. Washington's successor, the great American statesman John Adams, had some very pertinent things to say about this. According to him, a member of the "natural aristocracy of virtues and talents" was anyone who disposed not only of his own vote but, at the same time, of the votes of those whose opinions he influenced by his example, acknowledged authority, and persuasion. But since this is unfortunately true not only of the "natural aristocracy of virtues and talents" but of everybody who, by foul means or fair, influences the formation of political opinion, we must add the qualification that the unwritten plural franchise which actually exists in any democracy is the more justified the more we can rely on the existence and effectiveness of a genuine natural aristocracy. The latter therefore appears all the more indispensable.

Finally, we have to speak of science, whose leadership functions and responsibility are obvious. There can be no doubt that here, too, rights and duties are inextricably linked. Here, too, authority—and it is authority of the highest rank—has to be gained and held by achievement and character. But what, precisely, is the deontology of science, especially, in this context, of the social sciences?

Boswell has recorded an apposite remark by Samuel Johnson, that great eighteenth-century Englishman. Certain professions, Johnson said, principally the sailor's and the soldier's, had the dignity of danger. "Mankind reverence those who have got over fear, which is so general a weakness." Conversely, the honor of those professions whose dignity is danger cannot be more deeply wounded than by casting doubt on their courage.

The esteem in which science is held certainly does not rest on such a dignity of danger. We do not expect of a Sanskrit scholar the bravery of a soldier or sailor who, professionally, has to face physical danger of losing his life, but we do expect men of science to be courageous and intrepid in another sense, which we recognize when we have grasped that the "dignity of science" is truth.

68

This sounds a little pompous, but it is meant to express something very simple. It does not mean that science is respected because it has to offer "truth" like ripe plums. What we mean is this: just as much as fear, another universal human failing is a tendency to allow the prospect of advantages or the threat of disadvantages to deflect one from the pursuit of the "true" facts and, even more, from the free announcement of facts recognized as "true." The dignity of science is that its genuine apostles constantly have to overcome this human weakness of interested squinting at truth. Only those who fulfill this requirement can partake in the dignity of science. Only they discharge the obligation put upon them by the privilege of being the servants of science, and only they can hope to attain to natural nobility and to render to the community those services which it has a right to expect from them.

Since men of science, too, are generally neither saints nor heroes, it is no doubt hard for them to live up to this standard without faltering and occasional aberrations. It is hardest for those who, unlike the Sanskrit scholar, have chosen a field of knowledge which gives them occasion and indeed obliges them to defend the "dignity of truth" in the rough-and-tumble of interests and passions. Economic policy, of which we are treating here, is such a battlefield, and the scholars involved are the jurists and economists.[22] Economists also have this in common with jurists: their scientific authority, whose moral foundation is the "dignity of truth," is appealed to in controversial questions. Such activities by scholars are as old as the history of science and the universities; we have but to remember that in the fourteenth century Louis of Bavaria called on the famed scholars of the Universities of Bologna and Paris for opinions in his struggle with Pope John XXII. Curiously enough, this is not usually held against jurists, although the delicate nature of such a task is obvious. It always presents the man of science with a question of conscience which he must decide in the light of the "dignity of truth."

The answer should not be in doubt. Such a commission can be accepted—and indeed has point for the questioner—only if it is discharged in such a manner that the scholar's answer does not deviate in the slightest respect from that which he would have pronounced without the commission and without the ensuing advantages (which may include such things as enhanced prestige or public honors). The answer must be strictly in line with his scien-

[22] W. H. Hutt, *Economists and the Public* (London, 1936); Wilhelm Roepke, "Der wissenschaftliche Ort der Nationalökonomie," *Studium Generale*, July 1953.

tific convictions, and if there is the slightest doubt about this, the scholar should withdraw. The economist, in particular, should make it a rule to put his scientific work at the service of any precise commission, originating from the government or from international or nongovernmental organizations, only on condition that this work can serve his own convictions also and on the further condition that he may hope thereby to promote a good cause threatened by overwhelming forces. In the absence of these conditions, the economist has every reason to ask himself whether the counsel expected of him in the struggle of economic interests and social passions is not a mortgage on his conscience, considering the social function of his science.

If a task so undertaken also happens to involve some private interests, the economist can congratulate himself. Aims of economic policy which lack such a solid anchor have little prospect of being taken seriously in our world of overwhelming material interests and stormy passions. To take an important example, liberal trade policy would be in a bad way indeed if there did not, fortunately, exist groups which have a material interest in it and thereby form a natural counterweight to the fatal combination of protectionist interests and political passions such as nationalism and socialism. To help such groups may be regarded as a legitimate duty by the economist who weighs the opposing forces against each other.

The economist has all the less right to evade the duty of bringing his authority to bear on the controversies of economic policy since this duty has an important characteristic in common with every genuine duty. This is that it tends to be beset by vexations, and to withstand these vexations requires that same courage which is indispensable for defending the "dignity of truth." By putting his view onto one of the scales, he lessens the relative weight of the other, and the interest and passions involved on the other side will feel provoked. They have a perfect right to resist by trying to prove that the reasons, assumptions, and conclusions of the inconvenient scientific verdict are wrong and that the scientific judgment against them is a misjudgment. The scholar would be foolish if he thought himself in possession of objective truth, and it is no dishonor for him to be disproved. But he has a right to expect that his search for truth, his intellectual integrity, is not suspected. Like the judge, he has an absolute claim, which should be effectively protected, to the assurance that factual criticism of his sentence will not be replaced by an attempt to smear his reputation with accusations of bribery, cowardice, or political prejudice.

Bad experiences of this kind do not seem to have been spared even Adam Smith, the father of economics and contemporary of Samuel Johnson. In a famous passage of his *Wealth of Nations* (Book IV, Chapter 2), he says that anyone who opposes unconquerable private interests or has authority enough to be able to thwart them must expect that "neither the most acknowledged probity, nor the highest rank, nor the greatest public services can protect him from the most infamous abuse and detraction, from personal insults, nor sometimes from real danger."

TRUE CAPITALISM

Ludwig von Mises

from THE ANTI-CAPITALIST MENTALITY (1956)

The emergence of economics as a new branch of knowledge was one of the most portentous events in the history of mankind. In paving the way for private capitalistic enterprise it transformed within a few generations all human affairs more radically than the preceding ten thousand years had done. From the day of their birth to the day of their demise, the denizens of a capitalistic country are every minute benefited by the marvelous achievements of the capitalistic ways of thinking and acting.

The most amazing thing concerning the unprecedented change in earthly conditions brought about by capitalism is the fact that it was accomplished by a small number of authors and a hardly greater number of statesmen who had assimilated their teachings. Not only the sluggish masses but also most of the businessmen who, by their trading, made the laissez-faire principles effective failed to comprehend the essential features of their operation. Even in the heyday of liberalism only a few people had a full grasp of the functioning of the market economy. Western civilization adopted capitalism upon recommendation on the part of a small elite.

There were, in the first decades of the nineteenth century, many people who viewed their own unfamiliarity with the problems concerned as a serious shortcoming and were anxious to redress it. In the years between Waterloo and Sebastopol, no other books were more eagerly absorbed in Great Britain than treatises on economics. But the vogue soon subsided. The subject was unpalatable to the general reader.

Economics is so different from the natural sciences and technology on the one hand, and history and jurisprudence on the other hand, that it seems strange and repulsive to the beginner. Its heuristic singularity is viewed with suspicion by those whose research work is performed in laboratories or in archives and libraries. Its epistemological singularity appears nonsensical to the narrow-minded fanatics of positivism. People would like to find in an economics book knowledge that perfectly fits into their preconceived image of what economics ought to be, viz., a discipline shaped according to the logical structure of physics or of biology. They are bewildered and desist from seriously grappling with problems the analysis of which requires an unwonted mental exertion.

The result of this ignorance is that people ascribe all improvements in economic conditions to the progress of the natural sciences and technology. As they see it, there prevails in the course of human history a self-acting tendency toward progressing advancement of the experimental natural sciences and their application to the solution of technological problems. This tendency is irresistible, it is inherent in the destiny of mankind, and its operation takes effect whatever the political and economic organization of society may be. As they see it, the unprecedented technological improvements of the last two hundred years were not caused or furthered by the economic policies of the age. They were not an achievement of classical liberalism, free trade, laissez-faire, and capitalism. They will therefore go on under any other system of society's economic organization.

The doctrines of Marx received approval simply because they adopted this popular interpretation of events and clothed it with a pseudophilosophical veil that made it gratifying both to Hegelian spiritualism and to crude materialism. In the scheme of Marx the "material productive forces" are a superhuman entity independent of the will and the actions of men. They go their own way that is prescribed by the inscrutable and inevitable laws of a higher power. They change mysteriously and force mankind to adjust its social organization to these changes; for the material productive forces shun one thing: to be enchained by mankind's social organization. The essential content of history is the struggle of the material productive forces to be freed from the social bonds by which they are fettered.

Once upon a time, teaches Marx, the material productive forces

73

were embodied in the shape of the hand mill, and then they arranged human affairs according to the pattern of feudalism. When, later, the unfathomable laws that determine the evolution of the material productive forces substituted the steam mill for the hand mill, feudalism had to give way to capitalism. Since then the material productive forces have developed further, and their present shape imperatively requires the substitution of socialism for capitalism. Those who try to check the socialist revolution are committed to a hopeless task. It is impossible to stem the tide of historical progress.

The ideas of the so-called leftist parties differ from one another in many ways. But they agree in one point. They all look upon progressing material improvement as upon a self-acting process. The American union member takes his standard of living for granted. Fate has determined that he should enjoy amenities which were denied even to the most prosperous people of earlier generations and are still denied to non-Americans. It does not occur to him that the "rugged individualism" of big business may have played some role in the emergence of what he calls the "American way of life." In his eyes "management" represents the unfair claims of the "exploiters" who are intent upon depriving him of his birthright. There is, he thinks, in the course of historical evolution an irrepressible tendency toward a continuous increase in the "productivity" of his labor. It is obvious that the fruits of this betterment by rights belong exclusively to him. It is his merit that—in the age of capitalism—the quotient of the value of the products turned out by the processing industries divided by the number of hands employed tended toward an increase.

The truth is that the increase in what is called the productivity of labor is due to the employment of better tools and machines. A hundred workers in a modern factory produce per unit of time a multiple of what a hundred workers used to produce in the workshops of precapitalistic craftsmen. This improvement is not conditioned by higher skill, competence, or application on the part of the individual worker. (It is a fact that the proficiency needed by medieval artisans towered far above that of many categories of present-day factory hands.) It is due to the employment of more efficient tools and machines which, in turn, is the effect of the accumulation and investment of more capital.

The terms capitalism, capital, and capitalists were employed by Marx and are today employed by most people—also by the official propaganda agencies of the United States government—with an opprobrious connotation. Yet these words pertinently point toward the main factor whose operation produced all the marvelous achievements of the last two hundred years: the unprecedented improvement of the average standard of living for a continually increasing population. What distinguishes modern industrial conditions in the capitalistic countries from those of the precapitalistic ages as well as from those prevailing today in the so-called underdeveloped countries is the amount of the supply of capital. No technological improvement can be put to work if the capital required has not previously been accumulated by saving.

Saving, capital accumulation, is the agency that has transformed step by step the awkward search for food on the part of savage cave dwellers into the modern ways of industry. The pacemakers of this evolution were the ideas that created the institutional framework within which capital accumulation was rendered safe by the principle of private ownership of the means of production. Every step forward on the way toward prosperity is the effect of saving. The most ingenious technological inventions would be practically useless if the capital goods required for their utilization had not been accumulated by saving.

The entrepreneurs employ the capital goods made available by the savers for the most economical satisfaction of the most urgent among the not yet satisfied wants of the consumers. Together with the technologists, intent upon perfecting the methods of processing, they play, next to the savers themselves, an active part in the course of events that is called economic progress. The rest of mankind profit from the activities of these three classes of pioneers. But whatever their own doings may be, they are only beneficiaries of changes to the emergence of which they did not contribute anything.

The characteristic feature of the market economy is the fact that it allots the greater part of the improvements brought about by the endeavors of the three progressive classes—those saving, those investing the capital goods, and those elaborating new methods for the employment of capital goods—to the nonprogressive majority of people. Capital accumulation exceeding the increase in population raises, on the one hand, the marginal productivity of labor and, on the other hand, cheapens the products. The market process provides the common man with the opportunity to enjoy the fruits of other peoples' achievements. It forces the three progressive classes to serve the nonprogressive majority in the best possible way.

Everybody is free to join the ranks of the three progressive classes of a capitalist society. These classes are not closed castes. Membership in them is not a privilege conferred on the individual by a higher authority or inherited from one's ancestors. These classes are not clubs, and the ins have no power to keep out any newcomer. What is needed to become a capitalist, an entrepreneur, or a deviser of new technological methods is brains and will power. The heir of a wealthy man enjoys a certain advantage as he starts under more favorable conditions than others. But his task in the rivalry of the market is not easier, but sometimes even more wearisome and less remunerative than that of a newcomer. He has to reorganize his inheritance in order to adjust it to the changes in market conditions. Thus, for instance, the problems that the heir of a railroad "empire" had to face were, in the last decades, certainly more knotty than those encountered by the man who started from scratch in trucking or in air transportation.

The popular philosophy of the common man misrepresents all these facts in the most lamentable way. As John Doe sees it, all those new industries that are supplying him with amenities unknown to his father came into being by some mythical agency called progress. Capital accumulation, entrepreneurship, and technological ingenuity did not contribute anything to the spontaneous generation of prosperity. If any man has to be credited with what John Doe considers as the rise in the productivity of labor, then it is the man on the assembly line. Unfortunately, in this sinful world there is exploitation of man by man. Business skims the cream and leaves, as the Communist Manifesto points out, to the creator of all good things, to the manual worker, not more than "he requires for his maintenance and for the propagation of his race." Consequently, "the modern worker, instead of rising with the progress of industry, sinks deeper and deeper. . . . He becomes a pauper, and pauperism develops more rapidly than population and wealth." The authors of this description of capitalistic industry are praised at universities as the greatest philosophers and benefactors of mankind and their teachings are accepted with reverential awe by the millions whose homes, besides other gadgets, are equipped with radio and television sets.

The worst exploitation, say professors, "labor" leaders, and politicians, is effected by big business. They fail to realize that the characteristic mark of big business is mass production for the satisfaction of the needs of the masses. Under capitalism the workers themselves, directly or indirectly, are the main consumers of all those things that the factories are turning out.

In the early days of capitalism there was still a considerable time lag between the emergence of an innovation and its becoming accessible to the masses. About sixty years ago Gabriel Tarde was right in pointing out that an industrial innovation is the fancy of a minority before it becomes the need of everybody; what was considered first as an extravagance turns later into a customary requisite of all and sundry. This statement was still correct with regard to the popularization of the automobile. But big-scale production by big business has shortened and almost eliminated this time lag. Modern innovations can only be produced profitably according to the methods of mass production and hence become accessible to the many at the very moment of their practical inauguration. There was, for instance, in the United States no sensible period in which the enjoyment of such innovations as television, nylon stockings, or canned baby food was reserved to a minority of the well-to-do. Big business tends, in fact, toward a standardization of the peoples' ways of consumption and enjoyment.

Nobody is needy in the market economy because of the fact that some people are rich. The riches of the rich are not the cause of the poverty of anybody. The process that makes some people rich is, on the contrary, the corollary of the process that improves many peoples' want satisfaction. The entrepreneurs, the capitalists, and the technologists prosper as far as they succeed in best supplying the consumers.

*   *   *

In the universe there is never and nowhere stability and immobility. Change and transformation are essential features of life. Each state of affairs is transient; each age is an age of transition. In human life there is never calm and repose. Life is a process, not a perseverance in a *status quo*. Yet the human mind has always been deluded by the image of an unchangeable existence. The avowed aim of all utopian movements is to put an end to history and to establish a final and permanent calm.

The psychological reasons for this tendency are obvious. Every change alters the external conditions of life and well-being and forces people to adjust themselves anew to the modification of their environments. It hurts vested interests and threatens traditional ways of production and consumption. It annoys all those who are intellectually inert and shrink from revising their modes of thinking. Conservatism is contrary to the very nature of human acting. But it has always been the cherished program of the many, of the inert who dully resist every attempt to improve their own conditions which the minority of the alert initiate. In employing

77

the term *reactionary* one mostly refers only to the aristocrats and priests who called their parties conservative. Yet the outstanding examples of the reactionary spirit were provided by other groups: by the guilds of artisans blocking entrance into their field to newcomers; by the farmers asking for tariff protection, subsidies, and "parity prices"; by the wage earners hostile to technological improvements and fostering featherbedding and similar practices.

The vain arrogance of the literati and the Bohemian artists dismisses the activities of the businessmen as unintellectual moneymaking. The truth is that the entrepreneurs and promoters display more intellectual faculties and intuition than the average writer and painter. The inferiority of many self-styled intellectuals manifests itself precisely in the fact that they fail to recognize what capacity and reasoning power are required to develop and to operate successfully a business enterprise.

The emergence of a numerous class of such frivolous intellectuals is one of the least welcome phenomena of the age of modern capitalism. Their obtrusive stir repels discriminating people. They are a nuisance. It would not directly harm anybody if something would be done to curb their bustle or, even better, to wipe out entirely their cliques and coteries.

However, freedom is indivisible. Every attempt to restrict the freedom of the decadent troublesome literati and pseudo-artists would vest in the authorities the power to determine what is good and what is bad. It would socialize intellectual and artistic effort. It is questionable whether it would weed out the useless and objectionable persons; but it is certain that it would put insurmountable obstacles in the way of the creative genius. The powers that be do not like new ideas, new ways of thought, and new styles of art. They are opposed to any kind of innovation. Their supremacy would result in strict regimentation; it would bring about stagnation and decay.

The moral corruption, the licentiousness, and the intellectual sterility of a class of lewd would-be authors and artists is the ransom mankind must pay lest the creative pioneers be prevented from accomplishing their work. Freedom must be granted to all, even to base people, lest the few who can use it for the benefit of mankind be hindered. The license which the shabby characters of the *quartier Latin* enjoyed was one of the conditions that made possible the ascendance of a few great writers, painters, and sculptors. The first thing a genius needs is to breathe free air.

After all, it is not the frivolous doctrines of the Bohemians that

78

generate disaster, but the fact that the public is ready to accept them favorably. The response to these pseudo-philosophies on the part of the molders of public opinion and later on the part of the misguided masses is the evil. People are anxious to endorse the tenets they consider as fashionable lest they appear boorish and backward.

The most pernicious ideology of the last sixty years was Georges Sorel's syndicalism and his enthusiasm for the *action directe*. Generated by a frustrated French intellectual, it soon captivated the literati of all European countries. It was a major factor in the radicalization of all subversive movements. It influenced French royalism, militarism, and anti-Semitism. It played an important role in the evolution of Russian Bolshevism, Italian Fascism, and the German youth movement which finally resulted in the development of Nazism. It transformed political parties intent upon winning through electoral campaigns into factions which relied upon the organization of armed bands. It brought into discredit representative government and "bourgeois security," and preached the gospel both of civil and of foreign war. Its main slogan was: violence and again violence. The present state of European affairs is to a great extent an outcome of the prevalence of Sorel's teachings.

The intellectuals were the first to hail the ideas of Sorel; they made them popular. But the tenor of Sorelism was obviously anti-intellectual. He was opposed to cool reasoning and sober deliberation. What counts for Sorel is solely the deed, viz., the act of violence for the sake of violence. Fight for a myth whatever this myth may mean, was his advice. "If you place yourself on this ground of myths, you are proof against any kind of critical refutation."[1] What a marvelous philosophy, to destroy for the sake of destruction! Do not talk, do not reason, kill! Sorel rejects the "intellectual effort" even of the literary champions of revolution. The essential aim of the myth is "to prepare people to fight for the destruction of what exists."[2]

Yet the blame for the spread of the destructionist pseudo-philosophy rests neither with Sorel nor with his disciples, Lenin, Mussolini, and Rosenberg, nor with the hosts of irresponsible literati and artists. The catastrophe came because, for many decades, hardly anybody ventured to examine critically and to explode the trigger-consciousness of the fanatical desperadoes. Even those authors

[1] Cf. G. Sorel, *Réflexions sur la violence* (3rd ed.; Paris, 1912), p. 49.
[2] Cf. Sorel, *op. cit.*, p. 46.

who refrained from unreservedly endorsing the ideas of reckless violence were eager to find some sympathetic interpretation of the worst excesses of the dictators. The first timid objections were raised only when—very late, indeed—the intellectual abettors of these policies began to realize that even enthusiastic endorsement of the totalitarian ideology did not guarantee immunity from torture and execution.

There exists today a sham anti-Communist front. What these people who call themselves "anti-Communist liberals" and whom sober men more correctly call "anti-anti-Communists" are aiming at is Communism without those inherent and necessary features of Communism which are still unpalatable to Americans. They make an illusory distinction between Communism and socialism and—paradoxically enough—look for a support of their recommendation of non-Communist socialism to the document which its authors called The Communist Manifesto. They think that they have proved their case by employing such aliases for socialism as planning or the welfare state. They pretend to reject the revolutionary and dictatorial aspirations of the "Reds" and at the same time they praise in books and magazines, in schools and universities, Karl Marx, the champion of the Communist revolution and the dictatorship of the proletariat, as one of the greatest economists, philosophers, and sociologists and as the eminent benefactor and liberator of mankind. They want to make us believe that untotalitarian totalitarianism, a kind of a triangular square, is the patent medicine for all ills. Whenever they raise some mild objection to Communism, they are eager to abuse capitalism in terms borrowed from the objurgatory vocabulary of Marx and Lenin. They emphasize that they abhor capitalism much more passionately than Communism, and they justify all the unsavory acts of the Communists by referring to the "unspeakable horrors" of capitalism. In short: they pretend to fight Communism in trying to convert people to the ideas of the Communist Manifesto.

What these self-styled "anti-Communist liberals" are fighting against is not Communism as such, but a Communist system in which they themselves are not at the helm. What they are aiming at is a socialist, i.e., Communist, system in which they themselves or their most intimate friends hold the reins of government. It would perhaps be too much to say that they are burning with a desire to liquidate other people. They simply do not wish to be liquidated. In a socialist commonwealth, only the supreme autocrat and his abettors have this assurance.

An "anti-something" movement displays a purely negative attitude. It has no chance whatever to succeed. Its passionate diatribes virtually advertise the program that they attack. People must fight for something that they want to achieve, not simply reject an evil, however bad it may be. They must, without any reservations, endorse the program of the market economy.

Communism would have today, after the disillusionment brought by the deeds of the Soviets and the lamentable failure of all socialist experiments, but little chance of succeeding in the West if it were not for this faked anti-Communism.

What alone can prevent the civilized nations of Western Europe, America, and Australia from being enslaved by the barbarism of Moscow is open and unrestricted support of laissez-faire capitalism.

WHAT IS CAPITALISM?

Ayn Rand

from CAPITALISM: THE UNKNOWN IDEAL (1967)

The disintegration of philosophy in the nineteenth century and its collapse in the twentieth have led to a similar, though much slower and less obvious, process in the course of modern science.

Today's frantic development in the field of technology has a quality reminiscent of the days preceding the economic crash of 1929: riding on the momentum of the past, on the unacknowledged remnants of an Aristotelian epistemology, it is a hectic, feverish expansion, heedless of the fact that its theoretical account is long since overdrawn—that in the field of scientific theory, unable to integrate or interpret their own data, scientists are abetting the resurgence of a primitive mysticism. In the humanities, however, the crash is past, the depression has set in, and the collapse of science is all but complete.

The clearest evidence of it may be seen in such comparatively young sciences as psychology and political economy. In psychology, one may observe the attempt to study human behavior without reference to the fact that man is conscious. In political economy, one may observe. the attempt to study and to devise social systems without reference to man.

It is philosophy that defines and establishes the epistemological criteria to guide human knowledge in general and specific sciences in particular. Political economy came into prominence in the nineteenth century, in the era of philosophy's post-Kantian disintegration, and no one rose to check its premises or to challenge its base. Implicitly, uncritically, and by default, political economy accepted as its axioms the fundamental tenets of collectivism.

Political economists—including the advocates of capitalism—defined their science as the study of the management or direction or organization or manipulation of a "community's" or a nation's "resources." The nature of these "resources" was not defined; their communal ownership was taken for granted—and the goal of political economy was assumed to be the study of how to utilize these "resources" for "the common good."

The fact that the principal "resource" involved was man himself, that he was an entity of a specific nature with specific capacities and requirements, was given the most superficial attention, if any. Man was regarded simply as one of the factors of production, along with land, forests, or mines—as one of the less significant factors, since more study was devoted to the influence and quality of these others than to his role or quality.

Political economy was, in effect, a science starting in midstream: it observed that men were producing and trading, it took for granted that they had always done so and always would—it accepted this fact as the given, requiring no further consideration—and it addressed itself to the problem of how to devise the best way for the "community" to dispose of human effort.

There were many reasons for this tribal view of man. The morality of altruism was one; the growing dominance of political statism among the intellectuals of the nineteenth century was another. Psychologically, the main reason was the soul-body dichotomy permeating European culture: material production was regarded as a demeaning task of a lower order, unrelated to the concerns of man's intellect, a task assigned to slaves or serfs since the beginning of recorded history. The institution of serfdom had lasted, in one form or another, till well into the nineteenth century; it was abolished, politically, only by the advent of capitalism; politically, but not intellectually.

The concept of man as a free, independent individual was profoundly alien to the culture of Europe. It was a tribal culture down to its roots; in European thinking, the tribe was the entity, the unit, and man was only one of its expendable cells. This applied to rulers and serfs alike: the rulers were believed to hold their privileges only by virtue of the services they rendered to the tribe, services regarded as of a noble order, namely, armed force or military defense. But a nobleman was as much chattel of the tribe as a serf: his life and property belonged to the king. It must be remembered that the institution of private property, in the full, legal meaning of the term, was brought into existence only by capitalism. In the precapitalist eras, private property existed *de facto*, but not *de jure*, i.e., by custom and sufferance, not by right or by law. In law and in principle, all property belonged to the head of the tribe, the king, and was held only by his permission, which could be revoked at any time, at his pleasure. (The king could and did expropriate the estates of recalcitrant noblemen throughout the course of Europe's history.)

The American philosophy of the Rights of Man was never grasped fully by European intellectuals. Europe's predominant idea of emancipation consisted of changing the concept of man as a slave of the absolute state embodied by a king, to the concept of man as a slave of the absolute state embodied by "the people"— i.e., switching from slavery to a tribal chief into slavery to the tribe. A nontribal view of existence could not penetrate the mentalities that regarded the privilege of ruling material producers by physical force as a badge of nobility.

Thus Europe's thinkers did not notice the fact that during the nineteenth century, the galley slaves had been replaced by the inventors of steamboats, and the village blacksmiths by the owners of blast furnaces, and they went on thinking in such terms (such contradictions in terms) as "wage slavery" or "the antisocial selfishness of industrialists who take so much from society without giving anything in return"—on the unchallenged axiom that wealth is an anonymous, social, tribal product.

That notion has not been challenged to this day; it represents the implicit assumption and the base of contemporary political economy.

As an example of this view and its consequences, I shall cite the article on "Capitalism" in the *Encyclopaedia Britannica*. The article gives no definition of its subject; it opens as follows:

> CAPITALISM, a term used to denote the economic system that has been dominant in the western world since the breakup of feudalism. Fundamental to any system called capitalist are the relations between private owners of nonpersonal means of production (land, mines, *industrial plants*, etc., collectively known as capital) [italics mine] and free but capitalless workers, who sell their labour services to employers. . . . The resulting wage bargains determine the proportion in which the total product of society will be shared between the class of labourers and the class of capitalist entrepreneurs.[1]

[1] *Encyclopaedia Britannica*, 1964, Vol. IV, pp. 839–845.

(I quote from Galt's speech in *Atlas Shrugged*, from a passage describing the tenets of collectivism: "An industrialist—blank-out —there is no such person. A factory is a 'natural resource,' like a tree, a rock, or a mud-puddle.")

The success of capitalism is explained by the *Britannica* as follows:

Productive use of the "social surplus" was the special virtue that enabled capitalism to outstrip all prior economic systems. Instead of building pyramids and cathedrals, those in command of the social surplus chose to invest in ships, warehouses, raw materials, finished goods and other material forms of wealth. The social surplus was thus converted into enlarged productive capacity.

This is said about a time when Europe's population subsisted in such poverty that child mortality approached fifty percent, and periodic famines wiped out the "surplus" *population* which the precapitalist economies were unable to feed. Yet, making no distinction between tax-expropriated and industrially produced wealth, the *Britannica* asserts that it was the *surplus wealth* of that time that the early capitalists "commanded" and "chose to invest"—and that this investment was the cause of the stupendous prosperity of the age that followed.

What is a "social surplus"? The article gives no definition or explanation. A "surplus" presupposes a norm; if subsistence on a chronic starvation level is above the implied norm, what is the norm? The article does not answer.

There is, of course, no such thing as a "social surplus." All wealth is produced by somebody and belongs to somebody. And "the special virtue that enabled capitalism to outstrip all prior economic systems" was *freedom* (a concept eloquently absent from the *Britannica*'s account), which led, not to the expropriation, but to the *creation* of wealth.

I shall have more to say later about that disgraceful article (disgraceful on many counts, not the least of which is scholarship). At this point, I quoted it only as a succinct example of the tribal premise that underlies today's political economy. That premise is shared by the enemies and the champions of capitalism alike; it provides the former with a certain inner consistency, and disarms the latter by a subtle, yet devastating aura of moral hypocrisy—as witness their attempts to justify capitalism on the ground of "the common good" or "service to the consumer" or "the best allocation of resources." (*Whose* resources?)

If capitalism is to be understood, it is this *tribal premise* that has to be checked—and challenged.

Mankind is not an entity, an organism, or a coral bush. The entity involved in production and trade is *man*. It is with the study of man—not of the loose aggregate known as a "community"—that any science of the humanities has to begin.

This issue represents one of the epistemological differences between the humanities and the physical sciences, one of the causes of the former's well-earned inferiority complex in regard to the latter. A physical science would not permit itself (not yet, at least) to ignore or bypass the nature of its subject. Such an attempt would mean: a science of astronomy that gazed at the sky, but refused to study individual stars, planets, and satellites—or a science of medicine that studied disease, without any knowledge or criterion of health, and took, as its basic subject of study, a hospital as a whole, never focusing on individual patients.

A great deal may be learned about society by studying man; but this process cannot be reversed: nothing can be learned about man by studying society—by studying the interrelationships of entities one has never identified or defined. Yet that is the methodology adopted by most political economists. Their attitude, in effect, amounts to the unstated, implicit postulate: "Man is that which fits economic equations." Since he obviously does not, this leads to the curious fact that in spite of the practical nature of their science, political economists are oddly unable to relate their abstractions to the concretes of actual existence.

It leads also to a baffling sort of double standard or double perspective in their way of viewing men and events: if they observe a shoemaker, they find no difficulty in concluding that he is working in order to make a living; but as political economists, on the tribal premise, they declare that his purpose (and duty) is to provide society with shoes. If they observe a panhandler on a street corner, they identify him as a bum; in political economy, he becomes "a sovereign consumer." If they hear the Communist doctrine that all property should belong to the state, they reject it emphatically and feel, *sincerely,* that they would fight Communism to the death; but in political economy, they speak of the government's duty to effect "a fair redistribution of wealth," and they speak of businessmen as the best, most efficient trustees of the nation's "natural resources."

This is what a basic premise (and philosophical negligence) will do; this is what the tribal premise has done.

To reject that premise and begin at the beginning—in one's approach to political economy and to the evaluation of various social systems—one must begin by identifying man's nature, i.e., those essential characteristics which distinguish him from all other living species.

Man's essential characteristic is his rational faculty. Man's mind is his basic means of survival—his only means of gaining knowledge.

> Man cannot survive, as animals do, by the guidance of mere percepts. . , . He cannot provide for his simplest physical needs without a process of thought. He needs a process of thought to discover how to plant and grow his food or how to make weapons for hunting. His percepts might lead him to a cave, if one is available—but to build the simplest shelter, he needs a process of thought. No percepts and no "instincts" will tell him how to light a fire, how to weave cloth, how to forge tools, how to make a wheel, how to make an airplane, how to perform an appendectomy, how to produce an electric light bulb or an electronic tube or a cyclotron or a box of matches. Yet his life depends on such knowledge—and only a volitional act of his consciousness, a process of thought, can provide it.[2]

A process of thought is an enormously complex process of identification and integration, which only an individual mind can perform. There is no such thing as a collective brain. Men can learn from one another, but learning requires a process of thought on the part of every individual student. Men can cooperate in the discovery of new knowledge, but such cooperation requires the independent exercise of his rational faculty by every individual scientist. Man is the only living species that can transmit and expand his store of knowledge from generation to generation; but such transmission requires a process of thought on the part of the individual recipients. As witness, the breakdowns of civilization, the dark ages in the history of mankind's progress, when the accumulated knowledge of centuries vanished from the lives of men who were unable, unwilling, or forbidden to think.

In order to sustain its life, every living species has to follow a certain course of action required by its nature. The action required to sustain human life is primarily intellectual: everything man needs has to be discovered by his mind and produced by his effort. Production is the application of reason to the problem of survival.

[2] Ayn Rand, "The Objectivist Ethics," in *The Virtue of Selfishness.*

If some men do not choose to think, they can survive only by imitating and repeating a routine of work discovered by others—but those others had to discover it, or none would have survived. If some men do not choose to think or to work, they can survive (temporarily) only by looting the goods produced by others—but those others had to produce them, or none would have survived. Regardless of what choice is made, in this issue, by any man or by any number of men, regardless of what blind, irrational, or evil course they may choose to pursue—the fact remains that reason is man's means of survival and that men prosper or fail, survive or perish in proportion to the degree of their rationality.

Since knowledge, thinking, and rational action are properties of the individual, since the choice to exercise his rational faculty or not depends on the individual, man's survival requires that those who think be free of the interference of those who don't. Since men are neither omniscient nor infallible, they must be free to agree or disagree, to cooperate or to pursue their own independent course, each according to his own rational judgment. Freedom is the fundamental requirement of man's mind.

A rational mind does not work under compulsion; it does not subordinate its grasp of reality to anyone's orders, directives, or controls; it does not sacrifice its knowledge, its view of the truth, to anyone's opinions, threats, wishes, plans, or "welfare." Such a mind may be hampered by others, it may be silenced, proscribed, imprisoned, or destroyed; it cannot be forced; a gun is not an argument. (An example and symbol of this attitude is Galileo.)

It is from the work and the inviolate integrity of such minds— from the intransigent innovators—that all of mankind's knowledge and achievements have come. (See *The Fountainhead*.) It is to such minds that mankind owes its survival. (See *Atlas Shrugged*.)

The same principle applies to all men, on every level of ability and ambition. To the extent that a man is guided by his rational judgment, he acts in accordance with the requirements of his nature and, to that extent, succeeds in achieving a human form of survival and well-being; to the extent that he acts irrationally, he acts as his own destroyer.

The social recognition of man's rational nature—of the connection between his survival and his use of reason—is the concept of *individual rights*.

I shall remind you that "rights" are a moral principle defining and sanctioning a man's freedom of action in a social context, that they are derived from man's nature as a rational being and represent a necessary condition of his particular mode of survival. I shall remind you also that the right to life is the source of all rights, including the right to property.[3]

In regard to political economy, this last requires special emphasis: man has to work and produce in order to support his life. He has to support his life by his own effort and by the guidance of his own mind. If he cannot dispose of the product of his effort, he cannot dispose of his effort; if he cannot dispose of his effort, he cannot dispose of his life. Without property rights, no other rights can be practiced.

Now, bearing these facts in mind, consider the question of what social system is appropriate to man.

A social system is a set of moral-political-economic principles embodied in a society's laws, institutions, and government, which determine the relationships, the terms of association, among the men living in a given geographical area. It is obvious that these terms and relationships depend on an identification of man's nature, that they would be different if they pertain to a society of rational beings or to a colony of ants. It is obvious that they will be radically different if men deal with one another as free, independent individuals, on the premise that every man is an end in himself—or as members of a pack, each regarding the others as the means to his ends and to the ends of "the pack as a whole."

There are only two fundamental questions (or two aspects of the same question) that determine the nature of any social system: Does a social system recognize individual rights?—and: Does a social system ban physical force from human relationships? The answer to the second question is the practical implementation of the answer to the first.

Is man a sovereign individual who owns his person, his mind, his life, his work and its products—or is he the property of the tribe (the state, the society, the collective) that may dispose of him in any way it pleases, that may dictate his convictions, prescribe the course of his life, control his work, and expropriate his products? Does man have the right to exist for his own sake—or is he born in bondage, as an indentured servant who must keep buying his life by serving the tribe but can never acquire it free and clear?

This is the first question to answer. The rest is consequences

[3] For a fuller discussion of rights, I refer you to my articles "Man's Rights" in the Appendix to *Capitalism: The Unknown Ideal*, and "Collectivized 'Rights' " in *The Virtue of Selfishness*.

and practical implementations. The basic issue is only: Is man free?

In mankind's history, capitalism is the only system that answers: Yes.

Capitalism is a social system based on the recognition of individual rights, including property rights, in which all property is privately owned.

The recognition of individual rights entails the banishment of physical force from human relationships: basically, rights can be violated only by means of force. In a capitalist society, no man or group may *initiate* the use of physical force against others. The only function of the government, in such a society, is the task of protecting man's rights, i.e., the task of protecting him from physical force; the government acts as the agent of man's right of self-defense, and may use force only in retaliation and only against those who initiate its use; thus the government is the means of placing the retaliatory use of force under *objective control.*[4]

It is the basic, metaphysical fact of man's nature—the connection between his survival and his use of reason—that capitalism recognizes and protects.

In a capitalist society, all human relationships are *voluntary.* Men are free to cooperate or not, to deal with one another or not, as their own individual judgments, convictions, and interests dictate. They can deal with one another only in terms of and by means of reason, i.e., by means of discussion, persuasion, and *contractual* agreement, by voluntary choice to mutual benefit. The right to agree with others is not a problem in any society; it is *the right to disagree* that is crucial. It is the institution of private property that protects and implements the right to disagree—and thus keeps the road open to man's most valuable attribute (valuable personally, socially, and *objectively*): the creative mind.

This is the cardinal difference between capitalism and collectivism.

The power that determines the establishment, the changes, the evolution, and the destruction of social systems is philosophy. The role of chance, accident, or tradition, in this context, is the same as their role in the life of an individual: their power stands in inverse ratio to the power of a culture's (or an individual's) philosophical equipment, and grows as philosophy collapses. It is, therefore, by reference to philosophy that the character of a

[4] For a fuller discussion of this subject, see my article "The Nature of Government" in the Appendix to *Capitalism: The Unknown Ideal.*

social system has to be defined and evaluated. Corresponding to the four branches of philosophy, the four keystones of capitalism are: metaphysically, the requirements of man's nature and survival; epistemologically, reason; ethically, individual rights; politically, freedom.

This, in substance, is the base of the proper approach to political economy and to an understanding of capitalism—not the tribal premise inherited from prehistorical traditions.

The "practical" justification of capitalism does not lie in the collectivist claim that it effects "the best allocation of national resources." Man is not a "national resource" and neither is his mind—and without the creative power of man's intelligence, raw materials remain just so many useless raw materials.

The *moral* justification of capitalism does not lie in the altruist claim that it represents the best way to achieve "the common good." It is true that capitalism does—if that catch-phrase has any meaning—but this is merely a secondary consequence. The moral justification of capitalism lies in the fact that it is the only system consonant with man's rational nature, that it protects man's survival *qua* man, and that its ruling principle is: *justice.*

Every social system is based, explicitly or implicitly, on some theory of ethics. The tribal notion of "the common good" has served as the moral justification of most social systems—and of all tyrannies—in history. The degree of a society's enslavement or freedom corresponded to the degree to which that tribal slogan was invoked or ignored.

"The common good" (or "the public interest") is an undefined and undefinable concept: there is no such entity as "the tribe" or "the public"; the tribe (or the public or society) is only a number of individual men. Nothing can be good for the tribe as such; "good" and "value" pertain *only* to a living organism—to an individual living organism—not to a disembodied aggregate of relationships.

"The common good" is a meaningless concept, unless taken literally, in which case its only possible meaning is: the sum of the good of *all* the individual men involved. But in that case, the concept is meaningless as a moral criterion: it leaves open the question of what *is* the good of individual men and how does one determine it?

It is not, however, in its literal meaning that that concept is generally used. It is accepted precisely for its elastic, undefinable, mystical character, which serves, not as a moral guide, but as an escape from morality. Since the good is not applicable to the disembodied, it becomes a moral blank check for those who attempt to embody it.

When "the common good" of a society is regarded as something apart from and superior to the individual good of its members, it means that the good of some men takes precedence over the good of others, with those others consigned to the status of sacrificial animals. It is tacitly assumed, in such cases, that "the common good" means "the good of the majority" as against the minority or the individual. Observe the significant fact that that assumption is tacit: even the most collectivized mentalities seem to sense the impossibility of justifying it morally. But "the good of the majority," too, is only a pretense and a delusion: since, in fact, the violation of an individual's rights means the abrogation of all rights, it delivers the helpless majority into the power of any gang that proclaims itself to be "the voice of society" and proceeds to rule by means of physical force, until deposed by another gang employing the same means.

If one begins by defining the good of individual men, one will accept as proper only a society in which that good is achieved and achievable. But if one begins by accepting "the common good" as an axiom and regarding individual good as its possible but not necessary consequence (not necessary in any particular case), one ends up with such a gruesome absurdity as Soviet Russia, a country professedly dedicated to "the common good," where, with the exception of a minuscule clique of rulers, the entire population has existed in subhuman misery for over two generations.

What makes the victims and, worse, the observers accept this and other similar historical atrocities, and still cling to the myth of "the common good"? The answer lies in philosophy—in philosophical theories on the nature of moral values.

There are, in essence, three schools of thought on the nature of the good: the intrinsic, the subjective, and the objective. The intrinsic theory holds that the good is inherent in certain things or actions as such, regardless of their context and consequences, regardless of any benefit or injury they may cause to the actors and subjects involved. It is a theory that divorces the concept of "good" from beneficiaries, and the concept of "value" from valuer and purpose—claiming that the good is good in, by, and of itself.

The subjectivist theory holds that the good bears no relation to the facts of reality, that it is the product of a man's consciousness, created by his feelings, desires, "intuitions," or whims, and that it is merely an "arbitrary postulate" or an "emotional commitment."

The intrinsic theory holds that the good resides in some sort of reality, independent of man's consciousness; the subjectivist theory holds that the good resides in man's consciousness, independent of reality.

The *objective* theory holds that the good is neither an attribute of "things in themselves" nor of man's emotional states, but *an evaluation* of the facts of reality by man's consciousness according to a rational standard of value. (Rational, in this context, means: derived from the facts of reality and validated by a process of reason.) The objective theory holds that *the good is an aspect of reality in relation to man*—and that it must be discovered, not invented, by man. Fundamental to an objective theory of values is the question: Of value to whom and for what? An objective theory does not permit context-dropping or "concept-stealing"; it does not permit the separation of "value" from "purpose," of the good from beneficiaries, and of man's actions from reason.

Of all the social systems in mankind's history, *capitalism is the only system based on an objective theory of values.*

The intrinsic theory and the subjectivist theory (or a mixture of both) are the necessary base of every dictatorship, tyranny, or variant of the absolute state. Whether they are held consciously or subconsciously—in the explicit form of a philosopher's treatise or in the implicit chaos of its echoes in an average man's feelings—these theories make it possible for a man to believe that the good is independent of man's mind and can be achieved by physical force.

If a man believes that the good is intrinsic in certain actions, he will not hesitate to force others to perform them. If he believes that the human benefit or injury caused by such actions is of no significance, he will regard a sea of blood as of no significance. If he believes that the beneficiaries of such actions are irrelevant (or interchangeable), he will regard wholesale slaughter as his moral duty in the service of a "higher" good. It is the intrinsic theory of values that produces a Robespierre, a Lenin, a Stalin, or a Hitler. It is not an accident that Eichmann was a Kantian.

If a man believes that the good is a matter of arbitrary, subjective choice, the issue of good or evil becomes, for him, an issue of: *my* feelings or *theirs?* No bridge, understanding, or communication is possible to him. Reason is the only means of communication among men, and an objectively perceivable reality is their only common frame of reference; when these are invalidated (i.e., held to be irrelevant) in the field of morality, force becomes men's only way of dealing with one another. If the subjectivist wants to pursue some social ideal of his own, he feels morally entitled to force men "for their own good," since he *feels* that he is right and that there is nothing to oppose him but their misguided feelings.

Thus, in practice, the proponents of the intrinsic and the subjectivist schools meet and blend. (They blend in terms of their psycho-epistemology as well: by what means do the moralists of the intrinsic school discover their transcendental "good," if not by means of special, nonrational intuitions and revelations, i.e., by means of their feelings?) It is doubtful whether anyone can hold either of these theories as an actual, if mistaken, conviction. But both serve as a rationalization of power-lust and of rule by brute force, unleashing the potential dictator and disarming his victims.

The objective theory of values is the only moral theory incompatible with rule by force. Capitalism is the only system based implicitly on an objective theory of values—and the historic tragedy is that this has never been made explicit.

If one knows that the good is *objective*—i.e., determined by the nature of reality, but to be discovered by man's mind—one knows that an attempt to achieve the good by physical force is a monstrous contradiction which negates morality at its root by destroying man's capacity to recognize the good, i.e., his capacity to value. Force invalidates and paralyzes a man's judgment, demanding that he act against it, thus rendering him morally impotent. A value which one is forced to accept at the price of surrendering one's mind, is not a value to anyone; the forcibly mindless can neither judge nor choose nor value. An attempt to achieve the good by force is like an attempt to provide a man with a picture gallery at the price of cutting out his eyes. Values cannot exist (cannot be valued) outside the full context of a man's life, needs, goals, and *knowledge*.

The objective view of values permeates the entire structure of a capitalist society.

The recognition of individual rights implies the recognition of the fact that the good is not an ineffable abstraction in some supernatural dimension, but a value pertaining to reality, to this earth, to the lives of individual human beings (note the right to the pursuit of happiness). It implies that the good cannot be divorced from beneficiaries, that men are not to be regarded as interchangeable, and that no man or tribe may attempt to achieve the good of some at the price of the immolation of others.

94

The free market represents the *social* application of an objective theory of values. Since values are to be discovered by man's mind, men must be free to discover them—to think, to study, to translate their knowledge into physical form, to offer their products for trade, to judge them, and to choose, be it material goods or ideas, a loaf of bread or a philosophical treatise. Since values are established contextually, every man must judge for himself, in the context of his own knowledge, goals, and interests. Since values are determined by the nature of reality, it is reality that serves as men's ultimate arbiter: if a man's judgment is right, the rewards are his; if it is wrong, he is his only victim.

It is in regard to a free market that the distinction between an intrinsic, subjective, and objective view of values is particularly important to understand. The market value of a product is *not* an intrinsic value, not a "value in itself" hanging in a vacuum. A free market never loses sight of the question: Of value *to whom?* And, within the broad field of objectivity, the market value of a product does not reflect its *philosophically objective* value, but only its *socially objective* value.

By "philosophically objective," I mean a value estimated from the standpoint of the best possible to man, i.e., by the criterion of the most rational mind possessing the greatest knowledge, in a given category, in a given period, and in a defined context (nothing can be estimated in an undefined context). For instance, it can be rationally proved that the airplane is *objectively* of immeasurably greater value to man (to *man at his best*) than the bicycle— and that the works of Victor Hugo are *objectively* of immeasurably greater value than true-confession magazines. But if a given man's intellectual potential can barely manage to enjoy true confessions, there is no reason why his meager earnings, the product of *his* effort, should be spent on books he cannot read—or on subsidizing the airplane industry, if his own transportation needs do not extend beyond the range of a bicycle. (Nor is there any reason why the rest of mankind should be held down to the level of his literary taste, his engineering capacity, and his income. Values are not determined by fiat nor by majority vote.)

Just as the number of its adherents is not a proof of an idea's truth or falsehood, of an art work's merit or demerit, of a product's efficacy or inefficacy—so the free-market value of goods or services does not necessarily represent their philosophically objective value, but only their *socially objective* value, i.e., the sum of the individual judgments of all the men involved in trade at a given time, the sum of what *they* valued, each in the context of his own life.

Thus, a manufacturer of lipstick may well make a greater fortune than a manufacturer of microscopes—even though it can be rationally demonstrated that microscopes are scientifically more valuable than lipstick. But—valuable *to whom?*

A microscope is of no value to a little stenographer struggling to make a living; a lipstick is; a lipstick, to her, may mean the difference between self-confidence and self-doubt, between glamour and drudgery.

This does not mean, however, that the values ruling a free market are *subjective*. If the stenographer spends all her money on cosmetics and has none left to pay for the use of a microscope (for a visit to the doctor) *when she needs it,* she learns a better method of budgeting her income; the free market serves as her teacher: she has no way to penalize others for her mistakes. If she budgets rationally, the microscope is always available to serve her own specific needs *and no more,* as far as she is concerned: she is not taxed to support an entire hospital, a research laboratory, or a space ship's journey to the moon. Within her own productive power, she does pay a part of the cost of scientific achievements, *when and as she needs them.* She has no "social duty," her own life is her only responsibility—and the only thing that a capitalist system requires of her is the thing that *nature* requires: rationality, i.e., that she live and act to the best of her own judgment.

Within every category of goods and services offered on a free market, it is the purveyor of the best product at the cheapest price who wins the greatest financial rewards *in that field*—not automatically nor immediately nor by fiat, but by virtue of the free market, which teaches every participant to look for the *objective* best within the category of his own competence, and penalizes those who act on irrational considerations.

Now observe that a free market does not level men down to some common denominator—that the intellectual criteria of the majority do not rule a free market or a free society—and that the exceptional men, the innovators, the intellectual giants, are not held down by the majority. In fact, it is the members of this exceptional minority who lift the whole of a free society to the level of their own achievements, while rising further and ever further.

A free market is a *continuous process* that cannot be held still, an upward process that demands the best (the most rational) of every man and rewards him accordingly. While the majority have barely assimilated the value of the automobile, the creative minority introduces the airplane. The majority learn by demonstration, the minority is free to demonstrate. The "philosophically objective" value of a new product serves as the teacher for those who are willing to exercise their rational faculty, each to the extent of his ability. Those who are unwilling remain unrewarded—as well as those who aspire to more than their ability produces. The stagnant, the irrational, the subjectivist have no power to stop their betters.

(The small minority of adults who are *unable* rather than unwilling to work have to rely on voluntary charity; misfortune is not a claim to slave labor; there is no such thing as the *right* to consume, control, and destroy those without whom one would be unable to survive. As to depressions and mass unemployment, they are not caused by the free market, but by government interference into the economy.)

The mental parasites—the imitators who attempt to cater to what they think is the public's known taste—are constantly being beaten by the innovators whose products raise the public's knowledge and taste to ever higher levels. It is in this sense that the free market is ruled, not by the consumers, but by the producers. The most successful ones are those who discover new fields of production, fields which had not been known to exist.

A given product may not be appreciated at once, particularly if it is too radical an innovation; but, barring irrelevant accidents, it wins in the long run. It is in this sense that the free market is not ruled by the intellectual criteria of the majority, which prevail only at and for any given moment; the free market is ruled by those who are able to see and plan long-range—and the better the mind, the longer the range.

The economic value of a man's work is determined, on a free market, by a single principle: by the voluntary consent of those who are willing to trade him their work or products in return. This is the moral meaning of the law of supply and demand; it represents the total rejection of two vicious doctrines: the tribal premise and altruism. It represents the recognition of the fact that man is not the property nor the servant of the tribe, that *a man works in order to support his own life*—as, by his nature, he must —that he has to be guided by his own rational self-interest, and if he wants to trade with others, he cannot expect sacrificial victims, i.e., he cannot expect to receive values without trading commensurate values in return. The sole criterion of what is commensurate, in this context, is the free, voluntary, uncoerced judgment of the traders.

The tribal mentalities attack this principle from two seemingly opposite sides: they claim that the free market is "unfair" both to the genius and to the average man. The first objection is usually expressed by a question such as: "Why should Elvis Presley make more money than Einstein?" The answer is: Because men work in order to support and enjoy their own lives—and if many men find value in Elvis Presley, they are entitled to spend their money on their own pleasure. Presley's fortune is not taken from those who do not care for his work (I am one of them) nor from Einstein—nor does he stand in Einstein's way—nor does Einstein lack proper recognition and support in a free society, on an appropriate intellectual level.

As to the second objection, the claim that a man of average ability suffers an "unfair" disadvantage on a free market—

Look past the range of the moment, you who cry that you fear to compete with men of superior intelligence, that their mind is a threat to your livelihood, that the strong leave no chance to the weak in a market of voluntary trade. . . . When you live in a rational society, where men are free to trade, you receive an incalculable bonus: the material value of your work is determined not only by your effort, but by the effort of the best productive minds who exist in the world around you. . . .

The machine, the frozen form of a living intelligence, is the power that expands the potential of your life by raising the productivity of your time. . . . Every man is free to rise as far as he's able or willing, but it's only the degree to which he thinks that determines the degree to which he'll rise. Physical labor as such can extend no further than the range of the moment. The man who does no more than physical labor consumes the material value-equivalent of his own contribution to the process of production, and leaves no further value, neither for himself nor others. But the man who produces an idea in any field of rational endeavor—the man who discovers new knowledge—is the permanent benefactor of humanity. . . . It is only the value of an idea that can be shared with unlimited numbers of men, making all sharers richer at no one's sacrifice or loss, raising the productive capacity of whatever labor they perform. . . .

In proportion to the mental energy he spent, the man who creates a new invention receives but a small percentage of his value in terms of material payment, no matter what fortune he makes, no matter what millions he earns. But the man who works as a janitor in the factory producing that invention receives an enormous payment in proportion to the mental effort that his job requires of *him*. And the

98

same is true of all men between, on all levels of ambition and ability. The man at the top of the intellectual pyramid contributes the most to all those below him, but gets nothing except his material payment, receiving no intellectual bonus from others to add to the value of his time. The man at the bottom who, left to himself, would starve in his hopeless ineptitude, contributes nothing to those above him, but receives the bonus of all of their brains. Such is the nature of the "competition" between the strong and the weak of the intellect. Such is the pattern of "exploitation" for which you have damned the strong. [*Atlas Shrugged*]

And such is the relationship of capitalism to man's mind and to man's survival.

The magnificent progress achieved by capitalism in a brief span of time—the spectacular improvement in the conditions of man's existence on earth—is a matter of historical record. It is not to be hidden, evaded, or explained away by all the propaganda of capitalism's enemies. But what needs special emphasis is the fact that this progress was achieved by *nonsacrificial* means.

Progress cannot be achieved by forced privations, by squeezing a "social surplus" out of starving victims. Progress can come only out of *individual surplus*, i.e., from the work, the energy, the creative overabundance of those men whose ability produces more than their personal consumption requires, those who are intellectually and financially able to seek the new, to improve on the known, to move forward. In a capitalist society, where such men are free to function and to take their own risks, progress is not a matter of sacrificing to some distant future, it is part of the living present, it is the normal and natural, it is achieved as and while men live—and *enjoy*—their lives.

Now consider the alternative—the tribal society, where all men throw their efforts, values, ambitions, and goals into a tribal pool or common pot, then wait hungrily at its rim, while the leader of a clique of cooks stirs it with a bayonet in one hand and a blank check on all their lives in the other. The most consistent example of such a system is the Union of Soviet Socialist Republics.

Half a century ago, the Soviet rulers commanded their subjects to be patient, bear privations, and make sacrifices for the sake of "industrializing" the country, promising that this was only temporary, that industrialization would bring them abundance, and Soviet progress would surpass the capitalistic West.

Today, Soviet Russia is still unable to feed her people—while the rulers scramble to copy, borrow, or steal the technological achievements of the West. Industrialization is not a static goal; it is a dynamic process with a rapid rate of obsolescence. So the wretched serfs of a planned tribal economy, who starved while waiting for electric generators and tractors, are now starving while waiting for atomic power and interplanetary travel. Thus, in a "people's state," the progress of science is a threat to the people, and every advance is taken out of the people's shrinking hides.

This was not the history of capitalism.

America's abundance was not created by public sacrifices to "the common good," but by the productive genius of free men who pursued their own personal interests and the making of their own private fortunes. They did not starve the people to pay for America's industrialization. They gave the people better jobs, higher wages, and cheaper goods with every new machine they invented, with every scientific discovery or technological advance —and thus the whole country was moving forward and profiting, not suffering, every step of the way.

Do not, however, make the error of reversing cause and effect: the good of the country was made possible precisely by the fact that it was not forced on anyone as a moral goal or duty; it was merely an effect; the cause was a man's right to pursue his own good. It is this right—not its consequences—that represents the moral justification of capitalism.

But this right is incompatible with the intrinsic or the subjectivist theory of values, with the altruist morality and the tribal premise. It is obvious which human attribute one rejects when one rejects objectivity; and, in view of capitalism's record, it is obvious against which human attribute the altruist morality and the tribal premise stand united: against man's mind, against intelligence—particularly against intelligence applied to the problems of human survival, i.e., productive ability.

While altruism seeks to rob intelligence of its rewards, by asserting that the moral duty of the competent is to serve the incompetent and sacrifice themselves to anyone's need—the tribal premise goes a step further: it denies the existence of intelligence and of its role in the production of wealth.

It is morally obscene to regard wealth as an anonymous, tribal product and to talk about "redistributing" it. The view that wealth is the result of some undifferentiated, collective process, that we all did something and it's impossible to tell who did what, therefore some sort of equalitarian "distribution" is necessary—might have been appropriate in a primordial jungle with a savage horde moving boulders by crude physical labor (though even there someone had to initiate and organize the moving). To hold that view in an industrial society—where individual achievements are a matter of public record—is so crass an evasion that even to give it the benefit of the doubt is an obscenity.

Anyone who has ever been an employer or an employee, or has observed men working, or has done an honest day's work himself, knows the crucial role of ability, of intelligence, of a focused, competent mind—in any and all lines of work, from the lowest to the highest. He knows that ability or the lack of it (whether the lack is actual or volitional) makes a difference of life-or-death in any productive process. The evidence is so overwhelming—theoretically and practically, logically and "empirically," in the events of history and in anyone's own daily grind—that no one can claim ignorance of it. Mistakes of this size are not made innocently.

When great industrialists made fortunes on a *free* market (i.e., without the use of force, without government assistance or interference), they *created* new wealth—they did not take it from those who had *not* created it. If you doubt it, take a look at the "total social product"—and the standard of living—of those countries where such men are not permitted to exist.

Observe how seldom and how inadequately the issue of human intelligence is discussed in the writings of the tribal-statist-altruist theoreticians. Observe how carefully today's advocates of a mixed economy avoid and evade any mention of intelligence or ability in their approach to politico-economic issues, in their claims, demands, and pressure-group warfare over the looting of "the total social product."

It is often asked: Why was capitalism destroyed in spite of its incomparably beneficent record? The answer lies in the fact that the lifeline feeding any social system is a culture's dominant philosophy and that capitalism never had a philosophical base. It was the last and (theoretically) incomplete product of an Aristotelian influence. As a resurgent tide of mysticism engulfed philosophy in the nineteenth century, capitalism was left in an intellectual vacuum, its lifeline cut. Neither its moral nature nor even its political principles had ever been fully understood or defined. Its alleged defenders regarded it as compatible with government controls (i.e., government interference into the economy), ignoring the meaning and implications of the concept of laissez-faire. Thus, what existed in practice, in the nineteenth century, was not pure capitalism, but variously mixed economies. Since controls necessitate and breed further controls, it was the statist element of the mixtures that wrecked them; it was the free, capitalist element that took the blame.

Capitalism could not survive in a culture dominated by mysticism and altruism, by the soul-body dichotomy and the tribal premise. No social system (and no human institution or activity of any kind) can survive without a moral base. On the basis of the altruist morality, capitalism had to be—and was—damned from the start.[5]

For those who do not fully understand the role of philosophy in politico-economic issues, I offer—as the clearest example of today's intellectual state—some further quotations from the *Encyclopaedia Britannica's* article on capitalism.

> Few observers are inclined to find fault with capitalism as an engine of production. Criticism usually proceeds either from *moral* or *cultural* disapproval of certain features of the capitalist system, or from the short-run vicissitudes (crises and depressions) with which long-run improvement is interspersed. [Italics mine.]

The "crises and depressions" were caused by government interference, not by the capitalist system. But what was the nature of the "moral or cultural disapproval"? The article does not tell us explicitly, but gives one eloquent indication:

> Such as they were, however, both tendencies and realizations [of capitalism] bear the unmistakable stamp of the businessman's interests and still more the businessman's type of mind. Moreover it was not only policy but the philosophy of national and individual life, the scheme of cultural values, that bore that stamp. Its materialistic utilitarianism, its naive confidence in progress of a certain type, its actual achievements in the field of pure and applied science, the temper of its artistic creations, may all be traced to *the spirit of rationalism* that emanates from the businessman's office. [Italics mine.]

The author of the article, who is not "naive" enough to believe in a capitalistic (or *rational*) type of progress, holds, apparently, a different belief:

> At the end of the middle ages western Europe stood about where many underdeveloped countries stand in the 20th century. [This means that the culture of the Renaissance was about the equivalent of today's Congo; or else, it means that people's intellectual develop-

---

[5] For a discussion of the philosophers' default in regard to capitalism, see the title essay in my book *For the New Intellectual.*

ment has nothing to do with economics.] In underdeveloped economies the difficult task of statesmanship is to get under way a cumulative process of economic development, for once a certain momentum is attained, further advances appear to follow more or less automatically.

Some such notion underlies every theory of a planned economy. It is on some such "sophisticated" belief that two generations of Russians have perished, waiting for *automatic* progress.

The classical economists attempted a tribal justification of capitalism on the ground that it provides the best "allocation" of a community's "resources." Here are their chickens coming home to roost:

> The market theory of resource allocation within the private sector is the central theme of classical economics. The criterion for allocation between the public and private sectors is formally the same as in any other resource allocation, namely that the community should receive equal satisfaction from a marginal increment of resources used in the public and private spheres. . . . Many economists have asserted that there is substantial, perhaps overwhelming, evidence that total welfare in capitalist United States, for example, would be increased by a reallocation of resources to the public sector—more schoolrooms and fewer shopping centers, more public libraries and fewer automobiles, more hospitals and fewer bowling alleys.

This means that some men must toil all their lives without adequate transportation (automobiles), without an adequate number of places to buy the goods they need (shopping centers), without the pleasures of relaxation (bowling alleys)—in order that other men may be provided with schools, libraries, and hospitals.

If you want to see the ultimate results and full meaning of the tribal view of wealth—the total obliteration of the distinction between private action and government action, between production and force, the total obliteration of the concept of "rights," of an individual human being's reality, and its replacement by a view of men as interchangeable beasts of burden or "factors of production"—study the following:

> Capitalism has a bias against the public sector for two reasons. First, all products and income accrue [?] initially to the private sector while resources reach the public sector through the painful process of taxation. Public needs are met only by sufferance of consumers in their role as taxpayers [what about *producers*?], whose political representatives are acutely conscious of their constituents' tender feelings [!] about taxation. That people know better than governments what

103

to do with their income is a notion more appealing than the contrary one, that people get more for their tax money than for other types of spending. [By what theory of values? By whose judgment?] . . .

Second, the pressure of private business to sell leads to the formidable array of devices of modern salesmanship which influence consumer choice and bias consumer values toward private consumption . . . [This means that your desire to spend the money you earn rather than have it taken away from you, is a mere *bias*.] Hence, much private expenditure goes for wants that are not very urgent in any fundamental sense. [Urgent—to whom? Which wants are "fundamental," beyond a cave, a bearskin, and a chunk of raw meat?] The corollary is that many public needs are neglected because these superficial private wants, artificially generated, compete successfully for the same resources. [*Whose* resources?] . . .

A comparison of resource allocation to the public and private sectors under capitalism and under socialist collectivism is illuminating. [It is.] In a collective economy all resources operate in the public sector and are available for education, defense, health, welfare, and other public needs without any transfer through taxation. Private consumption is restricted to the claims that are *permitted* [by whom?] against the *social product*, much as public services in a capitalist economy are limited to the claims permitted against the private sector. [Italics mine.] In a collective economy public needs enjoy the same sort of built-in priority that private consumption enjoys in a capitalist economy. In the Soviet Union teachers are plentiful, but automobiles are scarce, whereas the opposite condition prevails in the United States.

Here is the conclusion of that article:

Predictions concerning the survival of capitalism are, in part, a matter of definition. One sees everywhere in capitalist countries a shifting of economic activity from the private to the public sphere. . . . At the same time [after World War II] private consumption appeared destined to increase in communist countries. [Such as the consumption of wheat?] The two economic systems seemed to be drawing closer together by changes converging from both directions. Yet significant differences in the economic structures still existed. It seemed reasonable to assume that the society which invested more in people would advance more rapidly and inherit the future. In this important respect capitalism, in the eyes of some economists, labours under a fundamental but not inescapable disadvantage in competition with collectivism.

The collectivization of Soviet agriculture was achieved by means of a government-planned famine—planned and carried out deliberately to force peasants into collective farms; Soviet Russia's enemies claim that fifteen million peasants died in that famine; the Soviet government admits the death of seven million.

At the end of World War II, Soviet Russia's enemies claimed that thirty million people were doing forced labor in Soviet concentration camps (and were dying of planned malnutrition, human lives being cheaper than food); Soviet Russia's apologists admit to the figure of twelve million people.

This is what the *Encyclopaedia Britannica* refers to as "investment in people."

In a culture where such a statement is made with intellectual impunity and with an aura of moral righteousness, the guiltiest men are not the collectivists; the guiltiest men are those who, lacking the courage to challenge mysticism or altruism, attempt to bypass the issues of reason and morality and to defend the only rational and moral system in mankind's history—capitalism—on any grounds other than rational and moral.

AMERICAN CAPITALISM

John Chamberlain

from THE ROOTS OF CAPITALISM (1968)

Capitalism presupposes an open society in which the ends are determined by individuals, or by voluntary associations of individuals. It is fundamentally incompatible with the idea of an all-encompassing state purpose, or a single official Manifest Destiny —though it is thoroughly compatible with a church whose own purposes are extragovernmental, either "not of this world" or, if of this world, devoted to leadership, mediation, and charity in the realms which do not belong to Caesar.

Theoretically, of course, it is quite conceivable that capitalism could flourish without a legal framework, either under pure anarchism, or under a beneficent landlordism, or with the blessings of a "let alone" monarch. But, as we shall see, it was James Madison, the scholar among the Founding Fathers, who put his finger unerringly on the need for a device which will put automatic checks on government if any freedoms are to flourish. Purely as a practical matter the institutions of an open society demand the safeguards of a limited government.

This is not to say that limited government is the *cause* of capitalism, or that it is the superstructure, either. It is merely to say that freedom is all of a piece. Government is necessary, for men, in Madison's phrase, are not angels. But since non-angelic men inevitably become the governors as well as the governed, the liberties of the individual, including the liberty to own, buy, and sell, must be protected from the possible cupidity, rapacity, and power-lust of officeholders. Capitalism, like any other manifestation of free choice, depends on the ability of a people to discover a political device, or a frame, which, in Professor John W. Burgess's famous phrase, will reconcile government with liberty.

To debate whether capitalism came before or after free government is a hen-egg proposition which can only lead to much scrambled history. All we can say for certain is that capitalism—the free application of energy and property to the making of things for trade in the open market—will grow wherever there is a cranny or a chink in a "planned" or controlled system. Once fairly started, it tends to eventuate in limited government. Venice, the dominant Mediterranean trading community of the later Middle Ages, was a republic. The free cities of northern Italy and the Hanseatic League operated outside of the lord-and-vassal relational pattern of feudalism, and the feudality was resisted whenever it tried to come inside the city gates. Conversely, when the Roman Republic became the Empire, and the Empire, in turn, started monkeying with fixed prices and a controlled bread-and-circuses economy, the decline came fast. And when the intendants of the French Bourbons tried to consolidate all decision-making, even to the extent of prescribing minutely for the operations of the textile trade, within the reach of government, the great explosion of 1789 was foreshadowed.

It was to get away from the all-encompassing purpose of king or dictator that colonists of all kinds fled to America. Dimly, they were all seeking the delineation of some realm of individual immunity against governmental power. The Pilgrims and early Puritans came to the shores of Massachusetts Bay to escape the this-worldly aegis of Archbishop Laud, who believed that state and church were the divinely ordained coextensive planners for society or the community. The Quakers journeyed to Penn's Woods on the Delaware because the inner light of their devotions clashed with the outer light of the court. As for the Cavaliers, they, too, were immunity-seekers once their Stuart patrons were in exile. They flocked to the southern colonies because, in John Milton's own phrase, the Cromwellian presbyter turned out to be "old priest writ large."

It is hardly to be denied that many of the newcomers to America backslid, some of them immediately. Their ideas of the proper boundaries of individual immunity frequently clashed. Some of them set up stringent this-worldly theocracies, persecuting the

107

dissenter, the Quaker, the agnostic, or the witch. When the lamp of resolution burned low, they acquiesced in arbitrary rule by colonial governors sent over from England to keep a stern hand on the controls. Nevertheless, despite the backsliding and the cross-purposes, the yeast of voluntary planning and individual choice was at work. America was becoming an open society, not a mere extension of a European state. In the course of a very few generations Puritan and Quaker and Cavalier—yes, and the indentured servants imported by all three—tended to coalesce, accepting the great home-country reconciliation that began with the Restoration of the Stuarts and continued with the Glorious Revolution of 1688, which made limited government its *sine qua non*.

We have seen that the colonists were the heirs of the thinking of John Locke, the philosopher of inalienable rights. But Locke, after all, was sophisticated stuff: his treatises on toleration and civil government were for the self-chosen leaders of the rebellion against George III. Since there were no Gallup polls at the time it is impossible to know how many colonists actually read Locke save as he happened to be "brokered" for the multitudes by popular pamphleteers. Of one thing, however, we may be sure: colonists of all sorts read the Bible.

As Rose Wilder Lane has pointed out, many of the colonists were children of men and women who had actually risked their necks to interpret the Scriptures for themselves. These sons and daughters of the Dissent didn't read the Bible as a substitute for Aristotle on Politics; they were thinking about their immortal souls. But what they imbibed, often unconsciously, was heady political stuff. They read about the God of the shepherd Abraham —a Single God who judged a man's rightness in living but made no attempt to force His say on human beings. Man, in the Old Testament, was left to control himself. The Ten Commandments of the God of Abraham were largely negatives: they told man what he should not do. But the negatives presupposed a positive creed.

Charles A. Beard, among others, has emphasized the continuity of Locke's thinking with that of Thomas Hooker, who, in turn, drew upon Thomas Aquinas. But one needs no paraphernalia of scholarship to know that the Commandment against murder is simply the other face of Locke's and Jefferson's "unalienable" right to life. "Thou shalt not steal" means that the Bible countenances private property—for if a thing is not owned in the first place it can scarcely be stolen. "Thou shalt not covet" means that it is sinful even to contemplate the seizure of another man's goods

—which is something which socialists, whether Christian or otherwise, have never managed to explain away. Furthermore, the prohibitions against false witness and adultery mean that contracts should be honored and double-dealing eschewed. As for the Commandment to "honor thy father and they mother that thy days may be long," this implies that the family, not the state, is the basic continuing unit and constitutive element of society.

By extension, or deduction, the Lockean creed is all here: the right to life, the right to the liberty and property necessary to sustain life, and the importance of the free family units as the guarantor, through its love and possessions, of "long" days in the land given by the Lord.

The Bible-reading colonists, then, had no actual need for the sophistications of late seventeenth-century political science. They were the children of antiquity, heirs to the oldest wisdom known to western man. The minds which they brought to the New World were no *tabula rasa*: the slate was colored by a tradition which antedated the medieval world by centuries. Even those Deists, the Jeffersonians, who thought of God as a vaguely impersonal Creator, derived their ideas of "natural law" from sources which had been approved by believers in a personal God throughout the ages.

But if the colonists brought with them a tradition, they had managed to shed all those social incrustations of the medieval world—the master-serf relationships of feudalism and a land-owning system made static by the device of entailing estates—which had almost caused the tradition to founder. In America there were no incrustations. There was merely an open world. Thus, though many of the colonists were hemmed in at first by the restrictions of Calvinism and its lip-service belief in the predestination of "God's elect," they were in a position to apply the Mosaic—or the Lockean—law *de novo*. They were not *compelled* men. Bound by no master plan, they moved outward from their individual freehold farms to meet their brothers in the marketplace—and capitalism, in its most primitive phases, was the natural result.

In recent years Professor R. H. Tawney (see his *Religion and the Rise of Capitalism*) has tried, at least by implication, to make it appear that capitalism was a mere by-product of the weakening of religious ties, an offshoot of the this-worldly aspects of Calvinism, which regarded a man's prosperity as the visible evidence of election by the Lord. But Tawney's effort to show that true Christianity is incompatible with freedom of choice in the economic sphere is a whopping *non sequitur*. The truth is that morality has no

109

redemptive virtue (and no Christian meaning) when it rests on compulsion. It is utterly incongruous to believe that one can be thrust or pulled into Heaven by a command which is wholly contemptuous of the individual's own will. As Hilaire Belloc, that most Christian man, has said, freedom and the exercise of one's will are aspects of the same thing—and a world which denies to an individual the right to choose the all-important means and methods of his own livelihood is a world without moral content.

Rightly interpreted, what Tawney—and Max Weber before him—actually prove is that Christianity tends to create a capitalistic mode of life whenever siege conditions do not prevail. (This is not to say that capitalism is Christian in and by itself, it is merely to say that capitalism is a material by-product of the Mosaic law.) In the early Middle Ages, which fostered the land-holding system which the Puritans, the Quakers, and the Cavaliers left behind them when they came to America, Western Europe was palpably under a state of siege. It was the time of the castle, the moat, the walled community. The Saracens had closed out the Mediterranean by seizing its littoral on three sides. The Roman world, retreating into the north, was robbed of its spaciousness and mobility; men gave up city life and huddled close to the "big house" of the armed lord, turning in their titles to freedom in exchange for the protections of the feudal order. As in any armed camp, rights and obligations were made reciprocal. A response to pressures from without, feudalism, with its emphasis on local strength, became the source of anarchistic quarrels between lord and lord within its own European orbit. There were sieges within sieges. The Christian church, growing up in a harsh atmosphere, performed its noble work by softening the rigors of a life that was essentially military; it stressed the spiritual duties of those implicated in a "relational" society and so prevented the feudal lord from becoming a crude caudillo. The church, as the protector of its flock, put a check on temporal government and thus saved each feudal locality from becoming a small totalitarian despotism. Far from being the source and protector of the political and economic institutions of the Middle Ages, the church was the buffer which defended the individual against the more abrasive trends of the times.

Naturally the church took a stand against usury in a period when there was no opportunity for money loans to expand into a fruitfulness that would reward both the borrower and the lender. Because money was quickly "used up" by the small-time medieval borrower, it seemed monstrous to Thomas Aquinas and other

Catholic philosophers to compel men to pay interest on what was no longer there. Money as something which had a "rental value," like land, would not readily be understood until the time had come when it could easily be turned into machinery or other capital goods, which had a continuing existence. The church also stood for a "just price" and for the manifold restrictions of the medieval guild because there was little room for adventurous competition in a society of closed manors which strained for protection from Saxon freebooter or Saracen raider, or merely for safety from the lusts of the baron on the other side of the river.

Once the enemy had been pushed back, however, the free will that is at the heart of the Christian order had its impact in the economic sphere. The Venetians, the Ragusans, and the Genoans adventured once again on the bosom of the Mediterranean. Freedoms which had flourished in the monotheistic Saracen world seeped back into Europe from the East and South as the frontiers of Christian energy expanded. Moreover, an energy that was capable of building cathedrals was capable of building clock towers to mark a purely mundane time. Even the monasteries themselves became centers of manufacture and trade. The monks made the best liqueurs, as all lovers of benedictine or cointreau can attest to this day.

In all of this, there was a belated continuity with the far past of the Judaic and Graeco-Roman civilizations. Actually, the continuity had hardly been submerged even during the most straitened medieval times. Recent revisionists of the Tawney-Max Weber thesis that our economic order grew out of the Calvinistic emphasis on saving and hard work have pointed out that capitalism, including the refinements of credit, first flourished in fourteenth-century Italian cities where Catholicism was at its crest. The Medici of Florence were business men. And banking was further elaborated in the Catholic cities of South Germany. This medieval banking escaped the category of usury for the simple reason that the creditors advanced money to enable people to earn money which blessed both lender and borrower alike.

In line with the revisionism of the Tawney-Max Weber notions, a lively controversy is now going on in the more esoteric economic journals. The Tawney thesis is being turned upside down by economists who argue that the medieval Catholic scholastics were wholly individualist in their approach to economics. The scholastics believed in Natural Law—and in the inalienable rights that must be deduced therefrom. Unlike the Calvinists of a later day, the scholastics did not believe in the divinity of work. Labor, to them, was the "curse of Adam," a necessary means of making a living. Consequently, they were never bemused into trying to elaborate a labor theory of value. They knew, as all sensible men must know, that value originates in the eye of the beholder. It achieves objective market expression in a price when two or more beholders clamor for the same thing. What the medieval scholastic philosophers stressed was the consumer's sovereignty and the ability of the market to decide value when one thing was offered for another. The medieval "just price," according to Emil Kauder, Murray Rothbard, and other "revisionists" of Tawney, was essentially the market price decided upon by individuals who were not under the duress of making "necessitous" bargains.

Even on Tawney's own showing, both Calvinism and Lutheranism, far from trying conscientiously to plow a furrow for capitalism, were reactions against the practices of a Christianity that seemed suddenly to let down the bars everywhere, even in its temporal headquarters in Rome. Calvin's own words on usury echo the thirteenth century. In early Calvinistic Massachusetts Puritans were put in the stocks for taking interest or for charging more than the going price. But the pull of the American earth was too strong for Calvinism. Even as in seventeenth-century England, the American Puritans gave up their strictness when it became apparent to the most committed of them that the Western world was no longer living in a state of siege. The defeat of the French and Indian menace on the frontier in the middle of the eighteenth century removed the last block which had kept the Puritan from becoming the Yankee. By the time of the Declaration of Independence Americans everywhere conceived themselves as defending an open society which they regarded as their Christian as well as their English birthright. The Ten Commandments and the natural rights philosophy which Locke took over from the medieval scholastics had had their way.

Obviously, an open society must be guaranteed against the tyranny of an individual, whether he be king or dictator. That, the colonists intended to do when they declared their independence. But the open society must also be made proof against the tyranny of a majority. "Planning," whether it is conducted in the name of a monarch or according to the decree of a mystical "general will" imposed by majority rule, comes in the end to the same thing: the minorities are sacrificed to the requirements of the plan. The colonists had had enough of such sacrifice, and at Philadelphia, in 1787, they proceeded to fashion themselves a document and a political structure which would, at least as far as they could foresee, be proof against any tyranny, whether of the One or the Many.

At this point it might be asked why, given thirteen state governments which had fought a successful war for the Lockean and Christian rights, a federal government was needed to supplant the existing Articles of Confederation. And, indeed, there is a school of critics and historians which holds that the thirteen states could have gone on managing for themselves. From Randolph Bourne to Professor Van Tyne, this school has insinuated that the Founders, in attempting to create or recover a federal consciousness, were meddling with freedom, not adding to its luster and scope.

Theoretically, of course, rights do not depend on the size of government. But the Founders had fought a war against an empire, and the fighting, as George Washington could well attest, had been rendered the more difficult because the sovereign American power had had thirteen heads. There had been the money difficulty—what with various state issues, all of them degenerating in value, and with the continental currency "not worth a continental," it had been next to impossible to satisfy the troops on pay day. There had also been the difficulty of getting New Englanders to fight in Jersey, or Jerseymen to carry on as the war moved toward Virginia. The money and enlistment parochialisms might have been fatal if British war-office bungling and the French fleet had not come to George Washington's rescue in time.

The Founders sensed that to survive in a world that was still dominated in 1787 by England, France, and Spain, all of whom had territory and territorial ambitions in the New World, a permanent union of states was needed. But how effectively to join the thirteen colonies? Madison sent to Jefferson for books: and the law and the history of confederations which he read about in those books demonstrated nothing but failure. The city-states of Greece had perished for want of an enduring principle of freedom-in-federation. Other "leagues" had done no better than the one which had been led by ancient Athens.

What the Founders wanted was a government which could take over the "power of the border" for all thirteen states, with enough sovereignty to conduct a unified diplomacy, to raise a federal army and pay it in good federal currency, and to deal with such matters as tariffs on a uniform basis. A single "power of the border" would keep Britain and Spain, for example, from trying to play off the Southern colonies against New England, and both of them against the Middle States. But if the need for a single diplomatic and military power was obvious to the generation of Washington, Hamilton, and Madison, the way to get it without sacrificing little Delaware to large Pennsylvania, or without surrendering the rights of the citizens to a possibly imperialist center, was not readily apparent.

Madison's theory, as expounded in No. 10 of The Federalist, was that in any great society "there will be rich and poor, creditors and debtors, a landed interest, a monied interest, a mercantile interest, a manufacturing interest." These interests, he continued, "may again be subdivided according to the different productions of different situations and soils . . ." Under pure majoritarian democracy, any combination of 51 percent of the people might gang up on "interests" which happened to be in a minority. "A pure democracy," said Madison in elaboration, "can admit no cure for the mischiefs of faction . . . there is nothing to check the inducements to sacrifice the weaker party. Hence it is that democracies have ever been found incompatible with personal security or the rights of property; and have, in general, been as short in their lives as they have been violent in their deaths."

Thus, well in advance of the French Revolution, Madison showed himself to be aware of the totalitarian poisons in Rousseau's theory of popular rule. The Constitution, which sought to set up internal bulwarks against the "passion of majorities," was a "social contract" (to use the French term), but it rejected Rousseau's contractural stipulation that "each of us places in common his person and his powers under the supreme direction of the general will." In common with most of his fellow-Founders, Madison wanted the compulsions of "general will" to be limited to specific, enumerated items.

"The great desideratum in Government is," he wrote, "so to modify the sovereignty as that it may be sufficiently neutral to controul one part from invading the rights of another, and at the same time sufficiently controuled itself from setting up an interest adverse to that of the entire Society."

Once that principle had been thoroughly grasped at Philadelphia, the rest was merely architecture. The Convention provided for the continuation of its representative organizing power by providing for ways in which the states or the citizens thereof would have the final say on amendments to the Constitution. As for setting up both state and individual immunities against the power of a federal majority, the Constitution put a whole sheaf of things beyond the reach of legislature and executive alike. There were prohibitions against retroactive law, against double jeopardy of life or limb, against trials not conducted before an impartial jury, against laws designed to curb freedom of speech and the press, and so on. From the economic standpoint three things must interest us here particularly. One is that the states were not permitted to put obstacles in the way of interstate commerce. A second is that the money standard was federalized. And the third was that the Bill of Rights (which should be considered as part of the original Constitution) contained a specific defense of private property. "No person," says the Fifth Amendment, "shall be ... deprived of life, liberty, or property, without due process of law; nor shall private property be taken for public use, without just compensation."

Finally, to keep the government from exceeding its powers, the Founders saw to it that the various functions of government should be separated, so as to check each other. A Supreme Court was created to keep both the law makers and the executive from invading the immunities guaranteed to the states and to individual citizens.

The Founders may have exceeded their authority (which was to "amend" the Articles of Confederation, not to throw everything into the hopper and make an entirely new beginning), but the people of at least eleven of the thirteen states did not object to the loose interpretation of mandate. We have had enough, perhaps, of the crude economic interpretation of the Constitution which stresses the plotting nature of Madison, Hamilton, and company. Charles A. Beard, who fathered the conspiracy theory, himself revolted against it in his old age when he came to Madison's defense in a noble book called *The Republic*. The original Beard thesis—that the Constitution was something put over by an undemocratic coup at the expense of the farmers and mechanics—does not survive the recent researches of Professor Robert E. Brown of Michigan State University. Professor Brown has demonstrated both the widespread nature of the franchise in eighteenth-century America (we had a "distributist" republic then, with some 90 percent of the families owning land) and its broadly honest representation at the Philadelphia convention and in the state ratifying conventions which followed.

The Constitution, on Professor Brown's voluminous evidence, was something which appealed to property holders of all kinds,

115

the farmers included. And the mechanics, who possessed the franchise without land ownership in many places, had a hand in voting its acceptance, too. Naturally, a generation which had fought a revolution for the sanctity of the Lockean triad of life, liberty, and property was interested in the whole scope of the due process guarantees of the Fifth Amendment. But if the property clause hadn't been there, the Constitution would hardly have been acceptable to a people which was even then pushing westward in a scramble to take up land.

The Founding Fathers did not succeed in making their document foolproof. Professor John W. Burgess of Columbia University, who makes the "reconciliation of government with liberty" dependent upon the continuing existence of an organizing power behind and antecedent to government itself, argues that the Founders should not have permitted either Congress or the state legislatures to have a hand in the amending process. Men holding political office, so Burgess observes, must be altogether too partial to amendments which serve to increase their power, not diminish it. To forestall the erosion of liberties through the aggrandizement of the political officers, amendments should in all circumstances be undertaken in representative convention by the people of the constituent states. They, after all, constitute the sovereign power whose consent made possible the original federal government.

The other flaws in the original Constitution were partly due to deliberate oversight (as in the decision to deny the blessings of liberty to Negro slaves), and partly due to the employment of loose language, as in the general welfare and the commerce clauses. Some one hundred and fifty years after the Founders had completed their labors, it was discovered that virtually anything at all can be done in the name of the general welfare and the right to "regulate commerce among the several states," even to the point of negating other parts of the Constitution. The Founders should have distinguished sharply between the particular welfare of groups and the general welfare, they should have tied the welfare clause to strictly enumerated powers, and they should have made plain that to regulate commerce does not mean to direct it or to control it. Finally, they should have forestalled in perpetuity the possibility of unchecked taxation—which, indeed, they thought they had done when they limited the levying of any *direct* tax to "proportion to the Census." The checks and balances of the federal system, the difficulty of amending the basic law, the fortunate internal division of our political parties and the fact that

Senate elections are staggered over a six-year period, all operate to prevent rule in most things by an unchecked majority. But ever since the passage of the income tax amendment in 1912 there has been no constitutional limit on what legislators can do with the people's income. A Congressional majority of 51 percent could vote *any* expropriation of any income-group that it chose, which means that, fiscally speaking, the citizen has no rightful immunity whatsoever in the realm wherein he makes his living.

Given what they knew, however, the Founders did consummately well. While they did not intend to legislate laissez-faire (Hamilton had his heart set on the encouragement and protection of infant industries by a system of bounties or tariffs), they began with the individual as a self-controlled and self-directed person. They established a large free-trade area under a uniform currency system. True, they imposed no check on the internal fiscal and economic policies of the several states, but the individual's right to move across state lines at will was sufficient of a guarantee against despotic measures in Albany, New York, say, or in Boston, Massachusetts. To this day a Boston citizen can dodge the Massachusetts inheritance laws by moving to Illinois or Florida; and a person who is irked by the New York State income tax can correct the imbalance by migrating for a few miles to Connecticut. Similarly, if a manufacturer doesn't like the labor laws or the business regulations of Michigan, he can move his plant to Indiana.

The Founders were not perfect men, and they certainly did not agree among themselves. Some feared the mob; some loved it. Some believed in paper money, some in a specie-backed central bank. Southerners among them wanted slavery perpetuated forever; some of the Virginians wanted to kill it by degrees; most of the Northerners would have liked to get rid of it overnight. The differences were multiple, but on one thing the Founders were agreed: they wanted to set up a republic in such a way that differences—and even basic inconsistencies—could be accepted and accommodated. The measure of their success is that they provided a framework which would permit lion and lamb, Hamiltonian and Jeffersonian, to go on living together without eating each other up. In all of this they had a big piece of luck: no state among the original thirteen was large enough or powerful enough to become cancerous, as the state of Prussia was to become the cancer in the late nineteenth-century German federation. Moreover, given equal representation in the Senate, it was a foregone conclusion that no Prussia would ever be allowed to develop in the future. Not even Texas is big enough or strong enough to become a Prussia.

The Founders could not foresee what the U.S. would become, economically speaking. Who among them could have prophesied that Eli Whitney's invention of the cotton gin would so strengthen the slave holding interests as to push the southern states to the folly of civil war? Who among them could foresee that the same Eli Whitney's elaboration of dies to make interchangeable parts would insure both northern manufacturing supremacy and victory in that civil war? Hamilton thought America would become a manufacturing nation but did not foresee the great westward push beyond the Alleghenies; Jefferson, on the other hand, anticipated the push, but thought the middle west would remain for a long time a purely agricultural empire. Neither Jefferson nor Hamilton could know that electric power and the fluidity of modern transport would mean that manufacturing could be decentralized to the point where "urban sores" would be wholly unnecessary, thus enabling the Jeffersonian to make the most of the Hamiltonian world, and vice versa.

But if the Founders could not possibly have blueprinted a future America, they knew that freedom would be equal to any contingency. They knew the connections between the great human rights of life, liberty, and property and an energy system that would function without impediment. Willy-nilly, they were good economists. Jefferson (who wasn't present in Philadelphia, but who saw to it that Madison got the literature he needed) was a friend and correspondent of J. B. Say, the Frenchman who first demonstrated, in his famous Law of Markets, that free production generates its own purchasing power. Jefferson knew the Physiocrats, but he was far from being a mere Physiocrat (a believer in simple agrarianism) himself, as his recommendation of Adam Smith's *Wealth of Nations* as being the "best" book on political economy attests. As Murray Rothbard points out, Jefferson was libertarian to the core, a believer in laissez-faire and hard money. (What he objected to in Hamilton's position was its emphasis on tariffs, which would force an *uneconomic* shift of resources from farming and trade into manufacturing.) As for Hamilton, he was, save in the instance of the tariff, a confirmed follower of Adam Smith: many passages in his famous reports on banking, currency, and manufacturers are paraphrases or even unacknowledged quotations from *Wealth of Nations*, as Louis Hacker has recently demonstrated. In the case of Madison himself, though he feared the

118

possible development of plutocracy, it was little Jamie, the "inimitable mixture of boyish fun ... and sedateness," who thought of property as the great reason for government.

Because the property right was protected in our basic document, free capitalism had the political climate it needed for expansion. Five years after the making of the Constitution, Hamilton's (and Tench Coxe's) famous report on Manufactures noted the existence of an American steel industry, a flourishing shipbuilding industry, and a copper and brass industry. The textile industry burgeoned quickly on these shores once Samuel Slater had slipped out of Britain with the blueprint of an Arkwright factory committed to memory. Protected by the limitation of government, and with the space of a continent in which to grow, the simple system of natural liberty had found its habitat. It was not to be seriously challenged for a hundred and fifty years.

PART II: CAPITALISM AND JUSTICE

"The bourgeoisie, by the rapid improvement of all instruments of production, by the immensely facilitated means of communication, draws all nations, even the most barbarian, into civilization."

KARL MARX
The Communist Manifesto

ECONOMIC MYTHS OF EARLY CAPITALISM

F. A. Hayek

from CAPITALISM AND THE HISTORIANS (1954)

There is . . . one supreme myth which more than any other has served to discredit the economic system to which we owe our present-day civilization and to the examination of which the present volume is devoted. It is the legend of the deterioration of the position of the working classes in consequence of the rise of "capitalism" (or of the "manufacturing" or the "industrial system"). Who has not heard of the "horrors of early capitalism" and gained the impression that the advent of this system brought untold new suffering to large classes who before were tolerably content and comfortable? We might justly hold in disrepute a system to which the blame attached that even for a time it worsened the position of the poorest and most numerous class of the population. The widespread emotional aversion to "capitalism" is closely connected with this belief that the undeniable growth of wealth which the competitive order has produced was purchased at the price of depressing the standard of life of the weakest elements of society.

That this was the case was at one time indeed widely taught by economic historians. A more careful examination of the facts has, however, led to a thorough refutation of this belief. Yet, a generation after the controversy has been decided, popular opinion still

123

continues as though the older belief had been true. How this belief should ever have arisen and why it should continue to determine the general view long after it has been disproved are both problems which deserve serious examination.

This kind of opinion can be frequently found not only in the political literature hostile to capitalism but even in works which on the whole are sympathetic to the political tradition of the nineteenth century. It is well represented by the following passage from Ruggiero's justly esteemed *History of European Liberalism*:

> Thus it was precisely at the period of intensest industrial growth that the condition of the labourer changed for the worse. Hours of labour multiplied out of all measure; the employment of women and children in factories lowered wages: the keen competition between the workers themselves, no longer tied to their parishes but free to travel and congregate where they were most in demand, further cheapened the labour they placed on the market: numerous and frequent industrial crises, inevitable at a period of growth, when population and consumption are not yet stabilized, swelled from time to time the ranks of the unemployed, the reserves in the army of starvation.[1]

There was little excuse for such a statement even when it appeared a quarter-century ago. A year after it was first published, the most eminent student of modern economic history, Sir John Clapham, rightly complained:

> The legend that everything was getting worse for the working man, down to some unspecified date between the drafting of the People's Charter and the Great Exhibition, dies hard. The fact that, after the price fall of 1820-1, the purchasing power of wages in general—not, of course, of everyone's wages—was definitely greater than it had been just before the revolutionary and Napoleonic wars, fits so ill with the tradition that it is very seldom mentioned, the works of statisticians of wages and prices being constantly disregarded by social historians.[2]

In so far as general public opinion is concerned, the position is scarcely better today, although the facts have had to be conceded even by most of those who had been mainly responsible for spreading the contrary opinion. Few authors have done more to create the belief that the early nineteenth century had been a time

[1] Guido de Ruggiero, *Storia del liberalismo europeo* (Bari, 1925), trans. R. G. Collingwood (London: Oxford University Press, 1927), p. 47, esp. p. 85. It is interesting that Ruggiero seems to derive his facts mainly from another supposedly liberal historian, Élie Halévy, although Halévy never expressed them so crudely.

[2] J. H. Clapham, *An Economic History of Modern Britain* (Cambridge, 1926), I, 7.

in which the position of the working class had become particularly bad than Mr. and Mrs. J. L. Hammond; their books are frequently quoted to illustrate this. But toward the end of their lives they admitted candidly that

> statisticians tell us that when they have put in order such data as they can find, they are satisfied that earnings increased and that most men and women were less poor when this discontent was loud and active than they were when the eighteenth century was beginning to grow old in a silence like that of autumn. The evidence, of course, is scanty, and its interpretation not too simple, but this general view is probably more or less correct.[3]

This did little to change the general effect their writing had had on public opinion. In one of the latest competent studies of the history of the Western political tradition, for instance, we can still read that, "like all the great social experiments, however, the invention of the labour market was expensive. It involved, in the first instance, a swift and drastic decline in the material standard of living of the working classes.[4]

I was going to continue here that this is still the view which is almost exclusively represented in the popular literature when the latest book by Bertrand Russell came to my hands in which, as if to confirm this, he blandly asserts:

> The industrial revolution caused unspeakable misery both in England and in America. I do not think any student of economic history can doubt that the average happiness in England in the early nineteenth century was lower than it had been a hundred years earlier; and this was due almost entirely to scientific technique.[5]

The intelligent layman can hardly be blamed if he believes that such a categorical statement from a writer of this rank must be true. If a Bertrand Russell believes this, we must not be surprised that the versions of economic history which today are spread in hundreds of thousands of volumes of pocket editions are mostly of the kind which spread this old myth. It is also still a rare exception when we meet a work of historical fiction which dispenses with the dramatic touch which the story of the sudden worsening of the position of large groups of workers provides.

[3] J. L. and Barbara Hammond, *The Bleak Age* (1934) (rev. ed.; London: Pelican Books, 1947), p. 15.

[4] Frederick Watkins, *The Political Tradition of the West* (Cambridge, Mass.: Harvard University Press, 1948), p. 213.

[5] Bertrand Russell, *The Impact of Science on Society* (New York: Columbia University Press, 1951), pp. 19-20.

The true fact of the slow and irregular progress of the working class which we now know to have taken place is of course rather unsensational and uninteresting to the layman. It is no more than he has learned to expect as the normal state of affairs; and it hardly occurs to him that this is by no means an inevitable progress, that it was preceded by centuries of virtual stagnation of the position of the poorest, and that we have come to expect continuous improvement only as a result of the experience of several generations with the system which he still thinks to be the cause of the misery of the poor.

Discussions of the effects of the rise of modern industry on the working classes refer almost always to the conditions in England in the first half of the nineteenth century; yet the great change to which they refer had commenced much earlier and by then had quite a long history and had spread far beyond England. The freedom of economic activity which in England had proved so favorable to the rapid growth of wealth was probably in the first instance an almost accidental by-product of the limitations which the revolution of the seventeenth century had placed on the powers of government; and only after its beneficial effects had come to be widely noticed did the economists later undertake to explain the connection and to argue for the removal of the remaining barriers to commercial freedom. In many ways it is misleading to speak of "capitalism" as though this had been a new and altogether different system which suddenly came into being toward the end of the eighteenth century; we use this term here because it is the most familiar name, but only with great reluctance, since with its modern connotations it is itself largely a creation of that socialist interpretation of economic history with which we are concerned. The term is especially misleading when, as is often the case, it is connected with the idea of the rise of the propertyless proletariat, which by some devious process have been deprived of their rightful ownership of the tools for their work.

The actual history of the connection between capitalism and the rise of the proletariat is almost the opposite of that which these theories of the expropriation of the masses suggest. The truth is that, for the greater part of history, for most men the possession of the tools for their work was an essential condition for survival or at least for being able to rear a family. The number of those who could maintain themselves by working for others, although they did not themselves possess the necessary equipment, was limited to a small proportion of the population. The amount of arable land and of tools handed down from one generation to the next limited

126

the total number who could survive. To be left without them meant in most instances death by starvation or at least the impossibility of procreation. There was little incentive and little possibility for one generation to accumulate the additional tools which would have made possible the survival of a larger number of the next, so long as the advantage of employing additional hands was limited mainly to the instances where the division of the tasks increased the efficiency of the work of the owner of the tools. It was only when the larger gains from the employment of machinery provided both the means and the opportunity for their investment that what in the past had been a recurring surplus of population doomed to early death was in an increasing measure given the possibility of survival. Numbers which had been practically stationary for many centuries began to increase rapidly. The proletariat which capitalism can be said to have "created" was thus not a proportion of the population which would have existed without it and which it had degraded to a lower level; it was an additional population which was enabled to grow up by the new opportunities for employment which capitalism provided. In so far as it is true that the growth of capital made the appearance of the proletariat possible, it was in the sense that it raised the productivity of labor so that much larger numbers of those who had not been equipped by their parents with the necessary tools were enabled to maintain themselves by their labor alone; but the capital had to be supplied first before those were enabled to survive who afterward claimed as a right a share in its ownership. Although it was certainly not from charitable motives, it still was the first time in history that one group of people found it in their interest to use their earnings on a large scale to provide new instruments of production to be operated by those who without them could not have produced their own sustenance.

Of the effect of the rise of modern industry on the growth of population, statistics tell a vivid tale. That this in itself largely contradicts the common belief about the harmful effect of the rise of the factory system on the large masses is not the point with which we are at present concerned. Nor need we more than mention the fact that, so long as this increase of the numbers of those whose output reached a certain level brought forward a fully corresponding increase in population, the level of the poorest fringe could not be substantially improved, however much the average might rise. The point of immediate relevance is that this increase of population and particularly of the manufacturing population had proceeded in England at least for two or three generations before the period of which it is alleged that the position of the workers seriously deteriorated.

The period to which this refers is also the period when the problem of the position of the working class became for the first time one of general concern. And the opinions of some of the contemporaries are indeed the main sources of the present beliefs. Our first question must therefore be how it came about that such an impression contrary to the facts should have become widely held among the people then living.

One of the chief reasons was evidently an increasing awareness of facts which before had passed unnoticed. The very increase of wealth and well-being which had been achieved raised standards and aspirations. What for ages had seemed a natural and inevitable situation, or even an improvement upon the past, came to be regarded as incongruous and seemed less justified, because general wealth was increasing faster than ever before. But this, of course, does not prove that the people whose fate was beginning to cause indignation and alarm were worse off than their parents or grandparents had been. While there is every evidence that great misery existed, there is none that it was greater than or even as great as it had been before. The aggregations of large numbers of cheap houses of industrial workers were probably more ugly than the picturesque cottages in which some of the agricultural laborers or domestic workers had lived; and they were certainly more alarming to the landowner or to the city patrician than the poor dispersed over the country had been. But for those who had moved from country to town it meant an improvement; and even though the rapid growth of the industrial centers created sanitary problems with which people had yet slowly and painfully to learn to cope, statistics leave little doubt that even general health was on the whole benefited rather than harmed.[6]

More important, however, for the explanation of the change from an optimistic to a pessimistic view of the effects of industrialization than this awakening of social conscience was probably the fact that this change of opinion appears to have commenced, not in the manufacturing districts which had firsthand knowledge of what was happening, but in the political discussion of the English metropolis which was somewhat remote from, and had little part it, the new development. It is evident that the belief about the "horrible" conditions prevailing among the manufacturing populations of the Midlands and the north of England was in

[6] Cf. M. C. Buer, *Health, Wealth and Population in the Early Days of the Industrial Revolution* (London: G. Routledge & Sons, 1926).

the 1830's and 1840's widely held among the upper classes of London and the south. It was one of the main arguments with which the landowning class hit back at the manufacturers to counter the agitation of the latter against the Corn Laws and for free trade. And it was from these arguments of the conservative press that the radical intelligentsia of the time, with little firsthand knowledge of the industrial districts, derived their views which were to become the standard weapons of political propaganda.

This position, to which so much even of the present-day beliefs about the effects of the rise of industrialism on the working classes can be traced, is well illustrated by a letter written about 1843 by a London lady, Mrs. Cooke Taylor, after she had for the first time visited some industrial districts of Lancashire. Her account of the conditions she found is prefaced by some remarks about the general state of opinion in London:

> I need not remind you of the statements put forward in the newspapers, relative to the miserable conditions of the operatives, and the tyranny of their masters, for they made such an impression on me that it was with reluctance that I consented to go to Lancashire; indeed these misrepresentations are quite general, and people believe them without knowing why or wherefore. As an instance: just before starting I was at a large dinner party, at the west end of the town, and seated next a gentleman who is considered a very clever and intelligent man. In the course of the conversation I mentioned that I was going to Lancashire. He stared and asked, "What on earth could take me there? That he would as soon think of going to St. Giles's; that it was a horrid place—factories all over; that the people, from starvation, oppression, and over-work, had almost lost the form of humanity; and that the mill-owners were a bloated, pampered race, feeding on the very vitals of the people." I answered that this was a dreadful state of things; and asked "In what part he had seen such misery?" He replied, that "he had never *seen* it, but had been *told* that it existed; and that for his part he never *had been* in the manufacturing districts, and that he *never would*." This gentleman was one of the very numerous body of people who spread reports without ever taking the trouble of inquiring if they be true or false.[7]

Mrs. Cooke Taylor's detailed description of the satisfactory state of affairs which to her surprise she found ends with the remark: "Now that I have seen the factory people at their work, in their cottages and in their schools, I am totally at a loss to account for

[7] This letter is quoted in "Reuben," *A Brief History of the Rise and Progress of the Anti-Corn-Law League* (London, [1845]). Mrs. Cooke Taylor, who appears to have been the wife of the radical Dr. Cooke Taylor, had visited the factory of Henry Ashworth at Turton, near Bolton, then still a rural district and therefore probably more attractive than some of the urban industrial districts.

the outcry that has been made against them. They are better clothed, better fed, and better conducted than many other classes of working people."[8]

But even if at the time itself the opinion which was later taken over by the historians was loudly voiced by one party, it remains to explain why the view of one party among the contemporaries, and that not of the radicals or liberals but of the Tories, should have become the almost uncontradicted view of the economic historians of the second half of the century. The reason for this seems to have been that the new interest in economic history was itself closely associated with the interest in socialism and that at first a large proportion of those who devoted themselves to the study of economic history were inclined toward socialism. It was not merely the great stimulus which Karl Marx's "materialist interpretation of history" undoubtedly gave to the study of economic history; practically all the socialist schools held a philosophy of history intended to show the relative character of the different economic institutions and the necessity of different economic systems succeeding each other in time. They all tried to prove that the system which they attacked, the system of private property in the means of production, was a perversion of an earlier and more natural system of communal property; and, because the theoretical preconceptions which guided them postulated that the rise of capitalism must have been detrimental to the working classes, it is not surprising that they found what they were looking for.

But not only those by whom the study of economic history was consciously made a tool of political agitation—as is true in many instances from Marx and Engels to Werner Sombart and Sidney and Beatrice Webb—but also many of the scholars who sincerely believed that they were approaching the facts without prejudice produced results which were scarcely less biased. This was in part due to the fact that the "historical approach" which they adopted had itself been proclaimed as a counterblast to the theoretical analysis of classical economics, because the latter's verdict on the popular remedies for current complaints had so frequently been unfavorable.[9] It is no accident that the largest and most in-

[8] *Ibid.*

[9] Merely as an illustration of the general attitude of that school a characteristic statement of one of its best-known representatives, Adolf Held, may be quoted. According to him, it was David Ricardo "in whose hand orthodox economics became the docile servant of the exclusive interests of mobile capital," and his theory of rent "was simply dictated by the hatred of the moneyed capitalist against the landowners" (*Zwei Bücher zur sozialen Geschichte Englands* [Leipzig: Duncker & Humbolt, 1881], p. 178).

fluential group of students of economic history in the sixty years preceding the first World War, the German Historical School, prided themselves also in the name of the "socialist of the chair" (*Kathedersozialisten*); or that their spiritual successors, the American "institutionalists," were mostly socialists in their inclination. The whole atmosphere of these schools was such that it would have required an exceptional independence of mind for a young scholar not to succumb to the pressure of academic opinion. No reproach was more feared or more fatal to academic prospects than that of being an "apologist" of the capitalist system; and, even if a scholar dared to contradict dominant opinion on a particular point, he would be careful to safeguard himself against such accusation by joining in the general condemnation of the capitalist system.[10] To treat the existing economic order as merely a "historical phase" and to be able to predict from the "laws of historical development" the emergence of a better future system became the hallmark of what was then regarded as the truly scientific spirit.

Much of the misrepresentation of the facts by the earlier economic historians was, in reality, directly traceable to a genuine endeavor to look at these facts without any theoretical preconceptions. The idea that one can trace the causal connections of any events without employing a theory, or that such a theory will emerge automatically from the accumulation of a sufficient amount of facts, is of course sheer illusion. The complexity of social events in particular is such that, without the tools of analysis which a systematic theory provides, one is almost bound to misinterpret them; and those who eschew the conscious use of an explicit and tested logical argument usually merely become the victims of the popular beliefs of their time. Common sense is a treacherous guide in this field, and what seem "obvious" explanations frequently are no more than commonly accepted superstitions. It may seem obvious that the introduction of machinery will produce a general reduction of the demand for labor. But persistent effort to think the problem through shows that this belief is the result of a logical fallacy, of stressing one effect of the assumed change and leaving out others. Nor do the facts give any support to the belief. Yet anyone who thinks it to be true is very likely to find what seems to him confirming evidence. It is easy enough to find in the early nineteenth century instances of extreme poverty

[10] A good account of the general political atmosphere prevailing among the German Historical School of economists will be found in Ludwig Pohle, *Die gegenwärtige Krise in der deutschen Volkswirtschaftslehre* (Leipzig, 1911).

and to draw the conclusion that this must have been the effect of the introduction of machinery, without asking whether conditions had been any better or perhaps even worse before. Or one may believe that an increase of production must lead to the impossibility of selling all the product and, when one then finds a stagnation of sales, regard this as a confirmation of the expectations, although there are several more plausible explanations than general "overproduction" or "underconsumption."

There can be no doubt that many of these misrepresentations were put forward in good faith; and there is no reason why we should not respect the motives of some of those who, to arouse public conscience, painted the misery of the poor in the blackest colors. We owe to agitation of this kind, which forced unwilling eyes to face unpleasant facts, some of the finest and most generous acts of public policy—from the abolition of slavery to the removal of taxes on imported food and the destruction of many intrenched monopolies and abuses. And there is every reason to remember how miserable the majority of the people still were as recently as a hundred or a hundred and fifty years ago. But we must not, long after the event, allow a distortion of the facts, even if committed out of humanitarian zeal, to affect our view of what we owe to a system which for the first time in history made people feel that this misery might be avoidable. The very claims and ambitions of the working classes were and are the result of the enormous improvement of their position which capitalism brought about.

CAPITALIST AND INTELLECTUAL

Bertrand de Jouvenel

from CAPITALISM AND THE HISTORIANS (1954)

The intellectual's hostility to the businessman presents no mystery, as the two have, by function, wholly different standards, so that the businessman's normal conduct appears blameworthy if judged by the criteria valid for the intellectual's conduct. Such judgment might be avoided in a partitioned society, avowedly divided in classes playing different parts and bound to different forms of honor. This, however, is not the case of our society, of which current ideas and the law postulate that it forms a single homogeneous field. Upon this field the businessman and the intellectual move side by side. The businessman offers to the public "goods" defined as anything the public will buy; the intellectual seeks to teach what is "good," and to him some of the goods offered are things of no value which the public should be discouraged from wanting. The world of business is to the intellectual one in which the values are wrong, the motivations low, the rewards misaddressed. A convenient gateway into the intellectual's inner courtyard where his judgments are rendered is afforded by his deficit preference. It has been observed that his sympathy goes to institutions which run at a loss, nationalized industries supported by the treasury, colleges dependent on grants and subsidies, newspapers which never get out of the red. Why is this? Because he knows from personal experience that, whenever he acts as he feels he should, there is unbalance between his effort

133

and its reception: to put it in economic jargon, the market value of the intellectual's output is far below factor input. That is because a really good thing in the intellectual realm is a thing which can be recognized as good by only a few. As the intellectual's role is to make people know for true and good what they did not previously recognize as such, he encounters a formidable sales resistance, and he works at a loss. When his success is easy and instantaneous, he knows it for an almost certain criterion that he has not truly performed his function. Reasoning from his experience, the intellectual suspects whatever yields a margin of profit of having been done, not from belief in and devotion to the thing, but because enough people could be found to desire it to make the venture profitable. You may plead with the intellectual and convince him that most things must be done this way. Still he will feel that those ways are not his. His profit-and-loss philosophy can be summed up in these terms: to him a loss is the natural outcome of devotion to a-thing-to-be-done, while a profit, on the other hand, is the natural outcome of deferring to the public.

The fundamental difference of attitude between the businessman and the intellectual can be pinned down by resort to a hackneyed formula. The businessman must say: "The customer is always right." The intellectual cannot entertain this notion. A bad writer is made by the very maxim which makes him a good businessman: "Give the public what it wants." The businessman operates within a framework of tastes, of value judgments, which the intellectual must ever seek to alter. The supreme activity of the intellectual is that of the missionary offering the Gospel to heathen nations. Selling spirits to them is a less dangerous and more profitable activity. Here the contrast is stark between offering "consumers" what they should have but do not want and offering them what they avidly accept but should not have. The trader who fails to turn to the more salable product is adjudged a fool, but the missionary who would so turn would be adjudged a knave.

Because we intellectuals are functionally teachers of truth, we are prone to take toward the businessman the very same attitude of moral superiority which was that of the Pharisee toward the Publican, and which Jesus condemned. It should be a lesson to us that the poor man lying by the wayside was raised by a merchant (the Samaritan) and not by the intellectual (the Levite). Dare we deny that the immense improvement which has occurred in the condition of the toiling many is chiefly the work of the businessmen?

We may rejoice that we minister to the highest wants of mankind; but let us be honestly fearful of this responsibility. Of the "goods" offered for profit, how many can we call positively harmful? Is it not the case of many more of the ideas we expound? Are there not ideas nefarious to the workings of the mechanisms and institutions which insure the progress and happiness of commonwealths? It is telling that all intellectuals agree to there being such ideas, though not all agree as to which are obnoxious. Far worse, are there not ideas which raise anger in the bosoms of men? Our responsibility is heightened by the fact that the diffusion of possibly mischievous ideas cannot and should not be stopped by the exertion of the temporal authority, while the merchandizing of harmful goods can be so stopped.

It is something of a mystery—and a promising field of investigation for historians and sociologists—that the intellectual community has waxed harsher in its judgments of the business community precisely while the business community was strikingly bettering the condition of the masses, improving its own working ethics, and growing in civic consciousness. Judged by its social fruits, by its mores, by its spirit, capitalism of today is immeasurably more praiseworthy than in previous days when it was far less bitterly denounced. If the change in the attitude of the intelligentsia is not to be explained by a turn for the worse in what they assess, is it not then to be explained by a change which has occurred in the intelligentsia itself?

This question opens a great realm of inquiry. It has for long been assumed that the great problem of the twentieth century is that of the industrial wage-earner's place in society; insufficient notice has been taken of the rise of a vast intellectual class, whose place in society may prove the greater problem. The intellectuals have been the major agents in the destruction of the ancient structure of Western society, which provides three distinct sets of institutions for the intellectuals, the warriors, and the producers. They have striven to render the social field homogeneous and uniform; the winds of subjective desires blow over it more freely; subjective appreciations are the criterion of all efforts. Quite naturally, this constitution of society puts a premium upon the "goods" which are most desired and brings to the forefront of society those who lead in the production of "goods." The intelligentsia has then lost to this "executive" class the primacy which it enjoyed when it stood as "the First Estate." Its present attitude may be to some degree explained by the inferiority complex it has acquired. Not only has the intelligentsia as a whole fallen to a less exalted sta-

135

tus, but, moreover, individual recognition tends to be determined by criteria of subjective appreciation by the public, which the intelligentsia rejects on principle; hence the countervailing tendency to exalt those intellectuals who are for intellectuals only.

We do not presume to explain, and the foregoing remarks are the merest suggestions. Our ambition is merely to stress that there is something to be explained and that it seems timely to undertake a study of the tensions arising between the intelligentsia and society.

MONOPOLY

Wilhelm Roepke

from ECONOMICS OF THE FREE SOCIETY (1963)

Now that we have established that the costs of production (in the sense already used and for the reasons we have indicated) constitutes in the long run the lower limit to which prices can fall, the question suggests itself whether and to what degree they can rise above this lower limit. That they can so rise is undeniable. It is, however, also clear that there is a powerful force which again pushes prices down to the level of costs, namely, the increased supply which results from the competition among the producers to sell at the higher price. The more ineffective this force becomes, the closer we approach *monopoly*. The resulting peculiarities we must now describe.

The characteristic feature of a monopoly, be it a single enterprise or a monopolistic combination of enterprises (cartel, syndicate, trust) is that it (or they) can freely determine the amount of supply; and where supply is sufficiently curtailed, prices can be held above the level of costs. If we proceed on what is probably the not unreal assumption that the monopolist seeks to maximize his profits, the question then is what price should he select to attain his goal? Should he choose a high price, his profit per unit will be high but his total sales small ("small turnover, large per unit profit"). Should he choose a low price, the profit per unit declines, while total sales increase ("large turnover, small profit per unit"). Confronted with these alternatives, the monopolist will select that price which, multiplied by the number of units sold, will yield the maximum net profit. He will seek by a series of experiments to establish the location of this maximum point. This will vary, of course, from firm to firm, and from plant to plant. The decisive factor here is the elasticity of demand; upon it will depend whether an increase in price will induce a sharp decrease in sales or whether a decrease in price will stimulate a sizable increase in sales. If the telephone company can count on a high elasticity of demand for telephone service, it will find that a reduction in its rates will result in an addition to its revenues which exceeds the total of the amounts lost on the bills of the individual subscribers. Thus, the greater is the elasticity of demand the lower is the monopoly price, and vice versa. From this it follows that a monopoly of foodstuffs may have extremely dangerous consequences for the community, especially a monopoly of grains.

Because of the importance of the elasticity of demand in the determination of monopoly price, the managements of monopolistic enterprises—railroads, electric power companies, the post office, state tobacco monopolies—must base their price policies primarily on this factor and have a fairly clear notion of what the coefficient of the elasticity of demand is in the given case. The monopolist must also take into account the fact that the elasticity of demand is decisively affected by possibilities available to consumers to turn to a substitute product (from the railroad to the automobile, from the gas stove to a coal or electric stove, etc.). On the other hand, there are cases where the elasticity of demand is low, e.g., matches or sewing thread, objects which though they possess slight value in themselves nevertheless have great practical importance. Expenditures for such items are imperceptible in contrast to expenditures with which they are associated (for heating and smoking, and for suiting material and tailoring, respectively), while their mass consumption assures to the manufacturers a large profit.

The position of the monopoly price point is further influenced by the structure of costs at different levels of supply. If costs are of the increasing type (i.e., if they increase as output increases), then a higher price is more advantageous for the monopolist; if costs are of the decreasing type, it would be wise to establish a lower price. Mining monopolies (where increasing costs are encountered) may incline to a policy of restricting supply and keeping prices high, while the publisher of a copyrighted book such as this one will find it to his advantage to fix its price as low as possible; the resultant broadening of the market enables him to benefit from the dominant tendency in book production, which is one of decreasing costs.

This last example suggests a further complication in the formation of monopoly price. If, for instance, the present book were a novel or a play, the publisher would have at his disposal still other means of increasing his profit. To begin with, he could publish a deluxe edition of several hundred copies, on imperial Japan paper and bound in vellum, "numbered and signed by the author." These he could sell to collectors at a high price. Next, he could bring out an ordinary edition at a medium price, and finally, a "popular" edition for the masses at a sensationally low price. For our publisher to have brought out the popular edition first would not only have entailed extra risks but a further obvious disadvantage in that those who might have been willing to pay a higher price for the ordinary edition, and even for the deluxe edition, would have profited from the lower price of the popular edition. By beginning with the more expensive type, our publisher puts to use his knowledge of the fact that a uniform price for the entire market establishes itself in accordance with the willingness to buy of the marginal buyers, i.e., those whose desire to buy is the weakest. Thus, the establishment of a single uniform price for a given commodity yields to all the buyers who otherwise would have paid a higher price for it a saving which they owe to the greater reluctance to buy of the marginal buyers. This saving, the counterpart of producers' profits, is designated as *consumers' surplus*, an expression to which, naturally, many will object since it refers not to a positive gain but only to a saving. It is understandable that the producers would cast a covetous eye on consumers' surplus; they are compelled, nonetheless, to cede this much to the buyers so long as a uniform price obtains for all the quantities of a good sold within a given time period. A prime function of competition, we may note, is to ensure, through an easily understood process, such price uniformity.

But the monopolist has the possibility, thanks to *price differentiation*, of increasing his profit at the cost of the consumers. This is accomplished in such a way that the whole of demand is ranged in different classes, according to the different degrees of surcharge possible. Next, prices are adapted to the several classes on the basis of what the traffic will bear in each case, as shown in our example of the different editions of the same book. In this example, price differentiation was rendered possible by artificially dividing the good in question into different qualities, the markets for each of these quality classifications being then successively exploited. The practice of selling a good first at a high price and then, following a progressive saturation of the higher strata of demand, at a low price, is usual even in the case of patented manufactured articles. Consider the example of the so-called zip fastener. When it first appeared on the market, it was regarded as an amazing innovation and commanded a high price. Today, the zipper is so cheap that it has been adapted to thousands of different uses. Similarly, most of the price phenomena connected with the production and sale of articles of fashion are explainable in terms of this principle.

There is an abundant assortment of examples that could be cited to illustrate the process by which a good is divided, artificially, into different subclasses. The transport industries afford a prime instance of such class divisions. The establishment, by the railroads, of a hierarchy of rates for passenger traffic enables the managements of such enterprises to leave to the passengers themselves the business of finding their appropriate classification according to the rates they can afford to pay. Customers in the upper classifications are drawn thereto by the greater comfort, but more especially by concern for their social position and by the less crowded condition of the compartments, things which are precisely the result of higher rates. In this and in analogous cases, (e.g., at the theatre), price classification becomes the equivalent of quality classification; this is true in every instance where the payment of a higher price carries with it a visible social distinction and procures the advantages which result from less crowding in the higher price classes. We shall find this tendency to be the more marked the more crowded are the lower priced accommodations. Otherwise, it would be necessary to install more amenities in the higher price classes. Hence, in the case of a railroad whose coaches are normally filled to capacity, there will be no need for the management to spend much on better equipment for the higher priced accommodations. Quite other considerations, again, must be taken into account to explain the differences in postal rates for letters and for printed matter and, similarly, in electricity rates for the home and for the factory.

The formation of prices on a purely competitive market or on a purely monopolistic one are, in reality, rare occurrences, for these "marginal cases" suppose the existence of conditions which are practically never completely fulfilled. Pure competition occurs only where the number of independent sellers is very great and where there is a perfect market, that is, a market where all the sellers and buyers are simultaneously and always aware of each other's offers and among whom, accordingly, a process of continual adjustment is going on. These conditions are most nearly realized, however, only on *organized markets*, in particular, on the most advanced type of an organized market, the stock market. If free or perfect competition exists anywhere, there is where it must be sought. Rather different is the situation on the *unorganized markets* of which we select retail trade as the best known example. When I enter a store to buy myself a hat, I enter, indeed, the "hat market" in the broad sense that I assert my demand for a hat, simultaneously with the rest of the hat demanders, against the total supply of hats available. But since total supply and total demand in this case coincide neither in time nor in place, a quick overall view of the market situation is lacking. I must have sought out many shops before being in a position to fairly judge hat prices; many customers must have left hat shops shrugging their shoulders before shop owners bring their prices down and in turn influence the hat manufacturers to do the same. It is to be noticed, then, that the entire mechanism of price formation functions in this instance slowly and hesitantly, a characteristic which explains the many monopoly-like peculiarities of price formation in retail trade.[1]

But the fact that free competition does not really exist in the chemically pure state, and that many prices contain a certain monopolistic element, must not lead us to conclude that our economic system rests, at bottom, no longer on competition but on mo-

[1] Perfect competition may be precisely defined as that situation which obtains when demand for the output of each producer is perfectly elastic. Otherwise expressed, under perfect competition no producer can ask more than another without risking the loss of all his customers; should he demand less than other producers, they would lose all their patronage to him. These being the prerequisites of perfect competition, it is understandable how rarely such a market situation occurs. In most cases, competition is in fact more or less imperfect. The ensuing problems are just those which have been most searchingly analyzed in recent economic literature. In particular, there has been much attention given to the importance of advertising as a cause of "imperfect (monopolistic) competition." See especially: E. Chamberlin, *The Theory of Monopolistic Competition* (Cambridge, Mass., 1933); J. Robinson, *The Economics of Imperfect Competition* (London, 1933); R. Triffin, *Monopolistic Competition and General Equilibrium* (Cambridge, Mass., 1940); A. Kozlik, "Monopol oder monopolistische Konkurrenz?" *Zeitschrift für Schweizerische Statistik und Volkswirtschaft*, 1941; W. Fellner, *Competition among the Few* (New York, 1950); *Monopoly and Competition and their Regulation*, ed. W. H. Chamberlin (London, 1953); F. Machlup, *The Economics of Sellers' Competition* (Baltimore, 1952).

nopoly. Such a conclusion would be quite wrong. It is to be observed, first, that pure monopoly is an even rarer phenomenon than pure competition. The most important instances in which the monopoly element prevails over the competitive element are: (1) *natural monopoly* where the few existing deposits of certain resources are owned by a single individual or group (e.g., the South African diamond syndicate); (2) *juridical monopoly* based on a grant by the state of an exclusive right to produce or sell a particular commodity (patents, copyrights, etc.), though such a right is usually valid only for a specified period; (3) *transportation monopoly* where the monopolist is protected within his production area against outside competition by the high costs of transport, a situation which may therefore also be termed *area monopoly* (for example, Pittsburgh steel manufacturers); (4) lastly, *trade name monopoly* arising from the susceptibility of consumers to advertisers' suggestions that a given product is unique of its kind (use of brand names). But even in these cases the monopolies, as a rule, must reckon with a number of contrarieties: the possibility that consumers will shift to a substitute product, the tendency for outsiders to move in as the monopoly operations become increasingly profitable, and finally and above all, foreign competition (insofar as the monopolist does not succeed in warding off the latter either by inducing the state to establish protective tariffs or import quotas, or by organizing an international cartel). Finally, the monopolists have to beware of employing their power in such ruthless fashion as to incite public opinion and the state to retaliate; this, however, is an obstacle which may be effectively overcome by the monopolists' skillful influencing of public opinion and of official bodies.

One of the particular accomplishments of modern economic science has been its investigation and definition of the several possible intermediary stages ("market forms") which may lie between pure monopoly and pure competition. But however useful such a procedure, it has had the unfortunate consequence of leading many to conclude that the concepts "monopoly" and "competition" are, for practical purposes, unusable since, in fact, only the intermediate forms exist. Such blurred distinctions serve not only the monopoly interests but also the collectivists who would view only with uneasiness the restoration of a genuinely competitive economy, inasmuch as they need monopoly as a sort of Exhibit A in their arguments for the establishment of a state monopoly as the only remaining solution to the problem. It is certainly possible to define competition and monopoly in such a way that competition can be shown to be unrealizable; consequently, every attempt to take active measures to restore this narrowly defined "competition" to life will be doomed to failure from the start. Such a definition is, however, meaningless. To supply a definition which makes sense, we must begin with what is a decisive question for the ordering of economic life, i.e., how the actual productive forces of the national economy should be allocated as among the several alternative uses. Then monopoly appears as that market form which frees the producer (to the extent to which he controls supply) from the influence of the consumer over the uses of the productive forces. This arbitrary power of the producer attains its maximum extension when production, in accordance with the collectivist program, is concentrated in the hands of the state which then becomes the most dangerous and most powerful of all monopolists. Not the least reason for fearing a state monopoly is the fact that this most powerful of monopolies is simultaneously the one easiest to disguise with slogans.

A criticism which, at the present writing especially, is very widespread is that our economic system is now and will continue to be dominated by monopolies. To this our emphatic reply must be that there is no necessity for such a development. Indeed, it is astonishing how, in every case, competition sooner or later triumphs over monopoly, if only it is given the chance. To say that "competitive capitalism" is necessarily "monopoly capitalism" is simply untrue. The truth is that there is hardly a monopoly worth the name at whose birth, in one way or another, the state has not acted as midwife. Indeed, the history of heavy industry monopolies in Germany has shown that even where the state directly intervened to establish a monopoly, vigorous coercive measures were necessary to force the several producers under one roof. There would probably be few monopolies in the world today if the state, for numerous reasons, had not intervened with all the weight of its authority, its juridical prestige, and its more or less monopoly-favoring economic policy (including the policy of restricting imports) against the natural tendency towards competition. Constant and vigorous assertion of this truth is necessary since an exactly opposite view is generally affirmed, and in a manner such as to suggest the inanity of further discussion of the point. Decades of Marxist propaganda have greatly contributed to the diffusion of this bias. The reigning ideology which enthuses over the "monumental" and the "grandiose," and which grows positively lyrical on the subject of "organizing" and "commanding" (at the expense of the natural and the spontaneous), is obviously an ideology favorable to monopoly. Neither do the monopolists fail to make the most of the state of mind of those who go about moaning that "capitalism" is dead or dying, that the competitive system is a contemptible and vulgar business which ought at the earliest opportunity to be replaced by a tightly organized economic system, and more of the same. Nothing, however, prevents governments from shaping their economic policies to the end that the natural tendency towards competition will once again be permitted to play its proper role in the economic system. Such action appears, at the moment, to be rather unlikely. This is certainly not the fault of "capitalism," but a consequence of the dominance of certain ideologies. We have as little reason to suspend the fight against these ideologies as we have to doubt the *economic noxiousness* of monopolies (in most cases) in their ultimate effects.

The principle charge that can be formulated against monopolies is that they do violence ... to the "business principle" and thus to one of the most essential principles of our economic system. Simultaneously, they introduce into economic life an element of arbitrary power which, in the extreme case of the complete and all-embracing state monopoly (collectivism), becomes absolute. Not only are monopolies in a position to reap superprofits (since competition alone can compel the rendering of a good or service equal in value to payment received) but they cause still further damage by gravely lessening the suppleness and adaptive power of our economic system.[2]

[2] To the list of the evils of monopoly already cited we can add still others to which reference will be made in a later chapter. At the same time, we ought not to lose sight of the fact that in a restricted number of cases monopoly is economically superior to competition. We refer here to those enterprises termed "public utilities." Such enterprises have a twofold character: on the one hand they serve to provide the public with goods and services of vital importance (electricity, gas, water, railroads, streetcars, busses, postal services, etc.); on the other, the very essence of these enterprises is such that to permit the establishment of competing units would be uneconomical, if not also technically impossible in view of the large amounts of capital involved as well as the complicated network of property rights which public utilities require (e.g., the underground conduits for wires and cables required by the telephone company).

The politico-economic problem of public utilities resides in the fact that while their monopoly character is more or less unavoidable, it is at the same time particularly dangerous since these enterprises serve to satisfy urgent (i.e., inelastic) public needs. For the solution of this problem there are two possibilities: either we allow the public utilities to exist as private enterprises, though still requiring them to submit to governmental regulation, or we establish in their place official state or community monopolies. Which of the two solutions would be the more purposeful

The full perniciousness of monopoly price formation becomes apparent when we remember that prices are the better able to fulfill their *regulatory function* in the economy the more flexible they are and the more faithfully they reflect the costs of production. Every price is a double appeal addressed to buyers and sellers: to the sellers an appeal to increase or restrict their supply; to the buyers an appeal to restrict or to increase their demand. Thus prices regulate simultaneously the use of the productive factors of the economy whose prices constitute, jointly, the production costs of a good. *To sum up, prices are nothing other than continuous appeals to the consumers to decide which of the economy's scarce production goods should or should not be, at any given moment, allocated to the various economic uses which can be made of them.* It stands to reason that prices will the better acquit themselves of the function the less they are manipulated by monopoly power or by interventions of the state.

Only in one case is that situation characterized by the word "monopoly" (which in the strict meaning of its Greek root means "single seller"), viz., the exclusive concentration of the supply of a commodity in a single hand, a consciously pursued objective of economic policy. This is the case of the government's fiscal monopoly by means of which a government (as in the well-known example of the tobacco monopolies of some countries [Austria and Italy]), having forcibly eliminated all competition, openly employs its resulting power to raise prices for the purpose of securing income for which it otherwise would be dependent on excise taxes on the commodity in question.

Precisely this special case makes clear that however much a monopoly position may be desirable from a purely egoistic point of view, it is something which from the standpoint of the general welfare is undesirable, or at least must be regarded with serious

---

can be determined only with difficulty, since much depends on the special circumstances obtaining in each country and on the particular type of public utility in question. The experience of the United States, where the system of regulated private monopoly prevails, has shown that efficacious supervision is difficult to realize and may well involve serious inconveniences. The overall disadvantages of state-managed enterprises, on the other hand, argue against the system of state monopolies. (We may note, however, that it is precisely in the case of [publicly operated] public utilities that management is subjected to a salutary scrutiny. The enterprises in question are daily and hourly in intimate and sensitive contact with the public. It is the prestige of the state or of the community which is at stake when complaints are directed against the public utilities of overcharging or poor service, while a well-administered public utility may prove to be a particularly effective advertisement of the virtues of public ownership of enterprise.)

145

misgivings. A consensus may be said to exist on the point that monopoly is basically undesirable because it involves the exercise of a degree of power in the economic and social life of the community which, even where the power is not consciously abused, appears incompatible with the ideals of freedom and justice and in addition creates the danger of disturbances of economic equilibrium and a lessening of productivity. Most people quite correctly associate with the concept of "monopoly" notions of exclusiveness, privilege, arbitrariness, excessive power, and exploitation. These characteristic attributes of monopoly are simultaneously the grounds for one of the most weighty and irrefutable objections to collectivism. As mentioned above, such as economic order, by its extreme concentration of production and distribution in the hands of the state, establishes a complete and all-embracing monopoly against which, in virtue of the apparatus of state coercion on which it rests, there is no appeal. The basic nature of such a system, moreover, is unaffected by possible decentralization of the governmental administration machinery or by the practice of inciting the state-run plants to compete with each other. The idea that in this case the state's exercise of monopoly power provides a guarantee that such power will be employed in the interest of the general welfare is revealed as a fiction.

In a few important instances, monopoly is to be recognized on technical or organizational grounds as superior or even as essential; such instances are the so-called "public utilities" (gas, electricity, water, telephone) in which it is all but impossible to permit the existence of competing firms. All the more unendurable in such cases would be monopoly left to its own devices, particularly since what is at stake here are services which are indispensable to the public. All the more necessary is it, in cases such as these where monopoly is practically unavoidable, to establish a system of control and supervision of the monopolistic enterprises. . . .

Recently, the attempt has been made (in particular, by Joseph A. Schumpeter in *Capitalism, Socialism, and Democracy*) to prove the advantages of monopoly by reference to the special case of public utilities. It is precisely the economic power and capital reserves of the large organization, so runs this argument, which favor technological innovation and progress. What is valid in this argument is that it cannot be known beforehand what use a monopolist will make of the power over which he disposes, whether he will merely extract profits from his enterprise, allowing it otherwise to stagnate behind the sheltering wall of market power, or whether he will seek to enter upon new paths of discovery and invention. What is true in any case is that the promotion of technological progress by means of monopoly can be expected only under specific, and for the most part only infrequently encountered conditions. The decisive fact remains that monopolists dispose of a degree of power over their markets and over the economy which a well-ordered, purposeful economic system based on a just relationship between performance and reward cannot tolerate. To the extent that technological progress is rooted in monopoly privilege, it is at least questionable whether the economic resources of the nation are being employed in accordance with the wishes of the consumer, such as these wishes would have manifested themselves in a context of effective competition.

At the same time, there is one consideration in this connection to which we must pay due regard if we are to arrive at usable definitions of monopoly and competition. Concepts of "pure" or "perfect" competition based on abstract mathematical models, whose assumptions must necessarily remain unrealized in the dynamic reality of economic life, should be replaced by the concept of "active" or "workable" competition in which the continuous striving of the producers for the favor of the consumers is emphasized as the essential note of competition. Where competition of this kind is maintained, it is probable that now one, now the other producer will advance ahead of others and thus acquire a special position. Such a situation is not to be described as "monopolistic" however, so long as other producers have "free entry" into the market in question and thereby the opportunity of themselves acquiring, in turn, such special positions. In this continuous testing and contesting of the protagonists in a given market, and in the incentives provided by the temporary advantages of market dominance, we see precisely that characteristic feature of competition which makes it such an extremely valuable institution. A position of dominance in the market need not be qualified as "monopoly" providing it is temporary and the leader is closely followed by competitors who are free to overtake him in turn. Hence, it does not follow that such progress as is promoted by the expectation and hope of taking the lead in a given industry should be attributed to monopoly. It is legitimate to speak of monopoly only where this competition for the "lead" is eliminated and the "lead" becomes a permanent position of privilege and power—a situation which is calculated more to hinder than to promote prog-

147

ress. On this reasoning, the state's legal sanction by a patent of the "lead," provided by an invention or innovation, constitutes not only just security for intellectual property rights, but also an indispensable economic incentive. Patent rights begin to be problematical, however, to the extent that competition is thereby hindered, and monopoly rights ending in abuses of market power are created.

Where competition is defined as a situation of continuous striving for the favor of the consumers, the concept of monopoly is correspondingly narrowed and limited to those cases in which this striving with its temporary positions of power is eliminated and replaced by a situation of permanently protected positions of power in the market. This makes it possible to set forth all the more unreservedly the evils brought upon the whole community by monopoly. They are found: (1) in the position of dominance of the producer over the consumer achieved in virtue of the elimination of the striving for the favor of consumers who, in turn, lose their appropriate economic role as the "sovereigns" of production; (2) in the resulting possibility of exploitation of consumers and the disruption of the just relationship between performance and reward (business principle), so that the monopoly price lacks the note of the "just price" peculiar to a competitive price; (3) in the weakening of the incentives inherent in competition to provide optimum supply in terms of both price and quality; (4) in the disturbance to the total economic order based on competition and free prices and in the resulting misallocation of resources; (5) in the creation of positions of power which seal off markets from new entrants, thereby depriving them of a fair chance at the economic and social opportunities which otherwise would have been available. Monopoly conditions may exist not only on commodities markets but also on the various individual labor markets in virtue of the power of strong labor unions to establish—by means of techniques such as the closed shop—exclusive control of the supply of labor. The resulting economic evils are analogous to those we have already described.

Applying what we have said thus far to the economic system which predominates in the free world, viz., the market economy, it is clear that such an economy, precisely on account of the central role played in it by competition, suffers a diminution both of its efficiency and its justice (in social terms) where it is plagued by monopoly. If it is desired to reap all those advantages of a market economy lacking in a collectivist economy, if what we

148

wish is a "social market economy" of the type so successfully maintained by the German government since 1948, then the fight against monopoly and the maintenance of effective competition must be recognized as one of the prime conditions thereof.

To properly evaluate the possibilities of a successful fight against monopolies, we must note first that the emergence and even more the duration of monopolies (in the realistic sense used here) are confined within much narrower limits than is popularly supposed and is maintained by social theories which aim at putting the nature of the free economy and its prospects in the most unfavorable light possible. Equally erroneous, we may add, is the view that the development of modern economic life and technological progress tend in ever increasing degree to favor monopolism. If there is an immanent tendency in the free economy it is, today as yesterday, a tendency in the direction of competition, not monopoly. This tendency has been in our time strengthened rather than weakened due precisely to the continuous revolutions in technology and improvements in transportation—with their market-enlarging effects—and the economic development of new areas. Everything is in movement as never before and he who is on top today, whether he be the greatest and most powerful, can maintain his place against his closely following rivals only with the most strenuous effort. If, notwithstanding, monopoly remains one of the greatest problems of our age, this is due not alone to the fact that the conditions favorable to competition are realized only with delay and in any event incompletely, but also to the manifold, often unconscious governmental interventions which frustrate competition. Perhaps the most serious of such interventions are those governmental measures aimed at eliminating foreign competition by means of restrictions on imports.

There is no question but that the outmoded old-liberal view that the desirable situation of free competition is self-perpetuating so long as the state refrains from economic interventions of any kind has been shown to be a fateful error. At the same time, there is a kernel of truth in the notion. Maximum international trade has been shown to be a highly effective corrective for monopolistic tendencies. But it would be unrealistic to count on the realization of this ideal, and even in such case it would be an unjustified simplification to regard the problem of modern monopolism as solved. Consequently, the governments of the free nations of the world cannot avoid the obligation of making the restraint and reduction of monopoly the object of a specific anti-monopoly policy.

149

The obligation is indeed one of the most urgent confronting those anxious to defend the free economy successfully against a collectivism whose appeal and propaganda are based largely on the alleged monopoly elements in "capitalism."

Since it happens only rarely that an individual producer can attain and maintain a more than temporary monopoly position (exception being made for the case of natural resources), the existence of monopoly generally supposes that a number of producers have joined together for the express purpose of eliminating competition among themselves (the principal form of such combination is the cartel, though it is to be observed that not all cartels are formed for the purpose of eliminating competition, in particular not such cartels whose interest is the promotion of more rational specialization, scientific research, and the exchange of technological information). In this case, freedom of contract is uniquely and illegitimately misused to restrict contractual freedom and hence economic freedom in general.

At the same time, the inherent difficulties and weaknesses of the cartel ought not be underestimated. As noted above, it is not easy to bring together the firms of a given industry and to keep them together in spite of their persistently divergent interests, and it is still less easy to deal effectively with the omnipresent threat of competition by outsiders who can destroy the cartel by selling below the cartel price. With the intent of overcoming such difficulties the cartels customarily resort to the technique of "compulsory membership," a procedure which must arouse the deepest misgivings. A further disturbing fact is that the difficulties attendant on the formation of cartels vary in severity in different industries (they are least important in those heavy industries which consist of a few large firms, whose fixed capital investments are large, and which are engaged in the production of homogeneous mass-produced commodities), with the result that the less "cartelizable" industries (finished goods industries such as the textile industry) are at a serious disadvantage.

Anti-monopoly policy is consequently essentially identical with the legal control of the cartel form of organization. Such control may take three forms. The mildest—and therefore also the least effective—form is the one under which cartels are admitted in principle and only their "abuse" prohibited (principle of prevention of abuse). The second possibility is the prohibition of cartels as such, enforced by the police power of the state (principle of prohibition on the model of the American antitrust legislation of

1890). The third and most desirable form of control is to make cartels subject not to criminal but civil prosecution and thereby to deprive a cartel agreement as an abuse of freedom of contract of the protection of the law (principle of denial of legal protection), without prejudice to the legal exceptions that might be made to such a general rule. There is ground for the expectation that the adoption of this form of control would solve the problem of monopolism satisfactorily and silently.

THE ALLEGED INJUSTICE

Ludwig von Mises

from THE ANTI-CAPITALIST MENTALITY (1956)

The most passionate detractors of capitalism are those who reject it on account of its alleged injustice.

It is a gratuitous pastime to depict what *ought* to be and is not because it is contrary to inflexible laws of the real universe. Such reveries may be considered as innocuous as long as they remain daydreams. But when their authors begin to ignore the difference between fantasy and reality, they become the most serious obstacle to human endeavors to improve the external conditions of life and well-being.

The worst of all these delusions is the idea that "nature" has bestowed upon every man certain rights. According to this doctrine nature is openhanded toward every child born. There is plenty of everything for everybody. Consequently, everyone has a fair inalienable claim against all his fellow men and against society that he should get the full portion which nature has allotted to him. The eternal laws of natural and divine justice require that nobody should appropriate to himself what by rights belongs to other people. The poor are needy only because unjust people have deprived them of their birthright. It is the task of the church and the secular authorities to prevent such spoliation and to make all people prosperous.

Every word of this doctrine is false. Nature is not bountiful but stingy. It has restricted the supply of all things indispensable for the preservation of human life. It has populated the world with animals and plants to whom the impulse to destroy human life and welfare is inwrought. It displays powers and elements whose operation is damaging to human life and to human endeavors to preserve it. Man's survival and well-being are an achievement of the skills with which he has utilized the main instrument with which nature has equipped him—reason. Men, cooperating under the system of the division of labor, have created all the wealth which the daydreamers consider as a free gift of nature. With regard to the "distribution" of this wealth, it is nonsensical to refer to an allegedly divine or natural principle of justice. What matters is not the allocation of portions out of a fund presented to man by nature. The problem is rather to further those social institutions which enable people to continue and to enlarge the production of all those things which they need.

The World Council of Churches, an ecumenical organization of Protestant churches, declared in 1948: "Justice demands that the inhabitants of Asia and Africa, for instance, should have the benefits of more machine production."[1] This makes sense only if one implies that the Lord presented mankind with a definite quantity of machines and expected that these contrivances will be distributed equally among the various nations. Yet the capitalistic countries were bad enough to take possession of much more of this stock than "justice" would have assigned to them and thus to deprive the inhabitants of Asia and Africa of their fair portion. What a shame!

The truth is that the accumulation of capital and its investment in machines, the source of the comparatively greater wealth of the Western peoples, are due exclusively to laissez-faire capitalism which the same document of the churches passionately misrepresents and rejects on moral grounds. It is not the fault of the capitalists that the Asiatics and Africans did not adopt those ideologies and policies which would have made the evolution of autochthonous capitalism possible. Neither is it the fault of the capitalists that the policies of these nations thwarted the attempts of foreign investors to give them "the benefits of more machine production." No one contests that what makes hundreds of millions in Asia and Africa destitute is that they cling to primitive methods of production and miss the benefits which the employment of better tools and up-to-date technological designs could bestow upon them. But there is only one means to relieve their distress—namely, the full adoption of laissez-faire capitalism. What they need is private

---

[1] Cf. *The Church and the Disorder of Society* (New York, 1948), p. 198.

153

enterprise and the accumulation of new capital, capitalists, and entrepreneurs. It is nonsensical to blame capitalism and the capitalistic nations of the West for the plight the backward peoples have brought upon themselves. The remedy indicated is not "justice" but the substitution of sound, i.e., laissez-faire, policies for unsound policies.

It was not vain disquisitions about a vague concept of justice that raised the standard of living of the common man in the capitalistic countries to its present height, but the activities of men dubbed as "rugged individualists" and "exploiters." The poverty of the backward nations is due to the fact that their policies of expropriation, discriminatory taxation, and foreign-exchange control prevent the investment of foreign capital while their domestic policies preclude the accumulation of indigenous capital.

All those rejecting capitalism on moral grounds as an unfair system are deluded by their failure to comprehend what capital is, how it comes into existence and how it is maintained, and what the benefits are which are derived from its employment in production processes.

The only source of the generation of additional capital goods is saving. If all the goods produced are consumed, no new capital comes into being. But if consumption lags behind production and the surplus of goods newly produced over goods consumed is utilized in further production processes, these processes are henceforth carried out by the aid of more capital goods. All the capital goods are intermediary goods, stages on the road that leads from the first employment of the original factors of production, i.e., natural resources and human labor, to the final turning out of goods ready for consumption. They all are perishable. They are, sooner or later, worn out in the processes of production. If all the products are consumed without replacement of the capital goods which have been used up in their production, capital is consumed. If this happens, further production will be aided only by a smaller amount of capital goods and will therefore render a smaller output per unit of the natural resources and labor employed. To prevent this sort of dissaving and disinvestment, one must dedicate a part of the productive effort to capital maintenance, to the replacement of the capital goods absorbed in the production of usable goods.

Capital is not a free gift of God or of nature. It is the outcome of a provident restriction of consumption on the part of man. It is created and increased by saving and maintained by the abstention from dissaving.

Neither have capital or capital goods in themselves the power to raise the productivity of natural resources and of human labor. Only if the fruits of saving are wisely employed or invested, do they increase the output per unit of the input of natural resources and of labor. If this is not the case, they are dissipated or wasted.

The accumulation of new capital, the maintenance of previously accumulated capital, and the utilization of capital for raising the productivity of human effort are the fruits of purposive human action. They are the outcome of the conduct of thrifty people who save and abstain from dissaving, viz., the capitalists who earn interest; and of people who succeed in utilizing the capital available for the best possible satisfaction of the needs of the consumers, viz., the entrepreneurs who earn profit.

Neither capital (or capital goods) nor the conduct of the capitalists and entrepreneurs in dealing with capital could improve the standard of living for the rest of the people, if these noncapitalists and nonentrepreneurs did not react in a certain way. If the wage earners were to behave in the way which the spurious "iron law of wages" describes and would know of no use for their earnings other than to feed and to procreate more offspring, the increase in capital accumulated would keep pace with the increase in population figures. All the benefits derived from the accumulation of additional capital would be absorbed by multiplying the number of people. However, men do not respond to an improvement in the external conditions of their lives in the way in which rodents and germs do. They know also of other satisfactions than feeding and proliferation. Consequently, in the countries of capitalistic civilization, the increase of capital accumulated outruns the increase in population figures. To the extent that this happens, the marginal productivity of labor is increased as against the marginal productivity of the material factors of production. There emerges a tendency toward higher wage rates. The proportion of the total output of production that goes to the wage earners is enhanced as against that which goes as interest to the capitalists and as rent to the land owners.[2]

To speak of the productivity of labor makes sense only if one refers to the marginal productivity of labor, i.e., to the deduction in net output to be caused by the elimination of one worker. Then

[2] Profits are not affected. They are the gain derived from adjusting the employment of material factors of production and of labor to changes occurring in demand and supply and solely depend on the size of the previous maladjustment and the degree of its removal. They are transient and disappear once the maladjustment has been entirely removed. But as changes in demand and supply again and again occur, new sources of profit emerge also again and again.

it refers to a definite economic quantity, to a determinate amount of goods or its equivalent in money. The concept of a general productivity of labor as resorted to in popular talk about an allegedly natural right of the workers to claim the total increase in productivity is empty and indefinable. It is based on the illusion that it is possible to determine the shares that each of the various complementary factors of production has physically contributed to the turning out of the product. If one cuts a sheet of paper with scissors, it is impossible to ascertain quotas of the outcome to the scissors (or to each of the two blades) and to the man who handled them. To manufacture a car one needs various machines and tools, various raw materials, the labor of various manual workers, and, first of all, the plan of a designer. But nobody can decide what quota of the finished car is to be physically ascribed to each of the various factors the cooperation of which was required for the production of the car.

For the sake of argument, we may for a moment set aside all the considerations which show the fallacies of the popular treatment of the problem and ask: Which of the two factors, labor or capital, caused the increase in productivity? But precisely if we put the question in this way, the answer must be: capital. What renders the total output in the present-day United States higher (per head of manpower employed) than output in earlier ages or in economically backward countries—for instance, China—is the fact that the contemporary American worker is aided by more and better tools. If capital equipment (per head of the worker) were not more abundant than it was three hundred years ago or than it is today in China, output (per head of the worker) would not be higher. What is required to raise, in the absence of an increase in the number of workers employed, the total amount of America's industrial output is the investment of additional capital that can only be accumulated by new saving. It is those saving and investing to whom credit is to be given for the multiplication of the productivity of the total labor force.

What raises wage rates and allots to the wage earners an ever increasing portion out of the output which has been enhanced by additional capital accumulation is the fact that the rate of capital accumulation exceeds the rate of increase in population. The official doctrine passes over this fact in silence or even denies it emphatically. But the policies of the unions clearly show that their leaders are fully aware of the correctness of the theory which they publicly smear as silly bourgeois apologetics. They are eager

156

to restrict the number of job seekers in the whole country by anti-immigration laws and in each segment of the labor market by preventing the influx of newcomers.

That the increase in wage rates does not depend on the individual worker's "productivity," but on the marginal productivity of labor, is clearly demonstrated by the fact that wage rates are moving upward also for performances in which the "productivity" of the individual has not changed at all. There are many such jobs. A barber shaves a customer today precisely in the same manner his predecessors used to shave people two hundred years ago. A butler waits at the table of the British prime minister in the same way in which once-butlers served Pitt and Palmerston. In agriculture some kinds of work are still performed with the same tools in the same way in which they were performed centuries ago. Yet the wage rates earned by all such workers are today much higher than they were in the past. They are higher because they are determined by the marginal productivity of labor. The employer of a butler withholds this man from employment in a factory and must therefore pay the equivalent of the increase in output which the additional employment of one man in a factory would bring about. It is not any merit on the part of the butler that causes this rise in his wages, but the fact that the increase in capital invested surpasses the increase in the number of hands.

All pseudoeconomic doctrines which depreciate the role of saving and capital accumulation are absurd. What constitutes the greater wealth of a capitalistic society as against the smaller wealth of a noncapitalistic society is the fact that the available supply of capital goods is greater in the former than in the latter. What has improved the wage earners' standard of living is the fact that the capital equipment per head of the men eager to earn wages has increased. It is a consequence of this fact that an ever-increasing portion of the total amount of usable goods produced goes to the wage earners. None of the passionate tirades of Marx, Keynes, and a host of less well-known authors could show a weak point in the statement that there is only one means to raise wage rates permanently and for the benefit of all those eager to earn wages—namely, to accelerate the increase in capital available as against population. If this be "unjust," then the blame rests with nature and not with man.

DISCRIMINATION

Milton Friedman

from CAPITALISM AND FREEDOM (1965)

It is a striking historical fact that the development of capitalism has been accompanied by a major reduction in the extent to which particular religious, racial, or social groups have operated under special handicaps in respect of their economic activities; have, as the saying goes, been discriminated against. The substitution of contract arrangements for status arrangements was the first step toward the freeing of the serfs in the Middle Ages. The preservation of Jews through the Middle Ages was possible because of the existence of a market sector in which they could operate and maintain themselves despite official persecution. Puritans and Quakers were able to migrate to the New World because they could accumulate the funds to do so in the market despite disabilities imposed on them in other aspects of their life. The Southern states after the Civil War took many measures to impose legal restrictions on Negroes. One measure which was never taken on any scale was the establishment of barriers to the ownership of either real or personal property. The failure to impose such barriers clearly did not reflect any special concern to avoid restrictions on Negroes. It reflected, rather, a basic belief in private property which was so strong that it overrode the desire to discriminate against Negroes. The maintenance of the general rules of private property and of capitalism have been a major source

158

of opportunity for Negroes and have permitted them to make greater progress than they otherwise could have made. To take a more general example, the preserves of discrimination in any society are the areas that are most monopolistic in character, whereas discrimination against groups of particular color or religion is least in those areas where there is the greatest freedom of competition.

. . . [O]ne of the paradoxes of experience is that, in spite of this historical evidence, it is precisely the minority groups that have frequently furnished the most vocal and most numerous advocates of fundamental alterations in a capitalist society. They have tended to attribute to capitalism the residual restrictions they experience rather than to recognize that the free market has been the major factor enabling these restrictions to be as small as they are.

We have already seen how a free market separates economic efficiency from irrelevant characteristics. . . . [T]he purchaser of bread does not know whether it was made from wheat grown by a white man or a Negro, by a Christian or a Jew. In consequence, the producer of wheat is in a position to use resources as effectively as he can, regardless of what the attitudes of the community may be toward the color, the religion, or other characteristics of the people he hires. Furthermore, and perhaps more important, there is an economic incentive in a free market to separate economic efficiency from other characteristics of the individual. A businessman or an entrepreneur who expresses preferences in his business activities that are not related to productive efficiency is at a disadvantage compared to other individuals who do not. Such an individual is in effect imposing higher costs on himself than are other individuals who do not have such preferences. Hence, in a free market they will tend to drive him out.

This same phenomenon is of much wider scope. It is often taken for granted that the person who discriminates against others because of their race, religion, color, or whatever, incurs no costs by doing so but simply imposes costs on others. This view is on a par with the very similar fallacy that a country does not hurt itself by imposing tariffs on the products of other countries.[1] Both are equally wrong. The man who objects to buying from or work-

---

[1] In a brilliant and penetrating analysis of some economic issues involved in discrimination, Gary Becker demonstrates that the problem of discrimination is almost identical in its logical structure with that of foreign trade and tariffs. See G. S. Becker, *The Economics of Discrimination* (Chicago: University of Chicago Press, 1957).

ing alongside a Negro, for example, thereby limits his range of choice. He will generally have to pay a higher price for what he buys or receive a lower return for his work. Or, put the other way, those of us who regard color of skin or religion as irrelevant can buy some things more cheaply as a result.

As these comments perhaps suggest, there are real problems in defining and interpreting discrimination. The man who exercises discrimination pays a price for doing so. He is, as it were, "buying" what he regards as a "product." It is hard to see that discrimination can have any meaning other than a "taste" of others that one does not share. We do not regard it as "discrimination"—or at least not in the same invidious sense—if an individual is willing to pay a higher price to listen to one singer than to another, although we do if he is willing to pay a higher price to have services rendered to him by a person of one color than by a person of another. The difference between the two cases is that in the one case we share the taste, and in the other case we do not. Is there any difference in principle between the taste that leads a householder to prefer an attractive servant to an ugly one and the taste that leads another to prefer a Negro to a white or a white to a Negro, except that we sympathize and agree with the one taste and may not with the other? I do not mean to say that all tastes are equally good. On the contrary, I believe strongly that the color of a man's skin or the religion of his parents is, by itself, no reason to treat him differently; that a man should be judged by what he is and what he does and not by these external characteristics. I deplore what seem to me the prejudice and narrowness of outlook of those whose tastes differ from mine in this respect and I think the less of them for it. But in a society based on free discussion, the appropriate recourse is for me to seek to persuade them that their tastes are bad and that they should change their views and their behavior, not to use coercive power to enforce my tastes and my attitudes on others.

FAIR EMPLOYMENT PRACTICES LEGISLATION

Fair employment practice commissions that have the task of preventing "discrimination" in employment by reason of race, color, or religion have been established in a number of states. Such legislation clearly involves interference with the freedom of individuals to enter into voluntary contracts with one another. It subjects any such contract to approval or disapproval by the state. Thus it is directly an interference with freedom of the kind that we would object to in most other contexts. Moreover, as is true with most other interferences with freedom, the individuals subjected to the law may well not be those whose actions even the proponents of the law wish to control.

For example, consider a situation in which there are grocery stores serving a neighborhood inhabited by people who have a strong aversion to being waited on by Negro clerks. Suppose one of the grocery stores has a vacancy for a clerk and the first applicant qualified in other respects happens to be a Negro. Let us suppose that as a result of the law the store is required to hire him. The effect of this action will be to reduce the business done by this store and to impose losses on the owner. If the preference of the community is strong enough, it may even cause the store to close. When the owner of the store hires white clerks in preference to Negroes in the absence of the law, he may not be expressing any preference or prejudice or taste of his own. He may simply be transmitting the tastes of the community. He is, as it were, producing the services for the consumers that the consumers are willing to pay for. Nonetheless, he is harmed, and indeed may be the only one harmed appreciably, by a law which prohibits him from engaging in this activity, that is, prohibits him from pandering to the tastes of the community for having a white rather than a Negro clerk. The consumers, whose preferences the law is intended to curb, will be affected substantially only to the extent that the number of stores is limited and hence they must pay higher prices because one store has gone out of business. This analysis can be generalized. In a very large fraction of cases, employers are transmitting the preference of either their customers or their other employees when they adopt employment policies that treat factors irrelevant to technical physical productivity as relevant to employment. Indeed, employers typically have an incentive, as noted earlier, to try to find ways of getting around the preferences of their consumers or of their employees if such preferences impose higher costs upon them.

The proponents of FEPC argue that interference with the freedom of individuals to enter into contracts with one another with respect to employment is justified because the individual who refuses to hire a Negro instead of a white, when both are equally qualified in terms of physical productive capacity, is harming

161

others, namely, the particular color or religious group whose employment opportunity is limited in the process. This argument involves a serious confusion between two very different kinds of harm. One kind is the positive harm that one individual does another by physical force, or by forcing him to enter into a contract without his consent. An obvious example is the man who hits another over the head with a blackjack. A less obvious example is stream pollution. . . . The second kind is the negative harm that occurs when two individuals are unable to find mutually acceptable contracts, as when I am unwilling to buy something that someone wants to sell me and therefore make him worse off than he would be if I bought the item. If the community at large has a preference for blues singers rather than for opera singers, they are certainly increasing the economic well-being of the first relative to the second. If a potential blues singer can find employment and a potential opera singer cannot, this simply means that the blues singer is rendering services which the community regards as worth paying for whereas the potential opera singer is not. The potential opera singer is "harmed" by the community's taste. He would be better off and the blues singer "harmed" if the tastes were the reverse. Clearly, this kind of harm does not involve any involuntary exchange or an imposition of costs or granting of benefits to third parties. There is a strong case for using government to prevent one person from imposing positive harm, which is to say, to prevent coercion. There is no case whatsoever for using government to avoid the negative kind of "harm." On the contrary, such government intervention reduces freedom and limits voluntary cooperation.

FEPC legislation involves the acceptance of a principle that proponents would find abhorrent in almost every other application. If it is appropriate for the state to say that individuals may not discriminate in employment because of color or race or religion, then it is equally appropriate for the state, provided a majority can be found to vote that way, to say that individuals must discriminate in employment on the basis of color, race, or religion. The Hitler Nuremberg laws and the laws in the Southern states imposing special disabilities upon Negroes are both examples of laws similar in principle to FEPC. Opponents of such laws who are in favor of FEPC cannot argue that there is anything wrong with them in principle, that they involve a kind of state action that ought not to be permitted. They can only argue that the particular

162

criteria used are irrelevant. They can only seek to persuade other men that they should use other criteria instead of these.

If one takes a broad sweep of history and looks at the kind of things that the majority will be persuaded of if each individual case is to be decided on its merits rather than as part of a general principle, there can be little doubt that the effect of a widespread acceptance of the appropriateness of government action in this area would be extremely undesirable, even from the point of view of those who at the moment favor FEPC. If, at the moment, the proponents of FEPC are in a position to make their views effective, it is only because of a constitutional and federal situation in which a regional majority in one part of the country may be in a position to impose its views on a majority in another part of the country.

As a general rule, any minority that counts on specific majority action to defend its interests is shortsighted in the extreme. Acceptance of a general self-denying ordinance applying to a class of cases may inhibit specific majorities from exploiting specific minorities. In the absence of such a self-denying ordinance, majorities can surely be counted on to use their power to give effect to their preferences, or if you will, prejudices, not to protect minorities from the prejudices of majorities.

To put the matter in another and perhaps more striking way, consider an individual who believes that the present pattern of tastes is undesirable and who believes that Negroes have less opportunity than he would like to see them have. Suppose he puts his beliefs into practice by always choosing the Negro applicant for a job whenever there are a number of applicants more or less equally qualified in other respects. Under present circumstances should he be prevented from doing so? Clearly the logic of the FEPC is that he should be.

The counterpart to fair employment in the area where these principles have perhaps been worked out more than any other, namely, the area of speech, is "fair speech" rather than free speech. In this respect the position of the American Civil Liberties Union seems utterly contradictory. It favors both free speech and fair employment laws. One way to state the justification for free speech is that we do not believe that it is desirable that momentary majorities decide what at any moment shall be regarded as appropriate speech. We want a free market in ideas, so that ideas get a chance to win majority or near-unanimous acceptance, even

163

if initially held only by a few. Precisely the same considerations apply to employment or more generally to the market for goods and services. Is it any more desirable that momentary majorities decide what characteristics are relevant to employment than what speech is appropriate? Indeed, can a free market in ideas long be maintained if a free market in goods and services is destroyed? The ACLU will fight to the death to protect the right of a racist to preach on a street corner the doctrine of racial segregation. But it will favor putting him in jail if he acts on his principles by refusing to hire a Negro for a particular job.

As already stressed, the appropriate recourse of those of us who believe that a particular criterion such as color is irrelevant is to persuade our fellows to be of like mind, not to use the coercive power of the state to force them to act in accordance with our principles. Of all groups, the ACLU should be the first both to recognize and proclaim that this is so.

RIGHT-TO-WORK LAWS

Some states have passed so-called "right to work" laws. These are laws which make it illegal to require membership in a union as a condition of employment.

The principles involved in right-to-work laws are identical with those involved in FEPC. Both interfere with the freedom of the employment contract, in the one case by specifying that a particular color or religion cannot be made a condition of employment; in the other, that membership in a union cannot be. Despite the identity of principle, there is almost 100 percent divergence of views with respect to the two laws. Almost all who favor FEPC oppose right to work; almost all who favor right to work oppose FEPC. As a liberal, I am opposed to both, as I am equally to laws outlawing the so-called "yellow-dog" contract (a contract making nonmembership in a union a condition of employment).

Given competition among employers and employees, there seems no reason why employers should not be free to offer any terms they want to their employees. In some cases employers find that employees prefer to have part of their remuneration take the form of amenities such as baseball fields or play facilities or better rest facilities rather than cash. Employers then find that it is more profitable to offer these facilities as part of their employment con-

164

tract rather than to offer higher cash wages. Similarly, employers may offer pension plans, or require participation in pension plans, and the like. None of this involves any interference with the freedom of individuals to find employment. It simply reflects an attempt by employers to make the characteristics of the job suitable and attractive to employees. So long as there are many employers, all employees who have particular kinds of wants will be able to satisfy them by finding employment with corresponding employers. Under competitive conditions the same thing would be true with respect to the closed shop. If in fact some employees would prefer to work in firms that have a closed shop and others in firms that have an open shop, there would develop different forms of employment contracts, some having the one provision, others the other provision.

As a practical matter, of course, there are some important differences between FEPC and right to work. The differences are the presence of monopoly in the form of union organizations on the employee side and the presence of federal legislation in respect of labor unions. It is doubtful that in a competitive labor market, it would in fact ever be profitable for employers to offer a closed shop as a condition of employment. Whereas unions may frequently be found without any strong monopoly power on the side of labor, a closed shop almost never is. It is almost always a symbol of monopoly power.

The coincidence of a closed shop and labor monopoly is not an argument for a right-to-work law. It is an argument for action to eliminate monopoly power regardless of the particular forms and manifestations which it takes. It is an argument for more effective and widespread antitrust action in the labor field.

Another special feature that is important in practice is the conflict between federal and state law and the existence at the moment of a federal law which applies to all the states and which leaves a loophole for the individual state only through the passage of a right-to-work law. The optimum solution would be to have the federal law revised. The difficulty is that no individual state is in a position to bring this about and yet people within an individual state might wish to have a change in the legislation governing union organization within their state. The right-to-work law may be the only effective way in which this can be done and therefore the lesser of evils. Partly, I suppose, because I am inclined to believe that a right-to-work law will not in and of itself have any great effect on the monopoly power of the unions, I do

165

not accept this justification for it. The practical arguments seem to me much too weak to outweigh the objection of principle.

SEGREGATION IN SCHOOLING

Segregation in schooling raises a particular problem not covered by the previous comments for one reason only. The reason is that schooling is, under present circumstances, primarily operated and administered by government. This means that government must make an explicit decision. It must either enforce segregation or enforce integration. Both seem to me bad solutions. Those of us who believe that color of skin is an irrelevant characteristic and that it is desirable for all to recognize this, yet who also believe in individual freedom, are therefore faced with a dilemma. If one must choose between the evils of enforced segregation or enforced integration, I myself would find it impossible not to choose integration.

The preceding chapter, written initially without any regard at all to the problem of segregation or integration, gives the appropriate solution that permits the avoidance of both evils—a nice illustration of how arrangements designed to enhance freedom in general cope with problems of freedom in particular. The appropriate solution is to eliminate government operation of the schools and permit parents to choose the kind of school they want their children to attend. In addition, of course, we should all of us, insofar as we possibly can, try by behavior and speech to foster the growth of attitudes and opinions that would lead mixed schools to become the rule and segregated schools the rare exception.

If a proposal like that of the preceding chapter were adopted, it would permit a variety of schools to develop, some all white, some all Negro, some mixed. It would permit the transition from one collection of schools to another—hopefully to mixed schools —to be gradual as community attitudes changed. It would avoid the harsh political conflict that has been doing so much to raise social tensions and disrupt the community. It would in this special area, as the market does in general, permit cooperation without conformity.[2]

[2] To avoid misunderstanding, it should be noted explicitly that . . . I am taking it for granted that the minimum requirements imposed on schools in order that vouchers be usable do not include whether the school is segregated or not.

166

The state of Virginia has adopted a plan having many features in common with that outlined in the preceding chapter. Though adopted for the purpose of avoiding compulsory integration, I predict that the ultimate effects of the law will be very different—after all, the difference between result and intention is one of the primary justifications of a free society; it is desirable to let men follow the bent of their own interests because there is no way of predicting where they will come out. Indeed, even in the early stages there have been surprises. I have been told that one of the first requests for a voucher to finance a change of school was by a parent transferring a child from a segregated to an integrated school. The transfer was requested not for this purpose but simply because the integrated school happened to be the better school educationally. Looking further ahead, if the voucher system is not abolished, Virginia will provide an experiment to test the conclusions of the preceding chapter. If those conclusions are right, we should see a flowering of the schools available in Virginia, with an increase in their diversity, a substantial if not spectacular rise in the quality of the leading schools, and a later rise in the quality of the rest under the impetus of the leaders.

On the other side of the picture, we should not be so naïve as to suppose that deep-seated values and beliefs can be uprooted in short measure by law. I live in Chicago. Chicago has no law compelling segregation. Its laws require integration. Yet in fact the public schools of Chicago are probably as thoroughly segregated as the schools of most Southern cities. There is almost no doubt at all that if the Virginia system were introduced in Chicago, the result would be an appreciable decrease in segregation, and a great widening in the opportunities available to the ablest and most ambitious Negro youth.

THE ROOTS OF WAR

Ayn Rand

from CAPITALISM: THE UNKNOWN IDEAL (1967)

It is said that nuclear weapons have made wars too horrible to contemplate. Yet every nation on earth feels, in helpless terror, that such a war might come.

The overwhelming majority of mankind—the people who die on the battlefields or starve and perish among the ruins—do not want war. They never wanted it. Yet wars have kept erupting throughout the centuries, like a long trail of blood underscoring mankind's history.

Men are afraid that war might come because they know, consciously or subconsciously, that they have never rejected the doctrine which causes wars, which has caused the wars of the past and can do it again—the doctrine that it is right or practical or necessary for men to achieve their goals by means of *physical force* (by *initiating* the use of force against other men) and that some sort of "good" can justify it. It is the doctrine that force is a proper or unavoidable part of human existence and human societies.

Observe one of the ugliest characteristics of today's world: the mixture of frantic war preparations with hysterical peace propaganda, and the fact that *both come from the same source*—from the same political philosophy. The bankrupt, yet still dominant, political philosophy of our age is *statism*.

Observe the nature of today's alleged peace movements. Professing love and concern for the survival of mankind, they keep screaming that the nuclear-weapons race should be stopped, that armed force should be abolished as a means of settling disputes among nations, and that war should be outlawed in the name of humanity. Yet these same peace movements do not oppose dictatorships; the political views of their members range through all shades of the statist spectrum, from welfare statism to socialism to fascism to Communism. This means that they are opposed to the use of coercion by one nation against another, but not by the government of a nation against its own citizens; it means that they are opposed to the use of force against *armed* adversaries, but not against the *disarmed*.

Consider the plunder, the destruction, the starvation, the brutality, the slave-labor camps, the torture chambers, the wholesale slaughter perpetrated by dictatorships. Yet *this* is what today's alleged peace-lovers are willing to advocate or tolerate—in the name of love for humanity.

It is obvious that the ideological root of statism (or collectivism) is the *tribal premise* of primordial savages who, unable to conceive of individual rights, believed that the tribe is a supreme, omnipotent ruler, that it owns the lives of its members and may sacrifice them whenever it pleases to whatever it deems to be its own "good." Unable to conceive of any social principles, save the rule of brute force, they believed that the tribe's wishes are limited only by its physical power and that other tribes are its natural prey, to be conquered, looted, enslaved, or annihilated. The history of all primitive peoples is a succession of tribal wars and intertribal slaughter. That this savage ideology now rules nations armed with nuclear weapons should give pause to anyone concerned with mankind's survival.

Statism is a system of institutionalized violence and perpetual civil war. It leaves men no choice but to fight to seize political power—to rob or be robbed, to kill or be killed. When brute force is the only criterion of social conduct, and unresisting surrender to destruction is the only alternative, even the lowest of men, even an animal—even a cornered rat—will fight. There can be no peace within an enslaved nation.

The bloodiest conflicts of history were not wars between nations, but *civil wars* between men of the same nation, who could find no peaceful recourse to law, principle, or justice. Observe that the history of all absolute states is punctuated by bloody uprisings—by violent eruptions of blind despair, without ideology, program, or goals—which were usually put down by ruthless extermination.

169

In a full dictatorship, statism's chronic "cold" civil war takes the form of bloody purges, when one gang deposes another—as in Nazi Germany or Soviet Russia. In a mixed economy, it takes the form of pressure-group warfare, each group fighting for legislation to extort its own advantages by force from all other groups.

The degree of statism in a country's political system, is the degree to which it breaks up the country into rival gangs and sets men against one another. When individual rights are abrogated, there is no way to determine who is entitled to what; there is no way to determine the justice of anyone's claims, desires, or interests. The criterion, therefore, reverts to the tribal concept of: one's wishes are limited only by the power of one's gang. In order to survive under such a system, men have no choice but to fear, hate, and destroy one another; it is a system of underground plotting, of secret conspiracies, of deals, favors, betrayals, and sudden, bloody coups.

It is not a system conducive to brotherhood, security, cooperation, and peace.

Statism—in fact and in principle—is nothing more than gang rule. A dictatorship is a gang devoted to looting the effort of the productive citizens of its own country. When a statist ruler exhausts his own country's economy, he attacks his neighbors. It is his only means of postponing internal collapse and prolonging his rule. A country that violates the rights of its own citizens will not respect the rights of its neighbors. Those who do not recognize individual rights will not recognize the rights of nations: a nation is only a number of individuals.

Statism *needs* war; a free country does not. Statism survives by looting; a free country survives by production.

Observe that the major wars of history were started by the more controlled economies of the time against the freer ones. For instance World War I was started by monarchist Germany and czarist Russia, who dragged in their freer allies. World War II was started by the alliance of Nazi Germany with Soviet Russia and their joint attack on Poland.

Observe that in World War II, both Germany and Russia seized and dismantled entire factories in conquered countries, to ship them home—while the freest of the mixed economies, the semicapitalistic United States, sent billions worth of lend-lease equipment, including entire factories, to its allies.[1]

[1] For a detailed, documented account of the full extent of Russia's looting, see Werner Keller, *East Minus West = Zero* (New York: G. P. Putnam's Sons, 1962).

170

Germany and Russia needed war; the United States did not and gained nothing. (In fact, the United States lost, economically, even though it won the war: it was left with an enormous national debt, augmented by the grotesquely futile policy of supporting former allies and enemies to this day.) Yet it is capitalism that today's peace-lovers oppose and statism that they advocate—in the name of peace.

Laissez-faire capitalism is the only social system based on the recognition of individual rights and, therefore, the only system that bans force from social relationships. By the nature of its basic principles and interests, it is the only system fundamentally opposed to war.

Men who are free to produce, have no incentive to loot; they have nothing to gain from war and a great deal to lose. Ideologically, the principle of individual rights does not permit a man to seek his own livelihood at the point of a gun, inside or outside his country. Economically, wars cost money; in a free economy, where wealth is privately owned, the costs of war come out of the income of private citizens—there is no overblown public treasury to hide that fact—and a citizen cannot hope to recoup his own financial losses (such as taxes or business dislocations or property destruction) by winning the war. Thus his own economic interests are on the side of peace.

In a statist economy, where wealth is "publicly owned," a citizen has no economic interests to protect by preserving peace—he is only a drop in the common bucket—while war gives him the (fallacious) hope of larger handouts from his masters. Ideologically, he is trained to regard men as sacrificial animals; he is one himself; he can have no concept of why foreigners should not be sacrificed on the same public altar for the benefit of the same state.

The trader and the warrior have been fundamental antagonists throughout history. Trade does not flourish on battlefields, factories do not produce under bombardments, profits do not grow on rubble. Capitalism is a society of *traders*—for which it has been denounced by every would-be gunman who regards trade as "selfish" and conquest as "noble."

Let those who are actually concerned with peace observe that *capitalism gave mankind the longest period of peace in history*— a period during which there were no wars involving the entire civilized world—from the end of the Napoleonic wars in 1815 to the outbreak of World War I in 1914.

It must be remembered that the political systems of the nineteenth century were not pure capitalism, but mixed economies. The element of freedom, however, was dominant; it was as close to a century of capitalism as mankind has come. But the element of statism kept growing throughout the nineteenth century, and by the time it blasted the world in 1914, the governments involved were dominated by statist policies.

Just as, in domestic affairs, all the evils caused by statism and government controls were blamed on capitalism and the free market—so, in foreign affairs, all the evils of statist policies were blamed on and ascribed to capitalism. Such myths as "capitalistic imperialism," "war-profiteering," or the notion that capitalism has to win "markets" by military conquest are examples of the superficiality or the unscrupulousness of statist commentators and historians.

The essence of capitalism's foreign policy is *free trade*—i.e., the abolition of trade barriers, of protective tariffs, of special privileges—the opening of the world's trade routes to free international exchange and competition among the private citizens of all countries dealing directly with one another. During the nineteenth century, it was free trade that liberated the world, undercutting and wrecking the remnants of feudalism and the statist tyranny of absolute monarchies.

> As with Rome, the world accepted the British empire because it opened world channels of energy for commerce in general. Though repressive (status) government was still imposed to a considerable degree on Ireland with very bad results, on the whole England's invisible exports were law and free trade. Practically speaking, while England ruled the seas any man of any nation could go anywhere, taking his goods and money with him, in safety.[2]

As in the case of Rome, when the repressive element of England's mixed economy grew to become her dominant policy and turned her to statism, her empire fell apart. It was not military force that had held it together.

Capitalism wins and holds its markets by free competition, at home and abroad. A market conquered by war can be of value (temporarily) only to those advocates of a mixed economy who seek to close it to international competition, impose restrictive

[2] Isabel Paterson, *The God of the Machine* (Caldwell, Idaho: The Caxton Printers, 1964), p. 121. Originally published by G. P. Putnam's Sons, New York, 1943.

172

regulations, and thus acquire special privileges by force. The same type of businessmen who sought special advantages by government action in their own countries, sought special markets by government action abroad. At whose expense? At the expense of the overwhelming majority of businessmen who paid the taxes for such ventures, but gained nothing. Who justified such policies and sold them to the public? The statist intellectuals who manufactured such doctrines as "the public interest" or "national prestige" or "manifest destiny."

The actual war profiteers of all mixed economies were and are of that type: men with political pull who acquire fortunes by government favor, during or after a war—*fortunes which they could not have acquired on a free market.*

Remember that private citizens—whether rich or poor, whether businessmen or workers—have no power to start a war. That power is the exclusive prerogative of a government. Which type of government is more likely to plunge a country into war: a government of limited powers, bound by constitutional restrictions—or an unlimited government, open to the pressure of any group with warlike interests or ideologies, a government able to command armies to march at the whim of a single chief executive?

Yet it is not a limited government that today's peace-lovers are advocating.

(Needless to say, unilateral pacifism is merely an invitation to aggression. Just as an individual has the right of self-defense, so has a free country if attacked. But this does not give its government the right to draft men into military service—which is the most blatantly statist violation of a man's right to his own life. There is no contradiction between the moral and the practical: a volunteer army is the most efficient army, as many military authorities have testified. A free country has never lacked volunteers when attacked by a foreign aggressor. But not many men would volunteer for such ventures as Korea or Vietnam. Without drafted armies, the foreign policies of statist or mixed economies would not be possible.)

So long as a country is even semi-free, its mixed-economy profiteers are not the source of its warlike influences or policies, and are not the primary cause of its involvement in war. They are merely political scavengers cashing-in on a public trend. The primary cause of that trend is the mixed-economy intellectuals.

Observe the link between statism and militarism in the intellectual history of the nineteenth and twentieth centuries. Just as the

173

destruction of capitalism and the rise of the totalitarian state were not caused by business or labor or any economic interests, but by the dominant statist ideology of the intellectuals—so the resurgence of the doctrines of military conquest and armed crusades for political "ideals" were the product of the same intellectuals' belief that "the good" is to be achieved by force.

The rise of a spirit of nationalistic imperialism in the United States did not come from the right, but from the left, not from big-business interests, but from the collectivist reformers who influenced the policies of Theodore Roosevelt and Woodrow Wilson. For a history of these influences, see *The Decline of American Liberalism* by Arthur A. Ekirch, Jr.[3]

> In such instances [writes Professor Ekirch] as the progressives' increasing acceptance of compulsory military training and of the white man's burden, there were obvious reminders of the paternalism of much of their economic reform legislation. Imperialism, according to a recent study of American foreign policy, was a revolt against many of the values of traditional liberalism. "The spirit of imperialism was an exaltation of duty above rights, of collective welfare above individual self-interest, the heroic values as opposed to materialism, action instead of logic, the natural impulse rather than the pallid intellect."[4]

In regard to Woodrow Wilson, Professor Ekirch writes:

> Wilson no doubt would have preferred the growth of United States foreign trade to come about as a result of free international competition, but he found it easy with his ideas of moralism and duty to rationalize direct American intervention as a means of safeguarding the national interest.[5]

And: "He [Wilson] seemed to feel that the United States had a mission to spread its institutions—which he conceived as liberal and democratic—to the more benighted areas of the world."[6] It was not the advocates of capitalism who helped Wilson to whip up a reluctant, peace-loving nation into the hysteria of a military crusade—it was the "liberal" magazine *The New Republic*. Its editor, Herbert Croly, used such arguments as: "The American nation needs the tonic of a serious moral adventure."

[3] New York: Longmans, Green & Co., 1955.
[4] *Ibid.*, p. 189. The quotation on "the spirit of imperialism" comes from R. E. Osgood, *Ideals and Self-Interest in America's Foreign Relations* (Chicago: University of Chicago Press, 1953), p. 47.
[5] *Ibid.*, p. 199.
[6] *Ibid.*

Just as Wilson, a "liberal" reformer, led the United States into World War I, "to make the world safe for democracy"—so Franklin D. Roosevelt, another "liberal" reformer, led it into World War II, in the name of the "Four Freedoms." In both cases, the "conservatives"—and the big-business interests—were overwhelmingly opposed to war but were silenced. In the case of World War II, they were smeared as "isolationists," "reactionaries," and "America-Firsters."

World War I led, not to "democracy," but to the creation of three dictatorships: Soviet Russia, Fascist Italy, Nazi Germany. World War II led, not to "Four Freedoms," but to the surrender of one-third of the world's population into Communist slavery.

If peace were the goal of today's intellectuals, a failure of that magnitude—and the evidence of unspeakable suffering on so large a scale—would make them pause and check their statist premises. Instead, blind to everything but their hatred for capitalism, they are now asserting that "poverty breeds wars" (and justifying war by sympathizing with a "material greed" of that kind). But the question is: *what breeds poverty?* If you look at the world of today and if you look back at history, you will see the answer: the degree of a country's freedom is the degree of its prosperity.

Another current catch-phrase is the complaint that the nations of the world are divided into the "haves" and the "have-nots." Observe that the "haves" are those who have freedom, and that it is freedom that the "have-nots" have not.

If men want to oppose war, it is *statism* that they must oppose. So long as they hold the tribal notion that the individual is sacrificial fodder for the collective, that some men have the right to rule others by force, and that some (any) alleged "good" can justify it— there can be no peace *within* a nation and no peace among nations.

It is true that nuclear weapons have made wars too horrible to contemplate. But it makes no difference to a man whether he is killed by a nuclear bomb or a dynamite bomb or an old-fashioned club. Nor does the number of other victims or the scale of the destruction make any difference to him. And there is something obscene in the attitude of those who regard horror as a matter of numbers, who are willing to send a small group of youths to die for the tribe, but scream against the danger to the tribe itself—and more: who are willing to condone the slaughter of defenseless victims, but march in protest against wars between the well-armed.

175

So long as men are subjugated by force, they will fight back and use any weapons available. If a man is led to a Nazi gas chamber or a Soviet firing squad, with no voices raised to defend him, would he feel any love or concern for the survival of mankind? Or would he be more justified in feeling that a cannibalistic mankind, which tolerates dictatorships, does not deserve to survive?

If nuclear weapons are a dreadful threat and mankind cannot afford war any longer, then *mankind cannot afford statism any longer.* Let no man of good will take it upon his conscience to advocate the rule of force—outside or *inside* his own country. Let all those who are actually concerned with peace—those who do love *man* and do care about his survival—realize that if war is ever to be outlawed, it is *the use of force* that has to be outlawed.

PROPERTY AND JUSTICE

Louis O. Kelso and Mortimer J. Adler

from THE CAPITALIST MANIFESTO (1958)

It has often been said that where there is no property, there can be neither justice nor injustice. The statement is usually meant to apply with complete generality to everything that belongs to a man by right—that which is his own or proper to him, whether innate or acquired.

As thus interpreted, the statement covers more than economic property and economic justice. We are here concerned only with the application of it to economic affairs, and especially to the distribution of wealth as that is related to the production of wealth. We are, therefore, excluding from consideration, as having no bearing on the justice of distribution, such wealth as a man obtains by charity or gift on which he has, prior to its receipt, no just claim, as well as the wealth he may obtain by seizure, theft, or other means by which he unjustly appropriates what does not belong to him.[1]

[1] Since property in things includes the right of control and disposition in any lawful manner, the laws relating to the transfer of property at death by will or by intestate distribution are merely regulative of special types of transfers of property by an owner. It is frequently said that the right to inherit or to receive property by will is purely artificial or statutory, meaning that it is not based on natural right. While no one has a natural right to receive property by will or inheritance (because no one, as a matter of justice, has a right to receive a gift), the owner of property does have a natural right to control and dispose of it. The justice of laws regulating transfers by will, and therefore of the laws regulating inheritance (which are by custom relied upon as substitutes for affirmative disposition by will), must be measured by the standards governing the relations of the state to the owners of property.

The question with which we are first of all concerned is how a man who already has some property—in the form of his own labor power, capital instruments, or both—can justly acquire additional property.

This question presupposes that if a man has no property at all—that is, if in violation of his natural rights, he is a chattel slave deprived of innate property in his labor power—he may justly claim to have that innate property restored to him; but until it is restored, he has no property whereby he can justly acquire further property.

The underlying proposition is twofold: on the one hand, when a man has no property rights in factors productive of particular wealth, he can have no basis for a just claim to property rights in the wealth so produced; on the other hand, when he owns as his property all of the instruments of production engaged in producing particular wealth, he can lay just claim to all the wealth so produced.

From this it follows that if several men together employ their respective property in the production of wealth, each man's just share in the distribution of the total wealth produced is proportionate to the contribution each has made by the use of his property toward the production of that wealth. It must be repeated once more that it is only through his productive property—his capital instruments or his labor power—that a man can participate in the production of wealth as an *independent* contributor. The slave whose labor power is owned and used by his master is not an *independent* contributor; hence he cannot, as a matter of strict justice, claim any share in the distribution of the wealth produced.

Two hypothetical cases will help us to clarify this basic point. They are stated in terms of the so-called Crusoe economy, a device so often used in the literature of economics.

(1) Imagine first the economy of Robinson Crusoe, before the advent of Friday but after he has taken possession of the island, domesticated a few animals, devised some hand tools, etc. All the further wealth he produces comes from the productive use of Crusoe's own capital and labor power. Part of Crusoe's output may be additional capital goods; the rest, consumables. To whom does it all belong? No one would hesitate for a second to give the one and only right answer: Crusoe. *A man is justly entitled to all the wealth he himself produces.*

(2) Imagine next the same island economy complicated by two additional factors. One is Friday, who, for the purposes of the

example, shall be Crusoe's chattel slave in violation of his natural rights. The other additional factor is another man, by the name of Smith, whom Crusoe does not enslave. Since Crusoe owns the island, all the capital goods thereon, and the one available slave, Smith enters into an arrangement with Crusoe whereby he will participate in the production of wealth by contributing his own labor power for which, after some bargaining, it is agreed that Smith shall receive some share in the distribution of the wealth produced.

The fact must be noted that the only way Smith can participate in the production of wealth is by using his own property—the only property he has, namely, his own labor power. Only by contributing his labor can Smith's participation in the production of wealth be the basis for a just claim to a share in the distribution of the wealth produced.

Crusoe's man Friday, his goat, his dog, his tools, and his land all more or less actively participate in the production of wealth. But since their participation does not involve any property on their part, it affords no basis for their claiming a share in the distribution of the wealth produced.

Crusoe gives his dog, his goat, and Friday enough to keep them alive and serviceable. Since they participate in production as Crusoe's property and not independently, he can rightfully claim as his all the wealth they produce. It is his to give them as he pleases or not. But since Smith participates in production, not as Crusoe's property used by Crusoe but independently and by the voluntary use of his own labor, he has a right to claim a share in the distribution, as Friday, for example, does not.

What is Smith's just share? Suppose, in this hypothetical case, that it could be known that the value of Smith's contribution to the total production of wealth was one-tenth of the value of the total final product, the other nine parts being contributed by Crusoe's own labor and capital (i.e., all the forms of productive property he owns). On that supposition, can there be any doubt at all that Smith's share in the distribution should be one-tenth of the total? If it is evident that a man is justly entitled to all the wealth he produces, does it not follow with equal clarity that, when several men jointly produce wealth, each is justly entitled to a distributive share that is proportionate to the value of the contribution each makes to the production of the wealth in question?

The foregoing hypothetical cases exemplify the principle of justice with regard to the distribution of wealth to those who have participated in its production by the use of their own productive property—their capital or labor power, or both. They show us concretely what it means to say that each independent participant is entitled to receive a distributive share of the total wealth produced; and that in each case the distributive share, to be just, must be strictly proportional to the contribution that each makes toward the production of the total wealth by the use of his own property.

This is the only principle whereby the distribution of the wealth produced can be justly grounded on the rights of property engaged in the production of wealth. It is furthermore the only distributive principle that is based on the recognition of the rights of property in productive factors, for the essence of such property lies in the right of the owner to receive the portion (or proportionate share) of the wealth which the productive factor owned by him produces.[2]

In order to apply this principle, we must be able to assess the economic value of the contribution made by each of the independent participants in production. How can their economic value be impartially or objectively determined, and determined in a way that is consonant with the institutions of a free society? More specifically, what assesses the value of the contribution to production made by factors A, B, and C, in terms of which the owners of such factors are entitled to receive proportionate shares of the total wealth produced?

Our answer, in brief, is: *free competition.*

Free Competition As the Determinant of Value

In the opening chapter of *Capital*, Karl Marx announces that, in elaborating on a theory advanced by Ricardo, he alone has solved a problem that Aristotle first raised but failed to solve; namely, the problem of finding an objective measure of the economic value of

[2] There are other distributive principles not based on justice or property rights. One is the principle of charity. To continue with the example we have been using, suppose Friday had a sister who became Smith's wife and bore him five children. If Smith's contribution to the production of wealth in the Crusoe economy continued to be no more than one-tenth of the value of the total annual output, his annual income would probably become woefully insufficient for the support of his household of seven. In that case, Crusoe might give him something to supplement the income he earned. Since Smith had not earned this additional wealth, it would represent a charitable distribution on Crusoe's part.

goods and services, so that a just exchange of commodities is possible.

Marx accepts Aristotle's principle of justice in exchange as requiring that the things exchanged be of equal value. He refers explicitly to the pages of Book V on Justice in Aristotle's *Ethics*, and especially to Chapter 5 where Aristotle raises the question of how we can equate the value of beds and houses so that a certain number of beds can be justly exchanged for a certain number of houses.

Aristotle recognized, Marx says, that we cannot equate qualitatively different commodities, unless they can somehow be made commensurable; but lacking any objective and common measure of their exchange value, he found that there was no way to commensurate qualitatively different things. Marx quotes Aristotle as declaring that "it is impossible that such unlike things can be commensurable"; and then adds that Aristotle "himself tells us what barred the way to his further analysis; it was the absence of any concept of value. What is that equal something, that common substance which admits of the value of the beds being expressed by a house? Such a thing, in truth, cannot exist, says Aristotle."[3]

At this point, Marx offers his own solution of the problem which, he says, Aristotle failed to solve. The objective and common measure of exchange value is human labor. According to the labor theory of value, two qualitatively different things can be made commensurable by measuring both by the amount of human labor involved in their production, and when thus measured, things of equivalent value can be justly exchanged.

Turning now to Book V, Chapter 5, of the *Ethics*, we find Aristotle saying, as Marx reports, that a just exchange of qualitatively different things requires that they be of equivalent value; and that this in turn requires some way of commensurating their value. "All goods," Aristotle declares, "must therefore be measured by some one thing," and "this unit," he then says, "is in truth demand, which holds all things together; for if men did not need one another's goods at all, or did not need them equally, there would

---

[3] *Capital*, Book I, Part I, Ch. 1, Sect. 3. "The brilliancy of Aristotle's genius," Marx tells us, "is that he discovered, in the expression of the value of commodities, a relation of equality. The peculiar conditions of the society in which he lived alone prevented him from discovering what, 'in truth,' was at the bottom of this equality." Living in a society that "was founded upon slavery, and had, therefore, for its natural basis, the inequality of men and of their labor powers," Aristotle, Marx thinks, was "prevented from seeing that to attribute value to commodities is merely a mode of expressing all labor as equal human labor."

be either no exchange or not an equal exchange."[4] Aristotle admits, as Marx says, that it is impossible for the qualitatively heterogeneous to be made perfectly commensurate; "but," he immediately adds, "with reference to demand they may become so sufficiently."[5]

So far as we know, Marx and Aristotle offer the only recorded solutions to the problem of how to commensurate the value of heterogeneous things in order to determine equivalents for the purpose of justice in exchange. If Marx's labor theory of value is false, as we contend it is, then Aristotle's solution is the only one available; and, as he says, it is sufficient for all practical purposes even if, under actual market conditions, it falls short of perfection.

The exchange value of goods and services is, in its very nature, a *matter of opinion*. Only where free and workable competition exists does the value set on things to be exchanged reflect the free play of the opinions of all, or at least many, potential buyers and sellers. Any other method of determining values must involve the imposition of an arbitrary opinion of value, an opinion held by one or more persons or an organized group; and such a determination of value, to be effective, must be imposed by force. We submit that the human mind can conceive of no other accurate, objective, and impartial determinant of economic value, once the fallacious labor theory of value has been discarded.

What has just been said about free competition as the only accurate, objective, and impartial means of measuring the equivalence of values for the purpose of justice in the exchange of heterogeneous commodities is equally applicable when the purpose is one of measuring the relative contribution of different factors in the production of wealth, in order to allocate a just distribution of the wealth produced among the owners of these productive forces.[6]

One further point should be observed in passing. If the labor theory of value were true—that is, if labor and labor alone were

---

[4] *Nicomachean Ethics*, Book V, Ch. 5, 1133ª27–29. We would say today not "demand" but "supply and demand," or "free competition." However, these are merely different expressions for the same thing.

[5] *Ibid.*, 1133ᵇ19–20. We might add that any variance between the absolutely just relative values of two things being exchanged and the values at which they are in fact exchanged in a particular market merely reflects variances from *perfect competition* in the market. Aristotle is in effect saying that the free and workable competition that is attainable in a market exempt from all monopolistic restraints results in a determination of values which makes goods and services sufficiently commensurable and makes just exchange possible.

[6] In a money economy, the unit of measurement of value is, of course, the unit of money employed.

the source of all value in economic goods and services—then labor would be entitled, in strict justice, to the whole of the wealth produced. According to this theory, labor, either in the form of living labor or, as Marx suggests, in the form of "congealed labor" (i.e., the labor that is accumulated and congealed in machines), contributes everything to the production of wealth except what nature itself affords. Hence, everything produced would belong to labor as a matter of just requital.[7]

Hence if the labor theory of value were true and if a just distribution of wealth were to be based upon it, there would be no problem of how to divide the wealth produced as between the owners of property in capital and the owners of property in labor power. Marx might then be right in arguing that capital property in private hands should be expropriated, and in recommending that the state, having "expropriated the expropriators," should operate all capital instruments for the general welfare of the working masses, to whom all the wealth produced should then be distributed according to their individual needs.[8]

Since, as we maintain, the labor theory of value is false, and capital is a producer of wealth in the same sense that labor is, all the consequences drawn from the labor theory are wholly without

---

[7] Twenty years before the *Communist Manifesto*, the Preamble of the Mechanics' Union of Trade Associations (Philadelphia, 1827) declared that labor was the source of all wealth, but instead of demanding all the wealth labor produced, they asked only for an equitable share of it, i.e., that which could be "clearly demonstrated to be a fair and full equivalent" for the productive services they rendered. That they did not think of a "fair and full equivalent" as *all* the wealth they produced is indicated by the following passage: "We are prepared to maintain that all who toil have a natural and unalienable right to reap the fruits of their own industry; and that they who by labor (the only source) are the authors of every comfort, convenience, and luxury are in justice entitled to an *equal participation*, not only in the meanest and coarsest, but likewise the richest and choicest of them all" (italics added). Equal participation left something for the owners of capital who did not, under this theory, contribute anything to the production of wealth. Marx was more consistent and thorough. He carried the labor theory of value to its logical conclusion; namely, that any return whatsoever to owners of capital who do not themselves work is *unearned increment* on their part, obtained unjustly by the exploitation of labor.

[8] It should be pointed out that even if the labor theory of value were true, and even if it justified placing all capital instruments in the hands of the state so that the wealth produced by "congealed labor" could be shared by all living laborers, it would not provide a just principle of distribution, useful in solving the problem of what shares individual workers would be entitled to receive relative to one another. This explains why Lenin argued against any system of distribution that is based on the rights of workers—equal rights or unequal rights—instead of upon their needs. See his tract entitled *The State and Revolution* (Moscow, 1949), Ch. 5, especially Sects. 3 and 4.

foundation. We are therefore confronted by a problem to be solved —one which, so far as we know, has not yet been solved. That is the problem of achieving a just distribution of the wealth produced in an industrial society, while at the same time (1) preserving the prosperity of the economy, (2) securing economic welfare by a satisfactory general standard of living for all, and (3) maintaining the economic and political freedom of the individual members of the society.

To that problem we now turn.

THE PROBLEM OF JUSTICE AND WELFARE IN AN INDUSTRIAL ECONOMY

If the increasing productiveness of labor were the sole source of the increasing output of wealth per man-hour employed, labor could justly claim a larger and larger distributive share of the total wealth produced, by virtue of contributing more and more to its production. An objective evaluation of the services of labor through free competition among all relevant factors in production would automatically award ever increasing wages as a just return for the services of labor. As the total wealth of the economy increased, the standard of living of those who worked for a living would rise.

But as we have already pointed out, the productiveness of sub-managerial and subtechnical labor is a relatively diminishing quantity as the productiveness of the whole economy increases with the introduction of productive forces other than human labor. If a competitive evaluation of the contribution of labor were then to set wages at a level which labor could justly claim as a return for its services, labor's standard of living might dwindle to bare subsistence or even fall below it.

Hence in an economy in which the wealth produced is distributed in accordance with the one principle of justice we have so far considered, that principle of distributive justice might work against the welfare of the great mass of men who work for a living, whose only income-bearing property is their own labor power, and whose only income takes the form of wages.

Such conflict would not necessarily occur in a pre-industrial economy, in which human labor was the chief productive factor and in which each man had property in his own labor power (i.e., no man being owned by another as a chattel slave). But the case of an industrial economy is exactly the opposite. As the machines of an industrial economy become more and more efficient in the production of wealth, the problem of the conflict between distributive justice and the welfare of workingmen becomes more and more aggravated.

Before we examine the problem further, let us be sure that the truth about the relatively diminishing productiveness of human labor is clearly seen. The comparison of two slave economies, one more and one less productive, will help us to compare pre-industrial with industrial economies, and less advanced with more advanced industrial economies. In each of these comparisons, the greater productiveness of one economy over the other will clearly be seen to result from productive factors other than mechanical labor.

Let us first consider the hypothetical case of a slave economy in which every man is either a master or a chattel slave. Let us further suppose that each slave owner participates in the production of wealth without any use of his own labor power, but only through the use of his capital property, including the slaves he owns. On this supposition, the total wealth produced would belong to the slave owners; and, other things being equal, more would go to a slave owner who used more land and slaves than to one who had less of such property to use in the production of wealth. Here we see a just distribution of wealth based on participation in production through the use of one's property, no part of which is one's own labor power.[9]

Now let us consider two slave economies, *Alpha* and *Beta,* and let us imagine them as differing in one respect and only one. The slave owners in *Alpha* own beasts of burden as well as human slaves, while the slave owners in *Beta* have slaves to use but no animals. All other productive factors are equal in the two economies, i.e., both have the same natural resources, the same hand tools, and the same type of slaves (i.e., the slaves in the two cases

[9] Questions about how the slave owner acquired the property he has at the beginning of a particular year may be relevant to other considerations, but not to the matter at hand. We are concerned here only with the total wealth produced in that particular year, at the start of which two slave owners differ in the productiveness of the capital they own. During that year, let us suppose that each employs his property to its fullest productive capacity, and neither contributes his own labor. At the end of that year, the man with the more highly productive capital employed is entitled to a larger share of the total wealth produced than the man with less productive capital involved, for his property has made a larger contribution toward its production.

have equal strength and skill); and, in addition, the slaves who are household stewards and supervise the work of other slaves are equally diligent and efficient.

In which of the two economies is more total annual wealth likely to be produced—*Alpha* with beasts of burden, or *Beta* without them? The answer is *Alpha,* of course.

Since the reason for this answer is that *Alpha* involves a productive factor (animal power) not involved in *Beta*, it is perfectly clear that one economy can be more productive than another without that greater production of wealth resulting from the greater productiveness of its human labor. And if that is clear, is it not equally clear, according to the principle of justice stated, that the distributive share to which labor is justly entitled does not necessarily increase with every increase in the total productiveness of the economy?

Now, then, substitute machines for animals; and for slaves, substitute men with property in their own labor power. With these substitutions, let *Alpha* be an industrial economy and *Beta* a non-industrial one. All other factors being equal, *Alpha* will annually produce more wealth than *Beta*; but the contribution of labor, as compared with all other forms of property, will be no greater in *Alpha* than in *Beta*.

The same relationships will hold if *Alpha* is an advanced industrial society with powerful and automatic machinery, and *Beta* is a relatively primitive industrial economy, with few machines and poor ones.

Hence we see that the greater productiveness of one economy as compared with another can be attributed to labor only if, all other productive factors being equal, one economy employs more man power than another, or if, with equal amounts of man power employed, there is some difference in its average skill or strength.

Where it cannot be attributed to mechanical labor, and where, in fact, such labor power makes a relatively diminishing contribution as compared with all capital instruments of production, men who participate in production only through the use of such labor power may be justly entitled to so small a share of the total wealth produced, and would receive on a competitive evaluation of their contribution so small a share, that it may become necessary for them to use the power of labor unions, supported by the countervailing power of government, in order to obtain a reasonable subsistence or, better, a decent standard of living.

Laboring men may thus get what they need, even if it is more than they have justly earned by their contribution to the production of the society's total wealth. And if they do get more than they have justly earned, the distributive share paid out to the owners of capital must necessarily be less than the productive use of their property has justly earned for them. When this occurs, the rights of private property in capital instruments have been invaded and eroded, just as much as the rights of private property in labor power are invaded and eroded whenever the owners of such productive property are forced to take less than a competitively determined wage.

We are, therefore, confronted with this critical problem. In an industrial economy such as ours, is it possible to order things so that (1) all families are in a position to earn what amounts to a decent standard of living, (2) by an organization of the economy which preserves and respects the rights of private property in capital instruments as well as in labor power, and which (3) distributes the wealth produced among those who contribute to its production in accordance with the principle of distributive justice stated above?

We know that Soviet Russia claims or hopes eventually to be able to give all its families a decent standard of living. But we also know that its economy is based on the abolition of private property in capital instruments, and that it violates the principle of distributive justice insofar as it gives to each according to his needs, not according to his deserts. State ownership of all capital instruments and the governmental distribution of wealth in a charitable fashion may be able to achieve human welfare so far as the general standard of living is concerned, but such concentration of economic and political power in the hands of the officials who manage and operate the machinery of the state cannot help infringing, thwarting, or destroying the freedom of all the rest.

We know that in the United States we have already accomplished what Soviet Russia eventually hopes it can do to provide a generally high standard of living. But we also know that the distribution of wealth in this country has largely been effected by the power of labor unions supported by the countervailing power of government, by redistributive taxation, and by government spending to promote full employment. While more than 90 percent of the wealth is produced by capital instruments, about 70 percent of the resulting income is distributed to labor. Hence while private property in capital instruments still exists nominally, property rights are attenuated or eroded by withholding from

187

the owners of capital the share of the wealth produced that is proportionate to the contribution their property makes.

The economy of the United States, or what some of its enthusiastic exponents call our "welfare capitalism," is hardly a system based on property rights and distributive justice. We may have succeeded in meeting requirement (1) of the three *desiderata* stated on the preceding page, but only at the expense of sacrificing requirements (2) and (3).

Can the problem be solved? We think it can be, in spite of the fact that, in an advanced industrial economy, the contribution of mechanical labor to the production of wealth has diminished to the point where the return to which it is justly entitled and which it could obtain in a freely competitive market might well fall below mere subsistence, not to mention a decent standard of living.

With every future phase of technological progress, the discrepancy between (a) the contribution of labor to the production of wealth and (b) the income needed by workers to maintain a desirable standard of living must necessarily widen. But with every technological advance, the increasing productiveness of capital instruments also makes the solution of the problem more feasible.

That solution is based on full respect for property rights and on principles of economic justice which not only respect such property rights but also recognize that each man (or, more accurately, each household) has a natural human right to participate in the production of wealth through the ownership and application of productive property (either property in labor or in capital instruments or in both) to a degree sufficient to earn for that household a decent standard of living.

So far we have stated only one of the three principles of justice that constitute the solution of the problem. By itself, it is inadequate, as will be seen when we show why it needs to be supplemented by the other two.[10]

[10] An industrial economy faces another problem, which is neither one of justice nor of charity in the distribution of wealth. It is the problem of maintaining a level of consumption adequate to ever-increasing levels of productiveness. If it fails to solve this problem, an industrial economy is prone to cycles of boom-and-bust in a mounting series of economic crises of the sort that Karl Marx predicted would bring about the eventual and inevitable collapse of capitalism. His prediction that capitalism will sow the seeds of its own destruction is based, of course, on his assumption that what he called the "capitalistic exploitation of labor" would persist in keeping wages at a bare subsistence level. Since the few who are capitalists can consume only a small proportion of the goods an industrial society is able to produce; and since the laboring masses kept at a bare subsistence level do not have enough purchasing power to consume the residue, Marx argued that mounting

The Three Relevant Principles of Justice

Justice, in its most general formulation, imposes the following moral duties or precepts upon men who are associated for the purposes of a common life: (1) to act for the common good of all, not each for his own private interest exclusively; (2) to avoid injuring one another; (3) to render to each man what is rightfully his due; and (4) to deal fairly with one another in the exchange of goods and in the distribution of wealth, position, status, rewards, and punishments.

The one principle of justice already stated in this chapter is a special application of the fourth precept to the distribution of shares in the wealth produced among those who have participated in its production. When, according to this principle, the distributive share rightfully due a participant in production is determined, the third precept becomes applicable, for it commands us to render unto a man whatever is his due.

As we pointed out, two more principles are needed to solve the problem stated in the preceding section. The second principle is a special application of the third precept alone for, quite apart from particular exchanges or distributions, it is concerned with the economic rights of individuals and with the obligation of society to see that every family gets its due in accordance with such rights. The third principle calls for whatever legislative regulation of economic activity may be needed to prevent some individuals from injuring others by pursuing their private interests in a way that violates the economic rights of others. It is a special application of

---

crises of overproduction and underconsumption are inevitable. Only the widely diffused purchasing power that represents a generally higher standard of living can solve this problem. No plan for the organization of an industrial economy, no matter how just, has any practical significance unless it also solves this problem of the economy's self-preservation. Granting that, we are confronted with these alternatives: (1) Can an industrial economy be saved from self-destruction by adopting principles of economic justice, with full respect for all human rights, including those of private property in capital as well as in labor? Or (2) must it resort to principles of charity and welfare in order to effect a generally higher standard of living, and in doing so violate certain principles of justice by invading the rights of private property in capital (as in the United States) or by abolishing them entirely (as in Soviet Russia)? We think that the first alternative is not only possible, but that it is also morally and humanly better than the second, because by a just organization of the economy it preserves political liberty and gives men individual freedom as well as the economic welfare that is necessary, though not sufficient, for a good life. But it will take the capitalistic revolution we are advocating to bring this about.

the second precept of justice given above, and indirectly of the first as well.

As applicable to the production and distribution of wealth, these three principles of justice can be briefly stated in the following manner:

1. THE PRINCIPLE OF DISTRIBUTION

   Among those who participate in the production of wealth, each should receive a share that is proportionate to the value of the contribution each has made to the production of that wealth.

   (It will be seen that this is another way of saying that each participant in production is rightfully entitled to receive the wealth he produces. Where all exchanges, including those which are part of the process of production and distribution itself, are impartially evaluated through free competition, the share received by each participant, paid in money, is the equivalent in value of the contribution he has made.)

2. THE PRINCIPLE OF PARTICIPATION

   Every man has a natural right to life, in consequence whereof he has the right to maintain and preserve his life by all rightful means, including the right to obtain his subsistence by producing wealth or by participating in the production of it.

   (It will be seen that this is another way of saying that everyone has a right to earn a living by participating in the production of wealth. Since a man who is not a slave can participate in the production of wealth only through the use of his own productive property, i.e., his own labor power or capital, the right to earn a living is a right to property in the means of production. The principle of participation, therefore, says that every man or, more exactly, every household or consumer unit must own property in the means of production *capable,* if employed with reasonable diligence, of earning by its contribution to the production of wealth a distributive share that is equivalent to a viable income.)

3. THE PRINCIPLE OF LIMITATION

   Since everyone has a right to property in the means of production sufficient for earning a living, no one has a right to so extensive an ownership of the means of production that it excludes others from the opportunity to participate in production to an extent capable of earning for themselves a viable income; and, consequently, the ownership of productive property by an individual or household must not be allowed to increase beyond the point where it injures others by excluding them from the opportunity to earn a viable income.

190

(It will be seen that this is another way of saying, first, that chattel slavery is unjust, for it makes men propertyless and thus deprives them of their natural right to earn a living by their ownership of any means of production; and, second, that, in an economy in which the private ownership of capital as well as labor is the basis of an effective participation in the production of wealth, injustice is done when the ownership of capital is so highly concentrated in the hands of some men or households that others are excluded from even that minimum degree of participation in production which would enable them justly to earn a viable income for themselves.)

If the meaning of these three principles is clear; if the relation of the second to the first and of the third to the second is also clear; if their special significance for an industrial as opposed to a nonindustrial economy is seen; and if it is understood how the operation of these three principles would solve the problem stated in the preceding section, the reader does not need the amplification which follows in the remainder of this chapter. It is offered to provide a commentary that may be needed. It sets forth, in the light of the foregoing principles, the conditions requisite for the just organization of any economy, and especially of a capitalist economy.

The Organization of a Just Economy

To show how the first principle is supplemented by the second, and the second by the third, we will discuss the three principles in the order named.

(1) *The Principle of Distribution.* While the fourth precept in the general formulation of justice is almost exclusively concerned with economic transactions so far as exchanges are concerned, it has both political and economic application with regard to distributions.

Exchangeable goods are largely economic goods—commodities and services which have exchange value. Here the rule of justice is the simple rule of equality: that in the exchange of heterogeneous goods, the things exchanged should be of equivalent value. On the other hand, as the fourth precept indicates, wealth is not the only thing that is subject to distribution among men.

Political status and position can be justly or unjustly distributed. The rule of justice here is that equals should be treated equally, and unequals unequally in proportion to their inequality. The application of this rule depends on the ascertainment of the facts of equality and inequality.

The fact that all men are by nature equal makes the democratic distribution of citizenship—universal and equal suffrage—just.[11] From this fact it also follows that all oligarchical restrictions of citizenship and suffrage are unjust for, in restricting this fundamental political status, to which all men are entitled, oligarchies treat equals unequally.

The other fact, that men are individually different and unequal in their innate talents and acquired virtues, calls for an unequal distribution of political offices or functions. Some men by their individual merits are better qualified than others to perform the special functions of government above the basic plane of political participation on which all men are equally entitled to operate as citizens. To the extent that a democracy selects men for its hierarchy of public offices or functions according to their merit, it distributes these posts justly; for it thereby treats unequals unequally and proportionately, placing men of greater ability in positions of greater responsibility. What we have called a "rotating aristocracy of leaders" is as essential to the political justice of a democracy as is the institution of equal suffrage for all men.

The foregoing brief statement of the principle of distributive justice, as applied to the basic political status of citizenship and the hierarchy of public offices, prepares us for the statement of an analogous application of the principle to the distribution of wealth among the households of a community.

Considering *only* those who are engaged in the production of wealth, and relying on free and workable competition as the only way to ascertain the facts about the equal or unequal value of the contributions made by each of a number of independent participants in production, distributive justice is done if the share (whether in the form of wages, dividends, rents, etc.) received by each participant in production is proportionate to the value of his contribution to production.

Concretely stated, this means that if A, B, C, and D are four persons or families in a society having only four independent participants in the production of wealth; and if, through the use of

---

[11] The assertion that all men are by nature equal means that all are alike in their natural possession of the dignity of being human and, as persons, of having the natural endowments of reason and freedom which confer on all the capacity for active participation in political life.

the productive property they own, A, B, and C contribute to the total wealth produced in the ratio 3, 2, 1, then the distributive shares they should receive, according to their just deserts, should also be in the ratio of 3, 2, 1. And if the contribution of D, the fourth member, is equal to that of A, B, or C, his distributive share should in justice be equal to that of A, B, or C.

We can now explain why this principle is by itself inadequate to solve our problem or to set up a just economy.

As stated, the principle does not take account of every man's natural economic right to share in the distribution of wealth as a result of participating in its production. It looks only at the actual facts of participation without questioning whether the existing state of affairs is just in other respects, i.e., whether it provides every household with the opportunity to participate in production to an extent capable of earning thereby a viable income.

Thus, for example, the principle of distributive justice might be operative in a pre-industrial slave economy even though that economy were unjust in other respects. It would be unjust insofar as it deprived the men whom it enslaved of their natural right to earn a living and, consequently, of their right to live itself. It would also be unjust insofar as the concentrated ownership of labor power by a small class of slave owners prevented other men who were not slaves from earning by their own labor a viable income for themselves or families. Nevertheless, under such unjust conditions, distributive justice would still be done if the slave owners, who were also the major landowners and owners of hand tools and beasts of burden, received the major share of the wealth produced because the major portion of that wealth had been produced by their property, i.e., the means of production (land, tools, labor, etc.) which they owned.

Before we turn to the second and third principles of justice—the principles of participation and limitation—it is necessary to remind the reader ... that these three principles of justice apply only to primary distribution, and not at all to secondary distributions, for it is only the primary distribution of wealth that directly results from participation in its production. It is also necessary to deal with a problem which may have arisen in the reader's mind with respect to the principle of distribution that we have been considering. Facing this problem here may not only prevent certain misunderstandings of that principle, but may also contribute to the understanding of the other two principles which are still to be discussed.

The problem to be faced arises from the consideration of those aspects of human society which contribute to the production of wealth where such contributions are not paid for. The most obvious of these things, especially from the point of view of an industrial society, is accumulated scientific knowledge together with the dissemination of it through the educational system. But other things can also be mentioned, such as good public roads, an efficient postal system, adequate care of public health, and other services of government which protect or facilitate productive activity.

If certain factors enter into the production of wealth for which no one is paid because these factors do not represent private property for the productive use of which anyone can justly claim a return out of the primary distribution of the wealth produced, then how can it be said that each participant in production receives a distributive share that is proportionate to the competitively determined value of his contribution? Is there not a leak here?

If in the primary distribution of the total wealth produced, that total is divided among those alone who, by their labor or capital, have participated in its production, do they not inevitably receive some portion of the wealth that unpaid-for factors have contributed to producing? And do not these unpaid-for contributions especially benefit the owners of capital instruments which embody scientific discoveries or inventions that have not been protected by copyrights or patents or upon which the statutory copyright or patent protection has lapsed? Does not the income they receive for the contribution made to production by such capital instruments contain and conceal an "unearned increment"—a payment to them for something they did not contribute? If it does, then there is something wrong or inadequate in our principle of distributive justice which asserts that the distributive shares should in every case be proportioned to the value of the contribution made by those who actually participate in production through their ownership of currently active productive property, whether capital or labor or currently furnished raw materials.

We contend that the principle of distributive justice as stated is neither wrong nor inadequate. To begin with, this can be clearly shown with regard to the contribution that scientific discoveries and inventions make to the inherent productiveness of a technologically advanced industrial society. What can be said on that score applies to all the other unpaid-for factors that have been mentioned as grounds for questioning the justice of the distributive

194

principle which should be operative in the primary distribution of wealth in a free society.

It is true that the construction and use of capital instruments and related techniques of production do involve the appropriation, from mankind's funded knowledge, of ideas without which we would still be obtaining our subsistence in the most primitive manner. It should be noted, in the first place, that the ideas thus appropriated come from knowledge that is the achievement of the human race as a whole, not just our own society; and noted, in the second place, that even where some specific new discovery or invention has been recently made within our own society, and is then technologically applied to the production of wealth, that recent discovery or invention invariably involves the appropriation and use of innumerable "old ideas" or elements of applicable knowledge that have been in mankind's possession for centuries, e.g., the wheel.

The present inventor of an electronic control instrument which would eliminate the human control of some widely used productive machinery may contribute something quite novel. It may even be patentable under existing patent laws which, if the inventor takes advantage of them, would give him for a limited length of time a right (i.e., a property right) to charge a royalty for the use of his invention; after which time, the idea becomes "public domain" and can be appropriated by anyone without payment of royalty to the inventor or his heirs. But this new invention, even if it is capable of being patented, depends of necessity upon the contributions of thousands of scientists, mathematicians, discoverers, and inventors in the past.

Readily granting the importance and propriety of laws that encourage inventors by enabling them to obtain, for a limited time, a property right in their contribution to production, there can be no question that all the technologically applicable knowledge that lies back of inventions, which can be protected by patent laws, properly belongs, upon the expiration of statutory patent rights and copyrights, in the public domain. It is the common inheritance of all men simply because they are men; *and precisely because it is common, all have an equal right to use it just as all have an equal opportunity to add to it.*

The equal right of every man to appropriate and use knowledge that belongs to all men in common certainly does not entitle those who make no use of such knowledge to share equally in the wealth produced by those who take advantage of their right to use it by putting it to work in a productive instrument or process. Yet that is the only distributive effect which could follow from supposing that, since the knowledge is the common possession of all, all should stand to profit equally from its use.

To recognize that injustice would be done by thus treating equally those who, with respect to knowledge in the public domain, have not made an equal effort to use it productively is to see that the principle of distributive justice, *as stated*, is neither wrong nor inadequate, even when we take into account the contribution to production that is made by the technologically applicable knowledge that is the common possession of mankind.

The equality of men with regard to useful knowledge is an equal right to the opportunity to master it, use it, and take advantage of it. Men who use the common knowledge that spoiled food may be poisonous do not share the illness of those who remain ignorant or fail to apply such knowledge. It is said that one of the great technological feats of mankind was the domestication of animals. Once that was achieved, did the men who had the opportunity to take advantage of it, but did nothing about it, have a just claim for sharing equally with those who captured and domesticated animals for use as instruments of production?

Society and the state may well have a duty to all men to afford them an equal opportunity to make use of the funded common knowledge of mankind. A system of universal, free public schooling goes a long way toward creating such equal opportunity for all. The existence of free public libraries is another step in the same direction. But society and the state cannot have a moral responsibility to see that those who take advantage of such opportunities to acquire knowledge which they then subsequently put to use in the production of wealth should share in the proceeds of production on an equal basis with those who, having the same opportunities, make no use of them. That would not be justice but rank injustice.

The production of wealth is a current activity for a current result. If a man produces something by his labor and sells the product in a free market, he has currently received the return for his efforts and has no further claim on any return from the use that is later made of the thing he has sold. If, subsequently, the purchaser makes a productive use of it, then it is the purchaser of the thing, not the original producer of it, to whom the current return must be made.[12] He acquired property rights in it, and so long as these are vested in him, he has sole right to claim a distributive return for contributions to production made by the employment of his productive property, even as, at an earlier moment, the original producer of the thing in question had sole right to claim a distributive return for the use of his labor power in producing it.

Hence those who take advantage of the common knowledge of mankind and use it in the production of wealth by capital instruments that incorporate such knowledge, as well as those who acquire by legal means property rights in capital instruments of this sort, have no obligation whatsoever to share their current returns from the economic productivity of their capital property even with those who made the discoveries therein incorporated (assuming they could be identified), except to the extent provided by patent laws or by specific contractual arrangements between those who made the discoveries or inventions and others who wish to make use of them.

There is even less of an obligation on the part of those who own capital instruments that incorporate elements from the funded common knowledge of mankind (which all capital instruments do) to share with all members of society all or even some portion of the wealth produced by these instruments. Justice is done if the benefit that each participant in production derives from the funded common knowledge of mankind depends on the specific use he makes of that knowledge in the current production of wealth. Those who currently contribute to the fund of man's technologically applicable knowledge can derive a current benefit from their contribution to whatever extent they can take advantage of the existing patent laws or enter into special contracts of advantage to themselves.

What has been said on the subject of useful knowledge holds for other aspects of man's social life which contribute to the production of wealth, but which are in the public domain and which, therefore, all men are equally entitled to use to their advantage. Those who do are then entitled to derive a benefit corresponding to the productive use they have made of the factor in question. But in the case of the economically useful services of government

[12] Of course, specific contractual arrangements, such as provisions for royalty payments on tools embodying patented inventions, may be the basis of a duty of an otherwise outright owner to pay for using his property in production.

another consideration enters. Such services, e.g., road building and maintenance, postal service, etc., which promote the production of wealth, are among the functions of government the costs of which are paid for by taxation.

Under an equitable system of taxation, all members of society contribute to defray the costs of government. All are equally entitled to take advantage of those services performed by government which are helpful to anyone engaged in producing wealth. Hence, here as before, there is no ground for maintaining that those who make use of this right are not entitled to the benefit derived from the use they have made. To think otherwise is either (a) to assert that all who pay taxes should share equally in the economic benefits derived from the services of government, regardless of whether they take advantage of them in the production of wealth, or (b) to admit that the availability of such useful services in the production of wealth can have no definite effect on its distribution.

(2) *The Principle of Participation.* In the fourfold formulation of the general meaning of justice with which we began, the third precept called for rendering to each man what is his due by right. When it is declared that life, liberty, and the pursuit of happiness are among man's natural and inalienable rights, criteria are laid down by which to measure the justice of the political and economic institutions of a society.

A just society is one which, by its constitutions, laws, and arrangements, recognizes and protects all of man's natural rights; and to the extent that society violates one or more of these, it is unjust in its organization. Some of these rights belong to man as a human being, e.g., the rights of life, liberty, and the pursuit of happiness; some belong to man as a civic person or member of the political community, e.g., the right to suffrage, the right of association, the right to form political parties; and some belong to man as an economic person or member of the economy, e.g., the rights of man as an owner of property and as a producer or consumer of wealth.[13]

We are here concerned with man's economic rights. Among these, two are of paramount importance for the just organization of an economy.

One is man's right to property in his own labor power. As we have seen, the injustice of chattel slavery or forced labor consists

[13] For an enumeration and classification of natural rights see Jacques Maritain, *The Rights of Man and Natural Law* (New York, 1951), Ch. 2, esp. pp. 73–114.

in the violation of this right. But while an economy which has abolished chattel slavery or forced labor grants all men the right to be independent participants in the production of wealth through the use of their own labor power, that by itself is not enough in any economy in which men who wish to *earn* a living by the use of their property are unable to do so.

We are thus brought to the consideration of a second basic right, which is complementary to man's right to produce the wealth he needs, or, what is the same thing, to share in the distribution of wealth as a result of earning his share.

This second right derives immediately from the most fundamental among all of man's natural rights—his right to life or existence. The right to life involves more than a right not to be murdered or maimed. Since a man cannot live for long without having the means of subsistence, the right to life is meaningless unless it involves a right to acquire subsistence by rightful means.

This right has sometimes been referred to as the "right to a living wage."[14] As that phrase indicates, it is a right to *earn* a living, not to receive it as a gift or to obtain it by theft. To say that it is a right to *earned* income is, therefore, to say that the share of wealth received must be proportioned to the contribution made.

The chattel slave may be given subsistence; but since he is deprived of all property—property in his life and liberty as well as labor power—he has, under these unjust conditions, no way of earning his living. A man who cannot find employment may be kept alive by private charity or by the public dole; but he, too, is unable to earn a living so long as he is unable to use the only property he has, his labor power, to participate in the production of wealth and thereby have a just claim upon a share in its distribution.

Thus we see that there are two conditions under which a man's life may be preserved and yet his right to subsistence denied, i.e., his right to obtain a living through the use of his own property. One is the condition of slavery, in which a man lacks any property through which he can participate in the production of wealth. The other is the condition of those who have productive property but whose property, under the prevailing economic circumstances, is rendered ineffective as a means of obtaining a viable income.

We are, therefore, required by justice to do more than abolish

[14] See Msgr. John A. Ryan, *A Living Wage: Its Ethical and Economic Aspects* (New York, 1906).

chattel slavery. We are required to organize the economy in such a way that every man or family can use his or its property to participate in the production of wealth in a way that earns a living for that man or family.

This principle of justice, which is based on the right of every man or family to obtain a viable income by *earning* it, is integrally connected with the principle of distributive justice already stated. The latter declares the right of every independent participant in the production of wealth to receive a share of that wealth proportionate to his contribution. It indicates that a man's right to an earned income is a conditional right; for it imposes upon him the duty to contribute by the use of his property to the production of wealth. Unless he does so, he cannot rightfully claim a share.

Unless a man exercises his right to earn a living by actual participation in production, he is not entitled to any distributive share. But the right to earn a living by participating in the production of wealth would be a wholly illusory right if the only means by which it could be exercised were in fact incapable of producing wealth or of making a large enough contribution toward its production to earn a viable distributive share. Hence the principle of distributive justice does not operate to guarantee the right to earn a living unless the economy is so organized that every man or family has or can readily obtain property which can be effectively used to participate in the production of wealth to an extent that justifies the claim to a share which constitutes a viable income for that man or family.[15]

When, relative to the increasing productive power of capital instruments, labor as a whole makes a progressively diminishing contribution to the production of wealth, the full employment of those whose only property is such labor power, even if that is accompanied by a just distribution to them of what they earn

[15] In any society, there cannot help being marginal cases of economic failure or economic incompetence. After justice has been done, private or public charity always remains as the remedy for those who are in dire need through no moral fault of their own. In the organization of the economy, justice takes precedence over charity. Only after every step has been taken to see that justice is done, and only after every rightful claim is requited, should charity become operative in response to those pressing human needs which even the most just organization of the production and distribution of wealth may fail to provide for. On this point, see W. Stark's essay *The Contained Economy* (Aquinas Paper No. 26 [London: Blackfriars Publications, 1956]). Stark points out that "however desirable a spirit of charity may be in social life, society can yet survive without it. But justice is not just an embellishment of human co-existence, it is the very basis of it, an indispensable precondition." Declaring that "a sin against justice is an attack on the social bond itself," Stark maintains that "a sin against justice is a very much more serious affair than a sin against charity" (*op. cit.*, p. 18).

through the contribution they make, would not provide such men and their families with a viable income.

Hence in an industrial economy, and especially in one that is technologically advanced, the right to obtain subsistence by earning it involves more than the right to work and the right to a just return for work done. It involves the right to participate effectively in the production of wealth by means consistent with the existing state of technology and with the greatest technological advances of which the economy is capable.

As labor becomes less and less productive of wealth, the ownership of nothing but labor power becomes less and less adequate to satisfy the principle of participation, on condition, of course, that the share of wealth labor receives is equivalent to the value of its contribution as competitively determined. When, for example, the state of automated production reaches a point where, at current levels of consumer demand (free from artificial stimulants designed to create "full employment"), the demand for labor is substantially less than the number of those whose only means of participating in production is through their labor, then for a large number of men the mere ownership of labor power may give them insufficient income-earning property to satisfy the second principle of justice. *When the great bulk of the wealth is produced by capital instruments, the principle of participation requires that a large number of households participate in production through the ownership of such instruments.*

To assert that every man has a right to obtain his living by earning it is not, therefore, the same as asserting everyone's right to a living wage. Under pre-industrial conditions, it might have been possible for those who had no property except their own labor power to have earned a living wage if their contribution to the production of wealth had been justly requited. But in an advanced industrial economy, in which most of the wealth is produced by capital and in which the ownership of capital is concentrated so that all but a few households are entirely dependent upon their ownership of labor for participation in production, it is apparent that labor—at least mechanical labor—would not earn a living wage if the contribution it makes, relative to that made by capital instruments, were justly requited; that is, if instead of being overpaid, the value of its services were objectively and impartially evaluated under conditions of free competition.

To contend that, under all conditions, men are justly entitled to a living wage is, therefore, equivalent to saying that men have a right to the continuance of the conditions under which wealth is produced primarily by labor. There is, of course, no such right; nor would men wish to see it implemented or enforced if there were. To speak of the right to a living wage is, therefore, an inaccurate statement of the right to earn a viable income by effective participation in the production of wealth. The principle of participation entails a right to produce wealth in a manner consistent with the way wealth is in fact being produced, taking full advantage of the existing state of technology.

In an industrial economy, there are two basic ways in which a man or a household may participate in the production of wealth to an extent sufficient to earn thereby a viable income. One is through the productive employment of the capital instruments in which one has property (normally represented by shares of capital stock, but capable of being represented by other forms of securities or by partnerships or other proprietary interests). A household may also participate in production through combinations of these two means.

In all three cases, the income is *earned* income, for it is earned by the productive use of one's private property, whether that is property in capital instruments or property in labor power.

The right to earn a viable income is thus seen as the right of every man or family to own property which, under the prevailing system of producing wealth, is capable of enabling its owner to contribute to the production of wealth to an extent that justly entitles him to receive in return an earned income to support a decent standard of living.

(3) *The Principle of Limitation.* This third principle is implied by the first and second, i.e., the principles of distribution and participation.

Capital instruments are productive of wealth in exactly the same sense that labor power is productive of wealth. In the absence of chattel slavery, the owernship of labor cannot be concentrated; on the contrary, it is completely diffused, each free man having proprietorship in his own labor. But it is possible for the ownership of capital to become highly concentrated. Such concentration is capable of reaching the point at which some men or households are either totally excluded from participation in production or excluded from participating to an extent sufficient to earn them a viable income or, as we sometimes say, a decent standard of living. It is at this point that the principle of limitation must become operative to prevent such concentrations of capital ownership as are injurious to the economic rights of others, i.e., their right of effective participation in production and to earn thereby a viable income in the form of the distributive share to which they are justly entitled by the value of their contribution.

This principle of limitation has significance only for an economy based on the institution of private property in the means of production and on the joint participation of a number of independent contributors to the production of wealth. If the size of the distributive share an individual receives bears no relation to the value of the contribution he makes; if, in other words, the principle of distribution is "from each according to his ability, and to each according to his needs," then the principle of limitation is without significance. On the contrary, if the distribution of wealth is based on a principle of charity divorced from property rights, instead of on a principle of justice in acknowledgment of property rights, then the distribution of wealth may be more effectively accomplished through the greatest possible concentration of capital ownership, e.g., its total ownership by the state.

As the methods by which an economy produces its wealth call for proportionately more capital and less labor, the opportunities to participate in the production of wealth increasingly rest on individual ownership of capital and decreasingly on individual ownership of labor. The concentration of capital ownership—a wholly normal process where the inherent productiveness of one factor is constantly increasing in relation to that of the other—will tend at some point to become a monopolization of the principal means of production by some members of the economy. When this happens, others will be excluded from opportunities to which they have a natural right.

To whatever extent the concentrated ownership of a society's capital stock excludes any portion of its members from effective participation in the production of wealth (i.e., effective in the sense of earning a viable income through the productive employment of their own property), such concentrated ownership is intrinsically unjust. It not only violates the common good but also does direct injury to those individuals who are deprived of their natural right to earn a viable income under a system of production in which it is impossible for them to earn a living wage by forms of labor whose contribution, competitively evaluated, would not justly entitle them to a decent standard of living for themselves or their families.

Accordingly, the concentration of ownership in the hands of some men or families must not be allowed to go beyond the point where, under a just system of distribution, it would prevent other men or families from earning a viable income by participating effectively in production. When the preponderant portion of the wealth is produced by capital, participation in the production of wealth must be preponderantly through the ownership of capital —a requirement which at some point, to be empirically determined, imposes a limit upon concentration in the ownership of capital.[16]

It is not our purpose here to anticipate the legislative deliberations which must precede the determination of the point at which, under given technological conditions and for any given general standard of living, the concentrated ownership of capital becomes destructive of the opportunities of others to participate effectively in the production of wealth. In the second part of this book, devoted to outlining a practical program for accomplishing the capitalist revolution, we will suggest what we believe to be a number of feasible ways of making the principle of limitation operative.[17] Suffice it to say here that *the principles of distribution and participation cannot be observed in the absence of laws designed to make the principle of limitation effective.*

The liberty of each man to pursue his private interests, so far as this can be done without injury to others or to the common good, would not be infringed by legislation preventing individual accumulations of capital from exceeding the amount at which they tend to prevent others from effectively participating in the production of wealth by their ownership of capital. If any line can be drawn between liberty and license, it is certainly at the point at which one individual seeks to do as he pleases even though he thereby invades the rights and liberties of other men. In his essay *On Liberty,* John Stuart Mill circumscribed the sphere of actions in which the individual is justly entitled to be free from interference or regulation on the part of society or government, by excluding from that sphere actions which injure others or work against the public interest.[18]

---

[16] It should be noted that the principle of limitation calls for no upper limit to the private ownership of nonproductive property, i.e., consumer goods.

[17] This is done in Chapter 13.

[18] "The object of this Essay," he declared, "is to assert one very simple principle, as entitled to govern absolutely the dealings of society with the individual in the way of compulsion and control. . . . That principle is, that the sole end for which mankind are warranted, individually or collectively, in interfering with the liberty of action of any of their number, is self-protection. That the only purpose for which power can be rightfully exercised over any member of a civilized community, against his will, is to prevent harm to others. . . . The only part of the conduct of anyone, for which he is amenable to society, is that which concerns others" (*op. cit.,* Ch. 1). And in Chapter 5 he reiterated that "for such actions as are prejudicial to the interests of others, the individual is accountable, and may be subjected either to social or legal punishment, if society is of opinion that the one or the other is requisite for its protection."

In Mill's terms, the principle of limitation we are here discussing calls for a justifiable limitation on individual liberty to acquire wealth in the form of capital goods. It limits such liberty by a just concern for the rights of others. It simply says, to paraphrase Mill, that no man's ownership of the most productive form of property in an industrial economy should be so extensive as to exclude others from an economically significant participation in the production of wealth, or as to reduce their participation below that minimum level where their competitively evaluated distributive share is a viable income for themselves or their families.

In a democratic polity, political freedom and justice are as widely diffused as citizenship. If one wishes freedom and justice, the thing to be in a democracy is a citizen. As one cannot now effectively participate in democratic self-government without suffrage, so in the fully mature industrialism of the future it may be impossible to participate effectively in the industrial production of wealth without owning capital.

It should not come as a surprise, therefore, that in a truly capitalist economy, economic freedom and justice will be as widely diffused as the ownership of capital. The thing to be in a capitalist democracy is a citizen-capitalist.

PART III: CAPITALISM AND FREEDOM

"The President of the United States, on January 6, 1942, stated that we seek 'everywhere in the world' the four old freedoms: freedom of speech and expression, freedom of religion, freedom from fear, freedom from want.

Soon thereafter I called attention to the fact that there is a Fifth Freedom—economic freedom—without which none of the other four freedoms will be realized."

HERBERT HOOVER
Addresses upon the American Road

ENFORCED FRATERNITY

Frederic Bastiat

from THE LAW (1848)

No legal plunder: this is the principle of justice, peace, order, stability, harmony, and logic. Until the day of my death, I shall proclaim this principle with all the force of my lungs (which alas! is all too inadequate).*

And, in all sincerity, can anything more than the absence of plunder be required of the law? Can the law—which necessarily requires the use of force—rationally be used for anything except protecting the rights of everyone? I defy anyone to extend it beyond this purpose without perverting it and, consequently, turning might against right. This is the most fatal and most illogical social perversion that can possibly be imagined. It must be admitted that the true solution—so long searched for in the area of social relationships—is contained in these simple words: *Law is organized justice.*

Now this must be said: When justice is organized by law—that is, by force—this excludes the idea of using law (force) to organize any human activity whatever, whether it be labor, charity, agriculture, commerce, industry, education, art, or religion. The organizing by law of any one of these would inevitably destroy the essential organization—justice. For truly, how can we imagine force

* Translator's note: At the time this was written, Mr. Bastiat knew that he was dying of tuberculosis. Within a year, he was dead.

being used against the liberty of citizens without it also being used against justice, and thus acting against its proper purpose?

The Seductive Lure of Socialism

Here I encounter the most popular fallacy of our times. It is not considered sufficient that the law should be just; it must be philanthropic. Nor is it sufficient that the law should guarantee to every citizen the free and inoffensive use of his faculties for physical, intellectual, and moral self-improvement. Instead, it is demanded that the law should directly extend welfare, education, and morality throughout the nation.

This is the seductive lure of socialism. And I repeat again: These two uses of the law are in direct contradiction to each other. We must choose between them. A citizen cannot at the same time be free and not free.

Mr. de Lamartine once wrote to me thusly: "Your doctrine is only the half of my program. You have stopped at liberty; I go on to fraternity." I answered him: "The second half of your program will destroy the first."

In fact, it is impossible for me to separate the word *fraternity* from the word *voluntary*. I cannot possibly understand how fraternity can be *legally* enforced without liberty being *legally* destroyed, and thus justice being *legally* trampled underfoot.

Legal plunder has two roots: One of them, as I have said before, is in human greed; the other is in false philanthropy.

At this point, I think that I should explain exactly what I mean by the word *plunder*.*

I do not, as is often done, use the word in any vague, uncertain, approximate, or metaphorical sense. I use it in its scientific acceptance—as expressing the idea opposite to that of property (wages, land, money, or whatever). When a portion of wealth is transferred from the person who owns it—without his consent and without compensation, and whether by force or by fraud—to anyone who does not own it, then I say that property is violated; that an act of plunder is committed.

I say that this act is exactly what the law is supposed to suppress, always and everywhere. When the law itself commits this

* Translator's note: The French word used by Mr. Bastiat is *spoliation*.

act that it is supposed to suppress, I say that plunder is still committed, and I add that from the point of view of society and welfare, this aggression against rights is even worse. In this case of legal plunder, however, the person who receives the benefits is not responsible for the act of plundering. The responsibility for this legal plunder rests with the law, the legislator, and society itself. Therein lies the political danger.

It is to be regretted that the word *plunder* is offensive. I have tried in vain to find an inoffensive word, for I would not at any time—especially now—wish to add an irritating word to our dissentions. Thus, whether I am believed or not, I declare that I do not mean to attack the intentions or the morality of anyone. Rather, I am attacking an *idea* which I believe to be false; a *system* which appears to me to be unjust; an injustice so independent of personal intentions that each of us profits from it without wishing to do so, and suffers from it without knowing the cause of the suffering.

THREE SYSTEMS OF PLUNDER

The sincerity of those who advocate protectionism, socialism, and communism is not here questioned. Any writer who would do that must be influenced by a political spirit or a political fear. It is to be pointed out, however, that protectionism, socialism, and communism are basically the same plant in three different stages of its growth. All that can be said is that legal plunder is more visible in communism because it is complete plunder; and in protectionism because the plunder is limited to specific groups and industries.[1] Thus it follows that, of the three systems, socialism is the vaguest, the most indecisive, and, consequently, the most sincere stage of development.

But sincere or insincere, the intentions of persons are not here under question. In fact, I have already said that legal plunder is based partially on philanthropy, even though it is a false philanthropy.

[1] If the special privilege of government *protection* against competition—a monopoly—were granted only to one group in France, the iron workers, for instance, this act would so obviously be legal plunder that it could not last for long. It is for this reason that we see all the protected trades combined into a common cause. They even organize themselves in such a manner as to appear to represent *all persons who labor*. Instinctively, they feel that legal plunder is concealed by generalizing it.

With this explanation, let us examine the value—the origin and the tendency—of this popular aspiration which claims to accomplish the general welfare by general plunder.

LAW IS FORCE

Since the law organizes justice, the socialists ask why the law should not also organize labor, education, and religion.

Why should not law be used for these purposes? Because it could not organize labor, education, and religion without destroying justice. We must remember that law is force, and that, consequently, the proper functions of the law cannot lawfully extend beyond the proper functions of force.

When law and force keep a person within the bounds of justice, they impose nothing but a mere negation. They oblige him only to abstain from harming others. They violate neither his personality, his liberty, nor his property. They safeguard all of these. They are *defensive*; they defend equally the rights of all.

LAW IS A NEGATIVE CONCEPT

The harmlessness of the mission performed by law and lawful defense is self-evident; the usefulness is obvious; and the legitimacy cannot be disputed.

As a friend of mine once remarked, this negative concept of law is so true that the statement, *the purpose of the law is to cause justice to reign*, is not a rigorously accurate statement. It ought to be stated that *the purpose of the law is to prevent injustice from reigning*. In fact, it is *injustice*, instead of justice, that has an existence of its own. Justice is achieved only when injustice is absent.

But when the law, by means of its necessary agent, force, imposes upon men a regulation of labor, a method or a subject of education, a religious faith or creed—then the law is no longer negative; it acts positively upon people. It substitutes the will of the legislator for their own wills; the initiative of the legislator for their own initiatives. When this happens, the people no longer need to discuss, to compare, to plan ahead; the law does all this for them. Intelligence becomes a useless prop for the people; they cease to be men; they lose their personality, their liberty, their property.

Try to imagine a regulation of labor imposed by force that is not a violation of liberty; a transfer of wealth imposed by force that is not a violation of property. If you cannot reconcile these contradictions, then you must conclude that the law cannot organize labor and industry without organizing injustice.

ECONOMIC CONTROL AND TOTALITARIANISM

Friedrich Hayek

from THE ROAD TO SERFDOM (1944)

The control of the production of wealth is the control of human life itself.

HILAIRE BELLOC

Most planners who have seriously considered the practical aspects of their task have little doubt that a directed economy must be run on more or less dictatorial lines. That the complex system of interrelated activities, if it is to be consciously directed at all, must be directed by a single staff of experts, and that ultimate responsibility and power must rest in the hands of a commander-in-chief, whose actions must not be fettered by democratic procedure, is too obvious a consequence of underlying ideas of central planning not to command fairly general assent. The consolation our planners offer us is that this authoritarian direction will apply "only" to economic matters. One of the most prominent American planners, Mr. Stuart Chase, assures us, for instance, that in a planned society "political democracy can remain if it confines itself to all but economic matters." Such assurances are usually accompanied by the suggestion that by giving up freedom in what are, or ought to be, the less important aspects of our lives, we shall obtain greater freedom in the pursuit of higher values. On this ground people who abhor the idea of a political dictatorship often clamor for a dictator in the economic field.

The arguments used appeal to our best instincts and often attract the finest minds. If planning really did free us from the less important cares and so made it easier to render our existence one of plain living and high thinking, who would wish to belittle such an ideal? If our economic activities really concerned only the inferior or even more sordid sides of life, of course we ought to endeavor by all means to find a way to relieve ourselves from the excessive care for material ends, and, leaving them to be cared for by some piece of utilitarian machinery, set our minds free for the higher things of life.

Unfortunately the assurance people derive from this belief that the power which is exercised over economic life is a power over matters of secondary importance only, and which makes them take lightly the threat to the freedom of our economic pursuits, is altogether unwarranted. It is largely a consequence of the erroneous belief that there are purely economic ends separate from the other ends of life. Yet, apart from the pathological case of the miser, there is no such thing. The ultimate ends of the activities of reasonable beings are never economic. Strictly speaking there is no "economic motive" but only economic factors conditioning our striving for other ends. What in ordinary language is misleadingly called the "economic motive" means merely the desire for general opportunity, the desire for power to achieve unspecified ends.[1] If we strive for money it is because it offers us the widest choice in enjoying the fruits of our efforts. Because in modern society it is through the limitation of our money incomes that we are made to feel the restrictions which our relative poverty still imposes upon us, many have come to hate money as the symbol of these restrictions. But this is to mistake for the cause the medium through which a force makes itself felt. It would be much truer to say that money is one of the greatest instruments of freedom ever invented by man. It is money which in existing society opens an astounding range of choice to the poor man, a range greater than that which not many generations ago was open to the wealthy. We shall better understand the significance of this service of money if we consider what it would really mean if, as so

[1] Cf. L. Robbins, *The Economic Causes of War*, 1939, Appendix.

215

many socialists characteristically propose, the "pecuniary motive" were largely displaced by "noneconomic incentives." If all rewards, instead of being offered in money, were offered in the form of public distinctions or privileges, positions of power over other men, or better housing or better food, opportunities for travel or education, this would merely mean that the recipient would no longer be allowed to choose, and that, whoever fixed the reward, determined not only its size but also the particular form in which it should be enjoyed.

* * *

Once we realize that there is no separate economic motive and that an economic gain or economic loss is merely a gain or a loss where it is still in our power to decide which of our needs or desires shall be affected, it is also easier to see the important kernel of truth in the general belief that economic matters affect only the less important ends of life, and to understand the contempt in which "merely" economic considerations are often held. In a sense this is quite justified in a market economy—but only in such a free economy. So long as we can freely dispose over our income and all our possessions, economic loss will always deprive us only of what we regard as the least important of the desires we were able to satisfy. A "merely" economic loss is thus one whose effect we can still make fall on our less important needs, while when we say that the value of something we have lost is much greater than its economic value, or that it cannot even be estimated in economic terms, this means that we must bear the loss where it falls. And similarly with an economic gain. Economic changes in other words, usually affect only the fringe, the "margin," of our needs. There are many things which are more important than anything which economic gains or losses are likely to affect, which for us stand high above the amenities and even above many of the necessities of life which are affected by the economic ups and downs. Compared with them, the "filthy lucre," the question whether we are economically somewhat worse or better off, seems of little importance. This makes many people believe that anything which, like economic planning, affects only our economic interests, cannot seriously interfere with the more basic values of life.

This, however, is an erroneous conclusion. Economic values are less important to us than many things precisely because in economic matters we are free to decide what to us is more, and what

less, important. Or, as we might say, because in the present society it is *we* who have to solve the economic problems of our
lives. To be controlled in our economic pursuits means to be
always controlled unless we declare our specific purpose. Or,
since when we declare our specific purpose we shall also have to
get it approved, we should really be controlled in everything.

The question raised by economic planning is, therefore, not
merely whether we shall be able to satisfy what we regard as our
more or less important needs in the way we prefer. It is whether
it shall be we who decide what is more, and what is less, important for us, or whether this is to be decided by the planner. Economic planning would not affect merely those of our marginal
needs that we have in mind when we speak contemptuously
about the merely economic. It would, in effect, mean that we as
individuals should no longer be allowed to decide what we regard
as marginal.

The authority directing all economic activity would control not
merely the part of our lives which is concerned with inferior
things; it would control the allocation of the limited means for all
our ends. And whoever controls all economic activity controls the
means for all our ends, and must therefore decide which are to be
satisfied and which not. This is really the crux of the matter.
Economic control is not merely control of a sector of human life
which can be separated from the rest; it is the control of the means
for all our ends. And whoever has sole control of the means must
also determine which ends are to be served, which values are to
be rated higher and which lower, in short, what men should believe and strive for. Central planning means that the economic
problem is to be solved by the community instead of by the individual; but this involves that it must also be the community, or
rather its representatives, who must decide the relative importance of the different needs.

The so-called economic freedom which the planners promise us
means precisely that we are to be relieved of the necessity of
solving our own economic problems and that the bitter choices
which this often involves are to be made for us. Since under
modern conditions we are for almost everything dependent on
means which our fellow men provide, economic planning would
involve direction of almost the whole of our life. There is hardly
an aspect of it, from our primary needs to our relations with our
family and friends, from the nature of our work to the use of our

leisure, over which the planner would not exercise his "conscious control." [2]

* * *

The power of the planner over our private lives would be no less complete if he chose not to exercise it by direct control of our consumption. Although a planned society would probably to some extent employ rationing and similar devices, the power of the planner over our private lives does not depend on this, and would be hardly less effective if the consumer were nominally free to spend his income as he pleased. The source of this power over all consumption which in a planned society the authority would possess would be their control over production.

Our freedom of choice in a competitive society rests on the fact that, if one person refuses to satisfy our wishes we can turn to another. But if we face a monopolist we are at his mercy. And an authority directing the whole economic system would be the most powerful monopolist conceivable. While we need probably not be afraid that such an authority would exploit this power in the manner in which a private monopolist would do so, while its purpose would presumably not be the extortion of maximum financial gain, it would have complete power to decide what we are to be given and on what terms. It would not only decide what commodities and services were to be available, and in what quantities; it would be able to direct their distribution between districts and groups and could, if it wished, discriminate between persons to any degree it liked. If we remember why planning is advocated by most people, can there be much doubt that this power would be used for the ends of which the authority approves and to prevent the pursuits of ends which it disapproves?

The power conferred by a control of production and prices is

[2] The extent of the control over all life that economic control confers is nowhere better illustrated than in the field of foreign exchanges. Nothing would at first seem to affect private life less than a state control of the dealings in foreign exchange, and most people will regard its introduction with complete indifference. Yet the experience of most continental countries has taught thoughtful people to regard this step as the decisive advance on the path to totalitarianism and the suppression of individual liberty. It is in fact the complete delivery of the individual to the tyranny of the state, the final suppression of all means of escape—not merely for the rich, but for everybody. Once the individual is no longer free to travel, no longer free to buy foreign books or journals, once all the means of foreign contact can be restricted to those of whom official opinion approves or for whom it is regarded as necessary, the effective control of opinion is much greater than that ever exercised by any of the absolutist governments of the seventeenth and eighteenth centuries.

almost unlimited. In a competitive society the prices we have to pay for a thing, the rate at which we can get one thing for another, depend on the quantities of other things of which, by taking one, we deprive the other members of society. This price is not determined by the conscious will of anybody. And if one way of achieving our ends proves too expensive for us, we are free to try other ways. The obstacles in our path are not due to somebody disapproving of our ends, but to the fact that the same means are also wanted elsewhere. In a directed economy, where the authority watches over the ends pursued, it is certain that it would use its powers to assist some ends and to prevent the realization of others. Not our own view, but somebody else's, of what we ought to like or dislike would determine what we should get. And since the authority would have the power to thwart any efforts to elude its guidance, it would control what we consume almost as effectively as if it directly told us how to spend our income.

* * *

Not only in our capacity as consumers, however, and not even mainly in that capacity, would the will of the authority shape and "guide" our daily lives. It would do so even more in our position as producers. These two aspects of our lives cannot be separated; and as for most of us the time we spend at our work is a large part of our whole lives, and as our job usually also determines the place where and the people among whom we live, some freedom in choosing our work is, probably, even more important for our happiness than freedom to spend our income during the hours of leisure.

No doubt it is true that even in the best of worlds this freedom will be very limited. Few people have ever an abundance of choice of occupation. But what matters is that we have some choice, that we are not absolutely tied to a particular job which has been chosen for us, or which we may have chosen in the past, and that if one position becomes quite intolerable, or if we set our heart on another, there is almost always a way for the able, some sacrifice at the price of which he may achieve his goal. Nothing makes conditions more unbearable than the knowledge that no effort of ours can change them; and even if we should never have the strength of mind to make the necessary sacrifice, the knowledge that we could escape if we only strove hard enough makes many otherwise intolerable positions bearable.

This is not to say that in this respect all is for the best in our

219

present world, or has been so in the most liberal past, and that there is not much that could be done to improve the opportunities of choice open to the people. Here as elsewhere the state can do a great deal to help the spreading of knowledge and information and to assist mobility. But the point is that the kind of state action which really would increase opportunity is almost precisely the opposite of the "planning" which is now generally advocated and practised. Most planners, it is true, promise that in the new planned world free choice of occupation will be scrupulously preserved or even increased. But there they promise more than they can possibly fulfil. If they want to plan they must control the entry into the different trades and occupations, or the terms of remuneration, or both. In almost all known instances of planning the establishment of such controls and restrictions was among the first measures taken. If such control were universally practised and exercised by a single planning authority, one needs little imagination to see what would become of the "free choice of occupation" promised. The "freedom of choice" would be purely fictitious, a mere promise to practise no discrimination where in the nature of the case discrimination must be practised, and where all one could hope would be that the selection would be made on what the authority believed to be objective grounds.

There would be little difference if the planning authority confined itself to fixing the terms of employment and tried to regulate numbers by adjusting these terms. By prescribing the remuneration it would no less effectively bar groups of people from entering many trades than by specifically excluding them. A rather plain girl who badly wants to become a saleswoman, a weakly boy who has set his heart on a job where his weakness handicaps him, as well as in general the apparently less able or less suitable are not necessarily excluded in a competitive society; if they value the position sufficiently, they will frequently be able to get a start by a financial sacrifice and will later make good through qualities which at first are not so obvious. But when the authority fixes the remuneration for a whole category and the selection among the candidates is made by an objective test, the strength of their desire for the job will count for very little. The person whose qualifications are not of the standard type, or whose temperament is not of the ordinary kind, will no longer be able to come to special arrangements with an employer whose dispositions will fit in with his special needs: the person who prefers irregular hours or even a happy-go-lucky existence with a small and perhaps uncertain income to a regular routine will no longer have

220

the choice. Conditions will be without exception what in some measure they inevitably are in a large organization—or rather worse, because there will be no possibility of escape. We shall no longer be free to be rational or efficient only when and where we think it worth while, we shall all have to conform to the standards which the planning authority must fix in order to simplify its task. To make this immense task manageable it will have to reduce the diversity of human capacities and inclinations to a few categories of readily interchangeable units and deliberately to disregard minor personal differences. Although the professed aim of planning would be that man should cease to be a mere means, in fact—since it would be impossible to take account in the plan of individual likes and dislikes—the individual would more than ever become a mere means, to be used by the authority in the service of such abstractions as the "social welfare" or the "good of the community."

* * *

That in a competitive society most things can be had at a price—though it is often a cruelly high price we have to pay, is a fact the importance of which can hardly be overrated. The alternative is not, however, complete freedom of choice, but orders and prohibitions which must be obeyed and, in the last resort, the favor of the mighty.

It is significant of the confusion prevailing on all these subjects that it should have become a cause for reproach that in a competitive society almost everything can be had at a price. If the people who protest against the higher values of life being brought into the "cash nexus" that we should not be allowed to sacrifice our lesser needs in order to preserve the higher values, and that the choice should be made for us, this demand must be regarded as rather peculiar and scarcely testifies to great respect for the dignity of the individual. That life and health, beauty and virtue, honor and peace of mind, can often be preserved only at considerable material cost, and that somebody must make the choice, is as undeniable as that we all are sometimes not prepared to make the material sacrifices necessary to protect those higher values against all injury. To take only one example: we could, of course, reduce casualties by motor accidents to zero if we were willing to bear the cost—if in no other way—by abolishing motor cars. And the same is true of thousands of other instances in which we are constantly risking life and health and all the fine values of the spirit, of ourselves and of our fellow men, to further what we at the same time contemptuously describe as our material comfort.

Nor can it be otherwise since all our ends compete for the same means; and we could not strive for anything but these absolute values if they were on no account to be endangered.

That people should wish to be relieved of the bitter choice which hard facts often impose upon them is not surprising. But few want to be relieved through the choice being made for them by others. People just wish that the choice should not be necessary at all. And they are only too ready to believe that the choice is not really necessary, that it is imposed upon them merely by the particular economic system under which we live. What they resent is in truth that there is an economic problem.

In their wishful belief that there is really no longer an economic problem people have been confirmed by irresponsible talk about "potential plenty"—which, if it were a fact, would indeed mean that there is no economic problem which makes the choice inevitable. But although this snare has served socialist propaganda under various names as long as socialism has existed, it is still as palpably untrue as it was when it was first used over a hundred years ago. In all this time not one of the many people who have used it has produced a workable plan of how production could be increased so as to abolish even in Western Europe what we regard as poverty—not to speak of the world as a whole. The reader may take it that whoever talks about potential plenty is either dishonest or does not know what he is talking about.[3] Yet it is this false hope as much as anything which drives us along the road to planning.

While the popular movement still profits by this false belief, the claim that a planned economy would produce a substantially

[3] To justify these strong words the following conclusions may be quoted at which Mr. Colin Clark, one of the best known among the younger economic statisticians, and a man of undoubted progressive views and a strictly scientific outlook, has arrived in his *Conditions of Economic Progress* (1940, pp. 3–4): The "oft-repeated phrases about poverty in the midst of plenty, and the problems of production having already been solved if only we understood the problem of distribution, turn out to be the most untruthful of all modern clichés. . . . The under-utilisation of productive capacity is a question of considerable importance only in the U.S.A., though in certain years also it has been of some importance in Great Britain, Germany and France, but for most of the world it is entirely subsidiary to the more important fact that, with productive resources fully employed, they can produce so little. The age of plenty will still be a long while in coming. . . . If preventable unemployment were eliminated throughout the trade cycle, this would mean a distinct improvement in the standard of living of the population of the U.S.A., but from the standpoint of the world as a whole it would only make a small contribution towards the much greater problem of raising the real income of the bulk of the world population to anything like a civilised standard."

larger output than the competitive system is being progressively abandoned by most students of the problem. Even a good many economists with socialist views who have seriously studied the problems of central planning are now content to hope that a planned society will equal the efficiency of a competitive system; they advocate planning no longer because of its superior productivity but because it will enable us to secure a more just and equitable distribution of wealth. This is, indeed, the only argument for planning which can be seriously pressed. It is indisputable that if we want to secure a distribution of wealth which conforms to some predetermined standard, if we want consciously to decide who is to have what, we must plan the whole economic system. But the question remains whether the price we should have to pay for the realization of somebody's ideal of justice is not bound to be more discontent and more oppression than was ever caused by the much-abused free play of economic forces.

* * *

We should be seriously deceiving ourselves if for these apprehensions we sought comfort in the consideration that the adoption of central planning would merely mean a return, after a brief spell of a free economy, to the ties and regulations which have governed economic activity through most ages, and that, therefore the infringements of personal liberty need not be greater than they were before the age of laissez-faire. This is a dangerous illusion. Even during the periods of European history when the regimentation of economic life went furthest, it amounted to little more than the creation of a general and semipermanent framework of rules within which the individual preserved a wide free sphere. The apparatus of control then available would not have been adequate to impose more than very general directions. And even where the control was most complete it extended only to those activities of a person through which he took part in the social division of labor. In the much wider sphere in which he then still lived on his own products he was free to act as he chose.

The situation is now entirely different. During the liberal era the progressive division of labor has created a situation where almost every one of our activities is part of a social process. This is a development which we cannot reverse since it is only because of it that we can maintain the vastly increased population at anything like present standards. But, in consequence, the substitution of central planning for competition would require central direction of a much greater part of our lives than was ever attempted before. It could not stop at what we regard as our economic activities, because we are now for almost every part of our lives dependent on somebody else's economic activities.[4] The passion for the "collective satisfaction of our needs," with which our socialists have so well prepared the way for totalitarianism, and which wants us to take our pleasures as well as our necessities at the appointed time and in the prescribed form, is, of course, partly intended as a means of political education. But it is also the result of the exigencies of planning, which consists essentially in depriving us of choice, in order to give us whatever fits best into the plan and that at a time determined by the plan.

It is often said that political freedom is meaningless without economic freedom. This is true enough, but in a sense almost opposite from that in which the phrase is used by our planners. The economic freedom which is the prerequisite of any other freedom cannot be the freedom from economic care which the socialists promise us and which can be obtained only by relieving the individual at the same time of the necessity and of the power of choice; it must be the freedom of our economic activity which, with the right of choice, inevitably also carries the risk and the responsibility of that right.

[4] It is no accident that in the totalitarian countries, be it Russia or Germany or Italy, the question of how to organise the people's leisure should have become a problem of planning. The Germans have even invented for this problem the horrible and self-contradictory name of *Freizeitgestaltung* (literally: the shaping of the use made of the people's free time) as if it were still "free time" when it has to be spent in the way ordained by authority.

THE AGE OF TYRANNY

Wilhelm Roepke

from INTERNATIONAL ECONOMIC DISINTEGRATION
(1942)

> My conception of the *terribles simplificateurs* who will come over
> our old Europe is not pleasant, and now and then in my imagination
> I can see these ruffians already in flesh and blood before my eyes. I
> will describe them to you when we drink our pint of beer in Sep-
> tember.
>
> JACOB BURCKHARDT
> letter to F. von Preen, July 24, 1889

The manuscript of this book had reached the present point
when the catastrophe of war fell upon Europe. Almost overnight
the question presented itself how the world picture sketched in
the preceding pages was affected by that disturbing event and
what the author, from his point of view, might contribute towards
establishing the deeper significance of the calamity.

The uncanny, nerve-racking thing about the present situation is
that not a single proved formula for interpreting experience holds
good any longer. The war which has come upon us is not of the
kind familiar in history nor a conflict in which the aims of both
sides are as clear as their opposing national fronts; it is almost—
though not completely—a world-wide civil war in which the horizontal and the vertical fronts criss-cross confusedly. The very
conduct of the war shows no longer any clear outline: the sole characteristic it would seem like developing is that of conforming to

225

no recognized norms. There can be no doubt, however, that this second world war is the manifestation of a stupendous social castastrophe that is working itself out in the whole Western world and can be understood only in the light of the special internal structure of certain countries.

What is that structure and how did it come about? To answer that question satisfactorily is to hold the key to any understanding of the pass to which the world has come today, and, therewith, to its lasting liberation and pacification.

E. Halévy, the great French historian and sociologist, in his interesting work, *L'ère des tyrannies*, maintains that since 1914 the Western world has entered upon "the age of tyrannies," and that, contrary to the liberal, humanitarian ideals of most socialists, it is socialism that has brought us, by a logic seemingly inexorable, along that road.

Quite deliberately, Halévy chose the word "tyranny" to characterize in the clearest possible way what seems essential in the structure of the new collectivist governments and to draw a sharp distinction between that state structure on the one hand and dictatorship or despotism on the other. If a fairly clear, widespread knowledge of the forms assumed by the Greek tyrannies, or even of the passages in which Aristotle describes them, might be taken for granted, then the expression chosen would certainly not be bad. The structure of the modern collectivist state has indeed a quite amazing resemblance to that of some city states of antiquity in the period of despotisms known to us as tyrannies, such as Corinth or Megara, in their geneses, their main characteristics and perhaps, too, in the way they came to an end.[1] In each case there is the same reckless, violent usurpation of the functions of the state by a minority rising from the masses and leaning upon them while flattering and at the same time intimidating them. This minority is headed by a "charismatic"[2] leader and, in contrast with

[1] The Swedish philologist, M. P. Nilsson, in his essay, *The Age of the Early Greek Tyrants* (Belfast, 1936), has recently contributed much to a better understanding of the social structure of tyranny in antiquity. The analogy between ancient and modern tyrannies must not, of course, be exaggerated, nor must it be overlooked that in ancient times it assumed very varied forms. The same applies to the well-known tyrants of the Italian Renaissance like Cola di Rienzi or Malatesta.

[2] The great German sociologist, Max Weber [*Wirtschaft und Gesellschaft, Grundriss der Sozialökonomik* (Tübingen, 1921), Vol. III, pp. 140-148], coined the term and analyzed the conception of the "charismatic Führer." This chapter of Max Weber on "charismatic" government remains a *locus classicus* for an understanding of the modern collectivist state, and is extraordinarily relevant today.

genuine dictatorship, considers its rule by force as the normal, permanent form of state organization, and not as a temporary mandate to be restored to the legitimate authority once the emergency for the state is over. It is, then, a very dangerous, though none the less prevalent, misuse of words to label the blatant instances of tyranny found today "dictatorship."

Every well-knit state comprises some more or less powerful elements of a hierarchic and authoritarian nature, and it would serve no useful purpose to consider as characteristic of the modern "ochlocratic" tyranny a peculiar form of authoritarian government like dictatorship. Kemal Atatürk, for instance, was certainly a dictator in the sense of being the head of a state that he governed practically without opposition. However, it would be quite false and a grave injustice, alike to that great man and to the Turkey he created, to place him, as so many unreflecting journalists have done, among the modern usurpers risen from the masses. His historical rôle is much more that of the "Dictator" of ancient Rome, as opposed to the real tyrants, Sulla or Caesar, who, significantly enough, gave themselves the title of "Dictator Perpetuus." Thus, after Kemal's death, the direction of the state could indeed pass without any breach of continuity into the intelligent, moderate hands of Ismet Inönü. In the Turkey of Kemal there is no praetorian guard, no hierarchic, exclusive party alone allowed to bear arms and insolently identifying itself with the state. Neither is there any high-pitched self-advertisement, no striving after new ways of stimulating the masses so as to prevent their slipping back to the humdrum daily round, to the balanced, normal, steady community life. This normal course of life is, indeed, rightly considered the gravest menace to a régime reposing on an ever intenser excitement of the people's nerves, an excitement which, as Max Weber discerns with great clarity in the passage already quoted, is the outstanding characteristic of "charismatic" government. Where, as in Turkey and in other modern dictatorships, such as Portugal or Greece, those essential signs are lacking, we cannot speak of tyranny, but at most of dictatorships, whether we refer to ancient or to modern times.[3]

[3] This necessary distinction between dictatorship ("commissarial" dictatorship, to be more exact) and tyranny disposes also of the pessimistic prophecy that a war against tyrannies would force the democracies, if they want to be equal to their opponents, to adopt collectivism (tyranny). It is obvious that in such a case of extreme emergency a more or less authoritative direction of the state becomes unavoidable, as the present experience proves. But between such a "commissarial" dictatorship and tyranny there is a world of difference.

If the ancient, like the modern tyrannies, are clearly different from dictatorship, it is not less false to confound them with the idea of a government that is hierarchic, aristocratic, or authoritarian or to set them up as the opposites of democracy. It is hard to imagine any more grave or fateful confusion. It is, of course, easy to understand—since modern democracy grew out of an ardent, passionate fight against arbitrary rule and despotism—that the idea of democracy should awaken in our minds certain associations that are not quite in accord with its real nature and inherent possibilities. Surely no one could read without the deepest emotion Abraham Lincoln's famous oration on the battlefield of Gettysburg, one worthy to rank with that Pericles pronounced two thousand years ago over the Athenian dead. And is it not real blasphemy for Oscar Wilde to parody Lincoln in the words: "bludgeoning of the people by the people for the people"? Surely with regard to Abraham Lincoln; but also with regard to the conception of pure democracy and to its inherent dangers? Tocqueville, John Stuart Mill, Calhoun, and many others who cannot be suspect of reactionary leanings, acknowledge that democracy can lead to the worst despotism and intolerance unless it is limited by other principles and institutions, and it is such limitations, taken as a whole, that may be called the liberal element of the state.[4] There is little need to recall the germs of the modern collectivist doctrine found in Rousseau or in the more extreme theorists among the Jacobins to explain why collectivism—the "tyranny," according to Halévy—is rooted in a democracy that is unrestricted and not sufficiently counterbalanced by liberalism, a genuine aristocracy, or federalism. The characteristic, in fact, of tyranny ancient or modern is that it is always borne along on the tide of great mass movements, and can only thus survive. Mobilizing all its energy, its inventiveness and propaganda technique to show itself to the masses in a favourable light, it adopts by preference the most plebeian methods, knowing well that in the long run its domination cannot be assured by even the most refined terrorism. It was,

[4] This is very clearly put in Benjamin Constant's pamphlet, *De l'ésprit de conquête et de l'usurpation* (1st ed., Hanover, 1814), which is as up to date now as when it was written. This astonishing piece of writing is a reliable guide through all the confusion of our time which—on an infinitely lower level, granted—has so much in common with the Napoleonic period and which may indeed be regarded as its ultimate consequence. Constant rightly draws attention to the fact that genuine democracy can thrive without degenerating only in a restricted circle, one that permits the active collaboration of all the citizens and an effective integration of society—hence the great importance of the federal organization of democracy and of local self-government.

then, not unreasonable to maintain, as did Ortega y Gasset, that tyranny is the form of government in which the revolt of the masses against the moral and intellectual *élite* finds expression. Wherever a tyranny has come to power it has governed with the masses, preferably with the *crapule,* against the *élite* that carries civilization on, and is on the lookout for their reactions in every slightest word or gesture. The antithesis of tyranny is not democracy—a word that only indicates where power is vested—but the liberal principle which, now as always, imposes on every government, however constituted, the limits required by tolerance and respect for inalienable rights of the individual. It is thus compatible with different forms of state structure: it is the principle symbolized in Magna Charta, in the Bill of Rights, and in the Declaration of the "droits de l'homme et du citoyen." That is doubtless what most people have in mind when they speak of democracy as the antithesis of tyranny, but it would be well that they should realize the dangers of the ambiguity. Clearly nobody would wish to expose himself to ridicule by arguing that the so-called democracies today are not the leading antagonists of tyranny: that they are, however, is due less to the democratic principle than to that other which is still best described as liberal. It would not, on the other hand, occur to us to speak of any tyranny as a democracy; but that we shrink from doing so is due far more to the absence of liberal than of democratic characteristics. The masses may well feel more or less at ease for a while under such a regime, but not the *élite.* Whether or not a given individual does feel at ease under it is purely and simply a question of whether he belongs really to the mass or to the *élite;* and those who know anything about sociology need not be told that "mass" minds may be found among university professors just as workers, artisans, and peasants may belong to the *élite.* If that be the case and if, in fact, tyranny strikes root among the masses and can do so only in a state of society that may, sociologically speaking, be called a mass-society, if in history tyranny invariably follows the maxim: "panem et circenses"—as who can doubt?—then we arrive at precisely the conclusion for which Halévy's thesis had prepared us, the intimate connexion between tyranny and socialism.

Finally the question arises wherein lies the difference between the tyrannies, old and new, and the despotic reign, let us say, of Louis XIV. That there must be a world of difference we cannot for a moment doubt. To begin with, the lack of liberty, seemingly common to both, must not only have been less in degree, but also

229

of quite a different kind. How otherwise explain the magnificent
blossoming of the arts and sciences in the one case and the striking sterility in the other? Some explanation of that difference in
spiritual atmosphere may be found in what has just been said
about the mass-society character of tyranny. Moreover, tyranny
differs fundamentally from all other forms of monarchist absolut-
ism in that it is an illegitimate, usurping power, and is consequently devoid of a certain feeling on which the most indolent or
incapable king can depend—the feeling of its being rooted in tradition.[5] It can proffer no sort of established legal title, and so must
regard as the supreme end of the whole art of government, an end
camouflaged in every word and deed, to find some substitute for
that legal title and for that hold on the affections of the governed
which the government entirely lacks. Hence the need to enforce
uniformity of opinion and the unscrupulous imposition of the
will of the state; hence, too, the nervous desire to please, the
continuous quest of ostensible success, and then the anxious
watching for the crowd's approbation; the absence of that calm
poise that is the appanage of legitimate government and excessive
susceptibility to approval and reproach, coupled with an inferiority complex overcompensated by bombast. Not less characteristic of all tyrannies is a weakness for dissimulating their illegitimate, ephemeral tenure of power in monuments which strain to
make up for the centuries they lack in the past, in architecture
suggesting magnificent centuries ahead. That is the source also of
their dread of routine, recognized so clearly by Max Weber and
familiar to every student of contemporary collectivism, their
search for ever-new contrivances to prevent the deliberately over-
stimulated population from calming down or looking at things
soberly with the eyes of common sense. So will a top maintain its
balance only so long as you keep it spinning round and round.[6]

So far we have followed Halévy; all that we have said about the
essence of tyranny is just a series of variations on the simple
thesis sketched in his book. It would appear, however, that there
still is lacking from the picture of tyranny one essential trait that

[5] See Constant's *De l'ésprit de conquête et de l'usurpation* for the best statement
of the distinction between the legitimate and the usurped authority of the state.

[6] "Un usurpateur est exposé à toutes les comparaisons que suggèrent les regrets,
les jalousies ou les espérances; il est obligé de justifier son élévation: il a contracté
l'engagement tacite d'attacher de grands résultats à une si grande fortune: il doit
craindre de tromper l'attente du public, qu'il a si puissamment éveillée. L'inaction
la plus raisonnable, la mieux motivée, lui devient un danger. *Il faut donner aux
Français tous les trois mois,* disait un homme qui s'y entend bien, *quelque chose
de nouveau:* il a tenu sa parole" (Constant, *op. cit.,* Part II, Chap. 2).

Halévy does not mention, although the experiences of his time had already taught a lesson. To the essential characteristics of tyranny that he observed must be added the complete disappearance of norms and ultimate values, without which our society or any society cannot in the long run survive—the pernicious moral anemia, the cynical caprice in the choice of means that for lack of genuine aims become an end in itself—in short, that attitude that can be deliberately called the political pragmatism characteristic of every real tyranny.

Everything breaks up and falls into ruin until at last there remains the one constant aim of tyranny to which are unscrupulously sacrificed all moral principles, all promises, treaties, guarantees and ideals: the naked lust of power ("libido dominandi" of Sallust—*Cataline War*, Chapter 1); the endeavor to keep and to increase the power that is for ever challenged and that, in the last resort, serves no other purpose than to be relished with unreserved gusto. That being so, there is no limit to the violence or falsehood to be expected of such a government. All the ideals and sentiments appealed to and precisely those deserving the deepest respect—social justice, the solidarity of the nation, peace, religion, the purity of family life, the well-being of the masses, the claims of international law, the return to simpler, more natural ways of life, the cultivation of art, science, and literature—all reveal themselves in the end only as glaringly painted and interchangeable coulisses of propaganda. The tyrant becomes the most unscrupulous publicity agent, always and only concerned with effect. The worst of it is perhaps that it soon changes no small part of the population into scoffing cynics—as Benjamin Constant has shown with striking clarity when dealing with the events of the Napoleonic era in the work already cited.[7] It is easy to understand why a form of government with the characteristics described thus far is at the same time the embodiment of such moral nihilism: no nation can fall a victim to such government until it is itself in an advanced stage of social and moral disintegration, and apparently only he can become a tyrant and maintain his power for long who is a political nihilist possessed of a searing *libido dominandi*.

[7] "Des sujets qui soupçonnent leurs maitres de duplicité et de perfidie se forment à la perfidie et à la duplicité: celui qui entend nommer le chef qui le gouverne un grand politique parce que chaque ligne qu'il publie est une imposture veut être à son tour un grand politique, dans une sphère plus subalterne; la vérité lui semble niaiserie, la fraude habilité. . . . Si cette contagion gagne un peuple essentiellement imitateur, un peuple où chacun craigne par-dessus tout de passer pour dupe, la morale privée tardera-t-elle à être engloutie dans le naufrage de la morale publique?" (Constant, *op. cit.*, Part I, Chap. 8).

Other qualities are, no doubt, required, but this is assuredly an essential condition. Thus considered, tyranny appears as the most appalling manifestation of the breakdown of the society it attacks. Any society that lets tyranny get into its system must already be extremely enfeebled, and once tyranny has the mastery it quickly transforms the moral decay into galloping consumption. If, then, the real tyranny is today in such evidence and so widespread that we can speak (with some exaggeration) of an "age of tyranny," we can realize now to its full extent the alarming character of this statement. For, after all, tyranny is clearly no more than the most naked manifestation of a process of moral dissolution whose origins reach very far back and which threatens to engulf our whole civilization. We must recognize that the countries that have fallen to tyranny are those which—for reasons still to be elucidated—first lost their inner cohesion whilst the others were still enjoying more or less considerable reserves that gave them the force to resist.[8] No one will nurse the illusion, however, that the process of disintegration is not going on everywhere or that anything short of the most vigorous reaction can possibly stave it off.

Now, there is no modern tyranny which—whether from the outset or in a slow development, or even while combating socialist ideas—has not subjected the economic life of the nation to a system which, if words are to retain their meaning, can only be called socialistic. More than that—these are the only countries in which socialism has so far been completely established. All the tyrannies of today are socialistic, and, conversely, complete socialism has never been realized anywhere if not in the form of a tyranny.

Is not that in itself a convincing proof of the thesis that complete socialism and modern tyranny are of necessity most closely related? Just here lies the inner tragedy of socialism, known to anybody who at any time of his life has shared socialist ideas, and torturing all socialists who are as sincere as they are intelligent. It is the tragedy of the insoluble inner contradiction inherent in a movement which wants to complete radically the liberation of men started by democracy and liberalism, but in doing so must

[8] It appears relevant to point out here that the extent of the exhaustion of the moral and spiritual reserves varies from one collectivist state to another—a fact which makes it possible to classify them in a certain descending order. The greater the moral and cultural reserves remaining, the greater the inner resistance of the population to the tyranny; the less uncompromising the nature of the tyranny, the greater its moderation in international affairs; and in consequence all the greater will appear the possibility of a smooth return to a more normal form of government.

transform the state into a Leviathan. In other words, complete socialism cannot but be anti-liberal in the worst and fullest sense of the term. While it wants to ensure for the individual complete emancipation, all that in reality it can do is to impose on him the most exacting and intolerable form of slavery.

Not all socialists are prepared, like the anti-democratic socialists, to get round this contradiction by pretending, with Lenin, that liberty is a bourgeois prejudice. For the liberal-democratic socialists, however, the antinomy of socialism is a real stumbling-block. They make every imaginable effort to refute the disagreeable truth, yet experience and reflection alike argue so irresistibly against them that it only remains for them, if they want to be honest with themselves, to choose between the liberal principle of freedom and the socialist principle of "organization" (and all that euphemism covers). The reasons for the dilemma have been put forward so often and clearly of late that we may confine ourselves here to a few observations.

It is necessary to start from the irrefutable proposition that complete socialism, of whatever shade, always involves a complete planned economy. The economy of what plan? we must at once ask. Who draws up the plan and who plans the planners? A plan for the whole national economy means that the productive forces of the community are disposed of in a certain way. That is to say, the plan decides in detail which goods shall be produced and in what quantity. In the present economic system, production (apart from the public sector) is essentially determined by those to whom this right cannot very well be denied, namely the consumers. The economic process based on the competitive market is, so to speak, a "plébiscite de tous les jours" in which every shilling spent by the consumer represents a ballot-paper and in which the producer, by advertising, does election propaganda for an undetermined number of parties (i.e., classes of goods). This consumers' democracy has, it is true, the disadvantage, largely remediable, however, of distributing the ballot-papers very inequitably; it has also the great advantage of securing complete proportional representation. The minority is not eliminated, each voting paper retaining its value. A socialist planned economy means nothing other than that the democracy of the consumers is done away with and replaced by command from above. Decision as to the use of the productive factors of the community would be transferred from the market to the office of a government authority and become a matter of politics. The unfortunate population would have to submit to such use of those factors as might be deemed right by the group dominating the state for the time being. Can it be seriously believed that not only the selection of this group, but also the millions of decisions to be taken can be done with democratic machinery and with respect for the liberty of each individual? Is it deemed possible to extend this method to gramophone records and hot-water bottles? Is it credible that a socialist government would expose its economic plans to the caprices of a changing majority? However categorically these questions may be answered in the negative, it is not less certain that such a dictatorship in charge of national production can only be acquired and maintained by a group resolved to use it unscrupulously to the utmost limit of its political power and to trample over all rights and liberties to maintain itself in power. "The probability of the people in power being individuals who would dislike the possession and exercise of power is on the level with the probability that an extremely tender-hearted person would get the job of whipping-master on a slave plantation."[9]

The impossibility of drawing up an economic plan by democratic methods is due not to technical reasons alone, but resides rather in the nature of the thing itself. Everybody knows that democracy can really function properly only when there is a certain minimum of agreement about all the essential problems of national life. Only on the basis of such "unitas in necessariis," such as unity between all classes, ranks, and parties in the essential national problems and in the ultimate aims of policy, are the consultations and discussions that are the characteristic of liberal democracy possible. If that essential integration of the nation no longer exists, democracy necessarily falls victim either to anarchy or to collectivism (tyranny). But how is it possible to reach even half-agreement about all the details of an economic plan affecting directly and painfully all private interests? Since the decisions to be taken always profit one group of interests and injure another—how can the democratic method effect the compromise called for? Those decisions cannot in fact be taken except in an authoritarian way, arbitrarily, that is to say, and under the pressure of an interested minority. But since the suspicion of arbitrariness or even of favoritism would injure the government's prestige, it adorns its decision with the halo of some principle and

[9] Frank H. Knight, in a review of Lippmann's book, *Journal of Political Economy*, December 1938, p. 869.

gets its propaganda going. It will do all it can to degrade in the public mind the victims of its arbitrary decisions and grossly abuse what it chooses to call the public interest.

But there is yet another and more decisive consideration. The competitive market system is a process made up of innumerable, individual economic acts. These are under the control of the market, which affords to those concerned indications for the most rational use of productive capacity. An automatic system of rewards and punishments in the form of profit and loss ensures early and rapid action on those indications. Our economic system punishes disobedience to market rules by sanctions extending from negligible losses to bankruptcy, that is to say, to the exclusion of the offender from the body of those responsible for the process of production. Socialism (collectivism or communism) implies that the democratic sovereign, the market, has been replaced by the autocratic sovereign, the state. This new sovereign assures respect for itself by the means proper to its political character: draconian penalties for a long list of "economic crimes," secret police, concentration camps, and executions. Actions which in the reign of the old sovereign were inoffensive from the penal point of view, since they carried within themselves their own very effective penalties, become the gravest of crimes. Suddenly hosts of "economic traitors," "profiteers," "parasites," people guilty of "sabotage," "devisen crooks," and other riff-raff are discovered. What is happening in reality is that the attraction of the old sovereign is so great that the new is at the utmost pains to ensure respect for his orders. If we recall how often in history—from Diocletian to the French revolution—capital punishment itself has proved incapable of combating rising prices, one will understand the extraordinary power of the old sovereign of economic life, the market. From all this might be drawn the conclusion, self-evident and confirmed by experience through history, that socialism is an economic system in which the headsman beats the time. The headsman is in fact for this economic system a figure quite as important as the bailiff in the economic system where the market is sovereign.[10]

There is no reasonable room for doubt. Socialism and tyranny are correlated to each other, notwithstanding all the emphasis of

[10] See especially Walter Lippmann, *The Good Society* (Boston, 1937); and F. A. Hayek, *Freedom and the Economic System* (Chicago, 1939). Similar considerations had been developed in my article, "Sozialismus und politische Diktatur," *Neue Zürcher Zeitung*, January 18-19, 1937.

socialist theorists who dream of realizing a socialist state without infringing liberty in any but the economic sphere and notwithstanding the promises of tyrants at the beginning of their career to preserve liberty at least in the economic sphere. Whether a state sets out from anti-tyrannical socialism or from anti-socialist tyranny, the natural logic of events will finally lead the two states to the same end: thorough-going tyranny that leaves its impress on every sphere of social life and has all the charming traits we have already described. Like peace, tyranny is indivisible, and in the long run economic dictatorship cannot any more exclude political and intellectual dictatorship, than the other way around. It is in fact unpardonable naïveté to believe that a state can be collectivist in economic matters without being so in political and spiritual matters also and vice versa. "If there are Governments armed with economic power, if in a word we are to have Industrial Tyrannies, then the last state of man will be worse than the first" (Oscar Wilde). Then what Hölderlin wrote a century ago would come true: in wishing to make the state paradise, man has made it hell.

The structure of tyranny and its close relations with socialism having been examined, it still remains to characterize briefly its relations with the war and with the international disintegration now in progress. If the connexion between socialism and tyranny is a reciprocal one, so is that which exists between tyranny and the present international disintegration. On the one hand it was the world war that ripened the seeds of modern tyranny; on the other—and this is more important still—the very structure of tyranny tends towards imperialistic expansions and finally to war, again notwithstanding all the more or less sincere assertions to the contrary. Indeed, each characteristic of tyranny that has been analyzed so far involves the inclination to war.

ECONOMIC AND POLITICAL FREEDOM

Milton Friedman

from CAPITALISM AND FREEDOM (1965)

It is widely believed that politics and economics are separate and largely unconnected; that individual freedom is a political problem and material welfare an economic problem; and that any kind of political arrangements can be combined with any kind of economic arrangements. The chief contemporary manifestation of this idea is the advocacy of "democratic socialism" by many who condemn out of hand the restrictions on individual freedom imposed by "totalitarian socialism" in Russia, and who are persuaded that it is possible for a country to adopt the essential features of Russian economic arrangements and yet to ensure individual freedom through political arrangements. The thesis of this chapter is that such a view is a delusion, that there is an intimate connection between economics and politics, that only certain combinations of political and economic arrangements are possible, and that in particular, a society which is socialist cannot also be democratic, in the sense of guaranteeing individual freedom.

Economic arrangements play a dual role in the promotion of a free society. On the one hand, freedom in economic arrangements is itself a component of freedom broadly understood, so economic freedom is an end in itself. In the second place, economic freedom is also an indispensable means toward the achievement of political freedom.

The first of these roles of economic freedom needs special emphasis because intellectuals in particular have a strong bias against regarding this aspect of freedom as important. They tend to express contempt for what they regard as material aspects of life, and to regard their own pursuit of allegedly higher values as on a different plane of significance and as deserving of special attention. For most citizens of the country, however, if not for the intellectual, the direct importance of economic freedom is at least comparable in significance to the indirect importance of economic freedom as a means to political freedom.

The citizen of Great Britain, who after World War II was not permitted to spend his vacation in the United States because of exchange control, was being deprived of an essential freedom not less than the citizen of the United States, who was denied the opportunity to spend his vacation in Russia because of his political views. The one was ostensibly an economic limitation on freedom and the other a political limitation, yet there is no essential difference between the two.

The citizen of the United States who is compelled by law to devote something like 10 percent of his income to the purchase of a particular kind of retirement contract, administered by the government, is being deprived of a corresponding part of his personal freedom. How strongly this deprivation may be felt and its closeness to the deprivation of religious freedom, which all would regard as "civil" or "political" rather than "economic," were dramatized by an episode involving a group of farmers of the Amish sect. On grounds of principle, this group regarded compulsory federal old-age programs as an infringement of their personal individual freedom and refused to pay taxes or accept benefits. As a result, some of their livestock were sold by auction in order to satisfy claims for social security levies. True, the number of citizens who regard compulsory old-age insurance as a deprivation of freedom may be few, but the believer in freedom has never counted noses.

A citizen of the United States who under the laws of various states is not free to follow the occupation of his own choosing unless he can get a license for it, is likewise being deprived of an essential part of his freedom. So is the man who would like to exchange some of his goods with, say, a Swiss for a watch but is prevented from doing so by a quota. So also is the Californian who was thrown into jail for selling Alka Seltzer at a price below that set by the manufacturer under so-called "fair trade" laws. So also is the farmer who cannot grow the amount of wheat he wants.

And so on. Clearly, economic freedom, in and of itself, is an extremely important part of total freedom.

Viewed as a means to the end of political freedom, economic arrangements are important because of their effect on the concentration or dispersion of power. The kind of economic organization that provides economic freedom directly, namely, competitive capitalism, also promotes political freedom because it separates economic power from political power and in this way enables the one to offset the other.

Historical evidence speaks with a single voice on the relation between political freedom and a free market. I know of no example in time or place of a society that has been marked by a large measure of political freedom, and that has not also used something comparable to a free market to organize the bulk of economic activity.

Because we live in a largely free society, we tend to forget how limited is the span of time and the part of the globe for which there has ever been anything like political freedom: the typical state of mankind is tyranny, servitude, and misery. The nineteenth century and early twentieth century in the Western world stand out as striking exceptions to the general trend of historical development. Political freedom in this instance clearly came along with the free market and the development of capitalist institutions. So also did political freedom in the golden age of Greece and in the early days of the Roman era.

History suggests only that capitalism is a necessary condition for political freedom. Clearly it is not a sufficient condition. Fascist Italy and Fascist Spain, Germany at various times in the last seventy years, Japan before World Wars I and II, tzarist Russia in the decades before World War I—are all societies that cannot conceivably be described as politically free. Yet, in each, private enterprise was the dominant form of economic organization. It is therefore clearly possible to have economic arrangements that are fundamentally capitalist and political arrangements that are not free.

Even in those societies, the citizenry had a good deal more freedom than citizens of a modern totalitarian state like Russia or Nazi Germany, in which economic totalitarianism is combined with political totalitarianism. Even in Russia under the Tsars, it was possible for some citizens, under some circumstances, to change their jobs without getting permission from political authority because capitalism and the existence of private property provided some check to the centralized power of the state.

The relation between political and economic freedom is complex and by no means unilateral. In the early nineteenth century, Bentham and the Philosophical Radicals were inclined to regard political freedom as a means to economic freedom. They believed that the masses were being hampered by the restrictions that were being imposed upon them, and that if political reform gave the bulk of the people the vote, they would do what was good for them, which was to vote for laissez-faire. In retrospect, one cannot say that they were wrong. There was a large measure of political reform that was accompanied by economic reform in the direction of a great deal of laissez-faire. An enormous increase in the well-being of the masses followed this change in economic arrangements.

The triumph of Benthamite liberalism in nineteenth-century England was followed by a reaction toward increasing intervention by government in economic affairs. This tendency to collectivism was greatly accelerated, both in England and elsewhere, by the two World Wars. Welfare rather than freedom became the dominant note in democratic countries. Recognizing the implicit threat to individualism, the intellectual descendants of the Philosophical Radicals—Dicey, Mises, Hayek, and Simons, to mention only a few—feared that a continued movement toward centralized control of economic activity would prove *The Road to Serfdom*, as Hayek entitled his penetrating analysis of the process. Their emphasis was on economic freedom as a means toward political freedom.

Events since the end of World War II display still a different relation between economic and political freedom. Collectivist economic planning has indeed interfered with individual freedom. At least in some countries, however, the result has not been the suppression of freedom, but the reversal of economic policy. England again provides the most striking example. The turning point was perhaps the "control of engagements" order which, despite great misgivings, the Labor party found it necessary to impose in order to carry out its economic policy. Fully enforced and carried through, the law would have involved centralized allocation of individuals to occupations. This conflicted so sharply with personal liberty that it was enforced in a negligible number of cases, and then repealed after the law had been in effect for only a short period. Its repeal ushered in a decided shift in economic policy, marked by reduced reliance on centralized "plans" and "programs," by the dismantling of many controls, and by increased emphasis on the private market. A similar shift in policy occurred in most other democratic countries.

The proximate explanation of these shifts in policy is the limited success of central planning or its outright failure to achieve stated objectives. However, this failure is itself to be attributed, at least in some measure, to the political implications of central planning and to an unwillingness to follow out its logic when doing so requires trampling rough-shod on treasured private rights. It may well be that the shift is only a temporary interruption in the collectivist trend of this century. Even so, it illustrates the close relation between political freedom and economic arrangements.

Historical evidence by itself can never be convincing. Perhaps it was sheer coincidence that the expansion of freedom occurred at the same time as the development of capitalist and market institutions. Why should there be a connection? What are the logical links between economic and political freedom? In discussing these questions we shall consider first the market as a direct component of freedom, and then the indirect relation between market arrangements and political freedom. A by-product will be an outline of the ideal economic arrangements for a free society.

As liberals, we take freedom of the individual, or perhaps the family, as our ultimate goal in judging social arrangements. Freedom as a value in this sense has to do with the interrelations among people; it has no meaning whatsoever to a Robinson Crusoe on an isolated island (without his Man Friday). Robinson Crusoe on his island is subject to "constraint," he has limited "power," and he has only a limited number of alternatives, but there is no problem of freedom in the sense that is relevant to our discussion. Similarly, in a society freedom has nothing to say about what an individual does with his freedom; it is not an all-embracing ethic. Indeed, a major aim of the liberal is to leave the ethical problem for the individual to wrestle with. The "really" important ethical problems are those that face an individual in a free society—what he should do with his freedom. There are thus two sets of values that a liberal will emphasize—the values that are relevant to relations among people, which is the context in which he assigns first priority to freedom; and the values that are relevant to the individual in the exercise of his freedom, which is the realm of individual ethics and philosophy.

The liberal conceives of men as imperfect beings. He regards the problem of social organization to be as much a negative problem of preventing "bad" people from doing harm as of enabling

241

"good" people to do good; and, of course, "bad" and "good" people may be the same people, depending on who is judging them.

The basic problem of social organization is how to coordinate the economic activities of large numbers of people. Even in relatively backward societies, extensive division of labor and specialization of function is required to make effective use of available resources. In advanced societies, the scale on which coordination is needed, to take full advantage of the opportunities offered by modern science and technology, is enormously greater. Literally millions of people are involved in providing one another with their daily bread, let alone with their yearly automobiles. The challenge to the believer in liberty is to reconcile this widespread interdependence with individual freedom.

Fundamentally, there are only two ways of coordinating the economic activities of millions. One is central direction involving the use of coercion—the technique of the army and of the modern totalitarian state. The other is voluntary cooperation of individuals—the technique of the marketplace.

The possibility of coordination through voluntary cooperation rests on the elementary—yet frequently denied—proposition that both parties to an economic transaction benefit from it, *provided the transaction is bilaterally voluntary and informed.*

Exchange can therefore bring about coordination without coercion. A working model of a society organized through voluntary exchange is a *free private-enterprise exchange economy*—what we have been calling competitive capitalism.

In its simplest form, such a society consists of a number of independent households—a collection of Robinson Crusoes, as it were. Each household uses the resources it controls to produce goods and services that it exchanges for goods and services produced by other households, on terms mutually acceptable to the two parties to the bargain. It is thereby enabled to satisfy its wants indirectly by producing goods and services for others, rather than directly by producing goods for its own immediate use. The incentive for adopting this indirect route is, of course, the increased product made possible by division of labor and specialization of function. Since the household always has the alternative of producing directly for itself, it need not enter into any exchange unless it benefits from it. Hence, no exchange will take place unless both parties do benefit from it. Cooperation is thereby achieved without coercion.

Specialization of function and division of labor would not go far if the ultimate productive unit were the household. In a modern

242

society, we have gone much farther. We have introduced enterprises which are intermediaries between individuals in their capacities as suppliers of service and as purchasers of goods. And similarly, specialization of function and division of labor could not go very far if we had to continue to rely on the barter of product for product. In consequence, money has been introduced as a means of facilitating exchange, and of enabling the acts of purchase and of sale to be separated into two parts.

Despite the important role of enterprises and of money in our actual economy, and despite the numerous and complex problems they raise, the central characteristic of the market technique of achieving coordination is fully displayed in the simple exchange economy that contains neither enterprises nor money. As in that simple model, so in the complex enterprise and money-exchange economy, cooperation is strictly individual and voluntary *provided:* (a) that enterprises are private, so that the ultimate contracting parties are individuals and (b) that individuals are effectively free to enter or not to enter into any particular exchange, so that every transaction is strictly voluntary.

It is far easier to state these provisos in general terms than to spell them out in detail, or to specify precisely the institutional arrangements most conducive to their maintenance. Indeed, much of technical economic literature is concerned with precisely these questions. The basic requisite is the maintenance of law and order to prevent physical coercion of one individual by another and to enforce contracts voluntarily entered into, thus giving substance to "private." Aside from this, perhaps the most difficult problems arise from monopoly—which inhibits effective freedom by denying individuals alternatives to the particular exchange—and from "neighborhood effects"—effects on third parties for which it is not feasible to charge or recompense them. . . .

So long as effective freedom of exchange is maintained, the central feature of the market organization of economic activity is that it prevents one person from interfering with another in respect of most of his activities. The consumer is protected from coercion by the seller because of the presence of other sellers with whom he can deal. The seller is protected from coercion by the consumer because of other consumers to whom he can sell. The employee is protected from coercion by the employer because of other employers for whom he can work, and so on. And the market does this impersonally and without centralized authority.

Indeed, a major source of objection to a free economy is precisely that it does this task so well. It gives people what they want instead of what a particular group thinks they ought to want. Underlying most arguments against the free market is a lack of belief in freedom itself.

The existence of a free market does not of course eliminate the need for government. On the contrary, government is essential both as a forum for determining the "rules of the game" and as an umpire to interpret and enforce the rules decided on. What the market does is to reduce greatly the range of issues that must be decided through political means, and thereby to minimize the extent to which government need participate directly in the game. The characteristic feature of action through political channels is that it tends to require or enforce substantial conformity. The great advantage of the market, on the other hand, is that it permits wide diversity. It is, in political terms, a system of proportional representation. Each man can vote, as it were, for the color of tie he wants and get it; he does not have to see what color the majority wants and then, if he is in the minority, submit.

It is this feature of the market that we refer to when we say that the market provides economic freedom. But this characteristic also has implications that go far beyond the narrowly economic. Political freedom means the absence of coercion of a man by his fellow men. The fundamental threat to freedom is power to coerce, be it in the hands of a monarch, a dictator, an oligarchy, or a momentary majority. The preservation of freedom requires the elimination of such concentration of power to the fullest possible extent and the dispersal and distribution of whatever power cannot be eliminated—a system of checks and balances. By removing the organization of economic activity from the control of political authority, the market eliminates this source of coercive power. It enables economic strength to be a check to political power rather than a reinforcement.

Economic power can be widely dispersed. There is no law of conservation which forces the growth of new centers of economic strength to be at the expense of existing centers. Political power, on the other hand, is more difficult to decentralize. There can be numerous small independent governments. But it is far more difficult to maintain numerous equipotent small centers of political power in a single large government than it is to have numerous centers of economic strength in a single large economy. But can there be more than one really outstanding leader, one person on whom the energies and enthusiasm of his countrymen are centered? If the central government gains power, it is likely to be at the expense of local governments. There seems to be something

244

like a fixed total of political power to be distributed. Consequently, if economic power is joined to political power, concentration seems almost inevitable. On the other hand, if economic power is kept in separate hands from political power, it can serve as a check and a counter to political power.

The force of this abstract argument can perhaps best be demonstrated by example. Let us consider first, a hypothetical example that may help to bring out the principles involved, and then some actual examples from recent experience that illustrate the way in which the market works to preserve political freedom.

One feature of a free society is surely the freedom of individuals to advocate and propagandize openly for a radical change in the structure of the society—so long as the advocacy is restricted to persuasion and does not include force or other forms of coercion. It is a mark of the political freedom of a capitalist society that men can openly advocate and work for socialism. Equally, political freedom in a socialist society would require that men be free to advocate the introduction of capitalism. How could the freedom to advocate capitalism be preserved and protected in a socialist society?

In order for men to advocate anything, they must in the first place be able to earn a living. This already raises a problem in a socialist society, since all jobs are under the direct control of political authorities. It would take an act of self-denial whose difficulty is underlined by experience in the United States after World War II with the problem of "security" among federal employees, for a socialist government to permit its employees to advocate policies directly contrary to official doctrine.

But let us suppose this act of self-denial to be achieved. For advocacy of capitalism to mean anything, the proponents must be able to finance their cause—to hold public meetings, publish pamphlets, buy radio time, issue newspapers and magazines, and so on. How could they raise the funds? There might and probably would be men in the socialist society with large incomes, perhaps even large capital sums in the form of government bonds and the like, but these would of necessity be high public officials. It is possible to conceive of a minor socialist official retaining his job although openly advocating capitalism. It strains credulity to imagine the socialist top brass financing such "subversive" activities.

The only recourse for funds would be to raise small amounts from a large number of minor officials. But this is no real answer. To tap these sources, many people would already have to be persuaded, and our whole problem is how to initiate and finance a campaign to do so. Radical movements in capitalist societies have never been financed this way. They have typically been supported by a few wealthy individuals who have become persuaded—by a Frederick Vanderbilt Field, or an Anita McCormick Blaine, or a Corliss Lamont, to mention a few names recently prominent, or by a Friedrich Engels, to go farther back. This is a role of inequality of wealth in preserving political freedom that is seldom noted— the role of the patron.

In a capitalist society, it is only necessary to convince a few wealthy people to get funds to launch any idea, however strange, and there are many such persons, many independent foci of support. And, indeed, it is not even necessary to persuade people or financial institutions with available funds of the soundness of the ideas to be propagated. It is only necessary to persuade them that the propagation can be financially successful; that the newspaper or magazine or book or other venture will be profitable. The competitive publisher, for example, cannot afford to publish only writing with which he personally agrees; his touchstone must be the likelihood that the market will be large enough to yield a satisfactory return on his investment.

In this way, the market breaks the vicious circle and makes it possible ultimately to finance such ventures by small amounts from many people without first persuading them. There are no such possibilities in the socialist society; there is only the all-powerful state.

Let us stretch our imagination and suppose that a socialist government is aware of this problem and is composed of people anxious to preserve freedom. Could it provide the funds? Perhaps, but it is difficult to see how. It could establish a bureau for subsidizing subversive propaganda. But how could it choose whom to support? If it gave to all who asked, it would shortly find itself out of funds, for socialism cannot repeal the elementary economic law that a sufficiently high price will call forth a large supply. Make the advocacy of radical causes sufficiently remunerative, and the supply of advocates will be unlimited.

Moreover, freedom to advocate unpopular causes does not require that such advocacy be without cost. On the contrary, no society could be stable if advocacy of radical change were costless, much less subsidized. It is entirely appropriate that men make sacrifices to advocate causes in which they deeply believe. Indeed, it is important to preserve freedom only for people who are willing to practice self-denial, for otherwise freedom degener-

246

ates into license and irresponsibility. What is essential is that the cost of advocating unpopular causes be tolerable and not prohibitive.

But we are not yet through. In a free-market society, it is enough to have the funds. The suppliers of paper are as willing to sell it to the *Daily Worker* as to the *Wall Street Journal*. In a socialist society, it would not be enough to have the funds. The hypothetical supporter of capitalism would have to persuade a government factory making paper to sell to him, the government printing press to print his pamphlets, a government post office to distribute them among the people, a government agency to rent him a hall in which to talk, and so on.

Perhaps there is some way in which one could overcome these difficulties and preserve freedom in a socialist society. One cannot say it is utterly impossible. What is clear, however, is that there are very real difficulties in establishing institutions that will effectively preserve the possibility of dissent. So far as I know, none of the people who have been in favor of socialism and also in favor of freedom have really faced up to this issue, or made even a respectable start at developing the institutional arrangements that would permit freedom under socialism. By contrast, it is clear how a free-market capitalist society fosters freedom.

A striking practical example of these abstract principles is the experience of Winston Churchill. From 1933 to the outbreak of World War II, Churchill was not permitted to talk over the British radio, which was, of course, a government monopoly administered by the British Broadcasting Corporation. Here was a leading citizen of his country, a Member of Parliament, a former cabinet minister, a man who was desperately trying by every device possible to persuade his countrymen to take steps to ward off the menace of Hitler's Germany. He was not permitted to talk over the radio to the British people because the BBC was a government monopoly and his position was too "controversial."

Another striking example, reported in the January 26, 1959 issue of *Time*, has to do with the "Blacklist Fadeout." Says the *Time* story:

> The Oscar-awarding ritual is Hollywood's biggest pitch for dignity, but two years ago dignity suffered. When one Robert Rich was announced as top writer for the *The Brave One*, he never stepped forward. Robert Rich was a pseudonym, masking one of about 150 writers ... blacklisted by the industry since 1947 as suspected Communists or fellow travelers. The case was particularly embarrassing because the Motion Picture Academy had barred any Communist or

247

Fifth Amendment pleader from Oscar competition. Last week both the Communist rule and the mystery of Rich's identity were suddenly rescripted.

Rich turned out to be Dalton (*Johnny Got His Gun*) Trumbo, one of the original "Hollywood Ten" writers who refused to testify at the 1947 hearings on Communism in the movie industry. Said producer Frank King, who had stoutly insisted that Robert Rich was "a young guy in Spain with a beard": "We have an obligation to our stockholders to buy the best script we can. Trumbo brought us *The Brave One* and we bought it.". . .

In effect it was the formal end of the Hollywood blacklist. For barred writers, the informal end came long ago. At least 15% of current Hollywood films are reportedly written by blacklist members. Said Producer King, "There are more ghosts in Hollywood than in Forest Lawn. Every company in town has used the work of blacklisted people. We're just the first to confirm what everybody knows."

One may believe, as I do, that Communism would destroy all of our freedoms, one may be opposed to it as firmly and as strongly as possible, and yet, at the same time, also believe that in a free society it is intolerable for a man to be prevented from making voluntary arrangements with others that are mutually attractive because he believes in or is trying to promote Communism. His freedom includes his freedom to promote Communism. Freedom also, of course, includes the freedom of others not to deal with him under those circumstances. The Hollywood blacklist was an unfree act that destroys freedom because it was a collusive arrangement that used coercive means to prevent voluntary exchanges. It didn't work precisely because the market made it costly for people to preserve the blacklist. The commercial emphasis, the fact that people who are running enterprises have an incentive to make as much money as they can, protected the freedom of the individuals who were blacklisted by providing them with an alternative form of employment, and by giving people an incentive to employ them.

If Hollywood and the movie industry had been government enterprises or if in England it had been a question of employment by the British Broadcasting Corporation it is difficult to believe that the "Hollywood Ten" or their equivalent would have found employment. Equally, it is difficult to believe that under those circumstances, strong proponents of individualism and private enterprise—or indeed strong proponents of any view other than the status quo—would be able to get employment.

Another example of the role of the market in preserving polit-

248

ical freedom, was revealed in our experience with McCarthyism. Entirely aside from the substantive issues involved, and the merits of the charges made, what protection did individuals, and in particular government employees, have against irresponsible accusations and probings into matters that it went against their conscience to reveal? Their appeal to the Fifth Amendment would have been a hollow mockery without an alternative to government employment.

Their fundamental protection was the existence of a private-market economy in which they could earn a living. Here again, the protection was not absolute. Many potential private employers were, rightly or wrongly, averse to hiring those pilloried. It may well be that there was far less justification for the costs imposed on many of the people involved than for the costs generally imposed on people who advocate unpopular causes. But the important point is that the costs were limited and not prohibitive, as they would have been if government employment had been the only possibility.

It is of interest to note that a disproportionately large fraction of the people involved apparently went into the most competitive sectors of the economy—small business, trade, farming—where the market approaches most closely the ideal free market. No one who buys bread knows whether the wheat from which it is made was grown by a Communist or a Republican, by a constitutionalist or a Fascist, or, for that matter, by a Negro or a white. This illustrates how an impersonal market separates economic activities from political views and protects men from being discriminated against in their economic activities for reasons that are irrelevant to their productivity—whether these reasons are associated with their views or their color.

As this example suggests, the groups in our society that have the most at stake in the preservation and strengthening of competitive capitalism are those minority groups which can most easily become the objects of the distrust and enmity of the majority—the Negroes, the Jews, the foreign-born, to mention only the most obvious. Yet, paradoxically enough, the enemies of the free market—the Socialists and Communists—have been recruited in disproportionate measure from these groups. Instead of recognizing that the existence of the market has protected them from the attitudes of their fellow countrymen, they mistakenly attribute the residual discrimination to the market.

PROGRESSIVE CAPITALISM

Gustav Stolper

from THIS AGE OF FABLE (1942)

The only alternative to "production for profit" is, we repeat, production by compulsion and terror. It is not enough, as we are so persuasively told, to have an economic general staff (which means practically nothing); nor is it enough that this general staff design a plan (which means practically more, because there the trouble starts). What really matters is the power with which that body is endowed to set the plan into action, to assure its thorough and minute execution, and to forestall foreseeable and unforeseeable disturbance and frustration. The gentle fable of the "economy for use" does not tell us about the inevitable bitter end.

Yet it is absurd to treat terror and fear as accidental, not as essential, to the success of an economic general staff. As long as every man decides for himself, directed by his best judgment on his personal advantage and limited by his moral standards, changeable social status, and such general laws as a democratic society sees fit to impose on him, he is guided by a somewhat reliable compass. As soon as he is deprived of this instrument he must be expressly instructed what to do and what not to do, and he must obey the instruction, because otherwise complete chaos would ensue. It is not enough for the planning authority to issue general orders. These orders must be specific in the extreme, to the minutest detail. Otherwise the plan cannot even start to work. It is therefore indispensable to create a substitute for such a general motive of individual behavior as individual material interest (the "profit motive") provides, and this substitute can only be fear of punishment. This fear must be kept alive, this fear must be all-pervasive, this fear must not be allowed to slacken. It is grotesque to expect that a dictatorship can ever become a kind, a lenient dictatorship. It cannot. In fact, it must be always extending and intensifying the terror because only thereby can the general discipline indispensable to any "planned economy" be maintained. You cannot put a policeman or an SA man or a Fascist militiaman behind every plant manager, every worker, every shopper, every railway engineer. But you can (and you do) put behind everybody the specter of that agent of the secret police with all that it threatens.

PROGRESSIVE CAPITALISM AND REACTIONARY PLANNING

Many view capitalism as a conservative, reactionary principle, and "planned economy" as a radical, progressive principle. Actually it is just the other way around. Capitalism is bent, for better or worse, on liberating forward-driving forces; a planned economy tends to put artificial restraints upon those forces and to crystallize them at a given point. Such a statement may arouse a storm of protest and many doubts; but one has to take risks in a rough outline of a problem so vast and complicated.

Any economy, and therefore also a capitalist economy, requires planning. Every businessman has to plan, and the larger his enterprise, the more careful and farsighted must his planning be. The management has to "plan" in the same way as the "planning commission" of a socialist community has to "plan," and it has very much the same data to work with.

The differences between the "planned" and the "capitalist" systems come down, rather, to the following:

1. Under capitalism the businessman makes a miscalculation at his own risk; at worst his mistake spells economic ruin for him. The errors of a planning commission are paid for by the community at large. (How many errors they commit we are never permitted to learn.)

2. If a hundred thousand businessmen are planning their way, each on his own account, the mathematical chances that smartness and folly will offset each other are incomparably greater than

251

when the decision as to the economic fate of a nation is entrusted to one central brain.

3 (and most important). Capitalism functions under an objective law made manifest through the market. Under capitalism the dictator is the consumer. In the long run production is determined by what the consumer is willing and able to buy. Such a dictator is subject to human influences like any other, and in principle it does not matter whether the influence is exerted through advertising, persuasion, party intrigues, or a pretty woman. No dictator lives in a vacuum; though a dictator, he is none the less a human being, responsive to all human motives. But he is also none the less a dictator. The capitalist businessman can never escape the dictatorship of the market, and the market, at least in countries where oversupply rather than undersupply is the rule, is in turn determined by the consumer.

In a socialist economy the dictator is not the consumer but the producer—the state or its agents. They prescribe how the consumer is to deport himself, what and how much he is to eat, what clothes he is to wear, where he is to live, what manner of life he is to follow. And the moment the socialist state acquires dictatorship over the consumer (in other words, over the citizen, who becomes forthwith a subject) it assumes control also over technical progress. And this spells the end of progress:

> For an innovation *is* a departure, and one which brings in its trains some incalculable disturbance of the behavior to which we have grown used and which seems "natural." As a recent writer has clearly shown, inventions have made their way insidiously; and because of some immediate convenience. If their effects, their long run consequences had been foreseen, it is safe to say that most of them would have been destroyed as wicked just as many of them were retarded in adoption because they were felt to be sacrilegious. In any case, we cannot think of their invention being the work of the state.[1]

The Reactionary Principle in Socialism

This may perhaps make clear why a socialist economy embodies a reactionary principle. An essential part of its very nature is a tendency to simplify things, to make them "manageable," and therefore to freeze everything at a given point.

[1] John Dewey, *The Public and Its Problems* (New York: Holt, 1927).

To illustrate, one need only consider the parallel developments in technical inventions and in manners of living during these past thirty years. Changes in dietary habits have revolutionized conditions in agriculture. The fact that women have come to wear lighter clothes has occasioned a crisis in cotton-growing. The radio and the talking picture, which today play a leading role in the lives of the masses, were in an experimental stage twenty years ago. The use of the automobile as a commonplace vehicle has transformed the manner in which Western people live more profoundly than any other technical innovation of the last hundred and fifty years. The invention of the safety razor should have put the barber out of business, but the women saved him; indeed the hairdresser's business has assumed an importance no one would have dreamed of. For all such developments there would be no place in a socialized "plan," for they have all been, as they will always remain, unforeseeable disturbances, owing their origin either to chance or to genius.

Differences of opinion are possible concerning the importance to be attached to all such factors. Here again final judgment does not fall within the economic sphere. Conceding the economic and technical superiority of capitalism, a person may still be a Communist because the Communist ideal as such, or the extinction of some defects of capitalism, may seem more important, more worth striving for. But that is not the decisive point. Decisive is whether individual freedom can exist apart from private property and freedom of consumption, and how highly one prizes individual freedom. For even were capitalism incurably afflicted with all the evils ascribed to it by its opponents, it would still be a blessing to be defended to the last ditch if it were the only thinkable economic system under which freedom—freedom not only in the material sphere but freedom of thought, speech, and movement— could be assured.

From an article in the London *New Statesman and Nation*, the brilliant and representative weekly of British Socialism, comes the following passage:

> The beautiful simplicity of nineteenth-century economic philosophy lay precisely in this, that the forces playing on the system were regarded as anonymous forces coming from outside. Along with the weather, new inventions, changes in taste and fashion, all the regions of consumer demand, indeed *the whole welter of influences affecting demand and supply were regarded as external data operating as it were out of the blue. People were expected to accept this*

253

ever-changing play of outside forces, and success lay precisely in the skill and speed of adjustment. Luck, it was realized, also played a part, but it was the luck of the game. *Suppose women change their minds about lipstick and powder, and decide to present shining faces to the world.* The cosmetic trade will slump and some embittered losers will curse the fickle jades. The smart ones will think out new nostrums for endowing women with clear natural complexions, and the unenterprising *will stagnate in a distressed industry.* The trade is fairly open to these risks. But *suppose a damfool imitation dictator in Whitehall puts a ban on lipstick and powder. The onus is no longer on the Almighty for having created a fickle sex.* The cosmetic industry will now have a target here on earth and it will pray, if not actively work, for the removal of its enemy. And here the awful thought occurs that *perhaps this is the secret of dictatorship; that its decrees are regarded as divine, that it can deal out economic fortune and misfortune arbitrarily and that its rulings are accepted* passively like changes in the physical weather. However, *we have not got to that stage in democratic countries* and people who will submit to the buffetings of fate will take up a very different attitude *when fate is discovered to be working through terrestrial lobbies.*[2]

The author of that article writes in a satirical, humorous mood. He does not take his own thesis too seriously. He seems to be willing to challenge "the weather." Somehow the democracies will master the "terrestrial lobbies" that shape the divine decrees of their governments. But the satire defeats itself by its contradictory assumptions. Once there is a "damfool dictator" in Whitehall (real, not imitation) people will submit much more passively to his decrres than they submit to weather in a democracy. Against bad weather you can seek shelter. But to seek shelter against the decrees of a dictator is high treason, penalized by death. His divinity may not be questioned. And incidentally, the humorous example referred to is not too far-fetched. Lipstick and powder were frowned on as foreign in the first "heroic" phase of Nazism; the underworld of the Brown Shirts that dominated the streets in those days determined moral and esthetic standards. They were the terrestrial lobby. Soon the ban was eased because the party leaders began to dictate the standards, and theirs were far from ascetic. The terrestrial lobbies consisted of the wives and mistresses of the arrivés. In Soviet Russia one of the highlights of the second Five Year Plan was the reappearance of beauty parlors, perfumes, and cosmetics. One divine decree commanded their use; another decree may abolish them tomorrow.

[2] *New Statesman and Nation*, Feb. 15, 1941. Italics ours.

PROSPERITY THROUGH FREEDOM

Lawrence Fertig

from PROSPERITY THROUGH FREEDOM (1961)

What are the virtues of a free-enterprise economy? Why is private capitalism of such great value to the American citizen that he should defend it to the death against Communism? It is the *only* system which can achieve the following objectives:

HUMAN FREEDOM

Any economic system which does not accomplish this is bad, no matter what advantages are claimed for it. For over five thousand years people have struggled to get their rulers off their backs, and it would be tragic if we retraced our steps. John Chamberlain in his *Roots of Capitalism* has stated the case well in the following paragraph: "There are so many spiritual implications in liberty that it deserves to be considered an end in itself. Even if state planning offered more material goods, people who have known and cherished liberty would rather live as free human beings on a more modest standard of living then sell their birthright for a mess of totalitarian pottage. But no such alternative exists. The fruits of totalitarianism are for the state, at most for a limited class."

The basic principle of traditional liberalism has always been,

Beware of the encroachments of the state! The mammoth growth of centralized power has always robbed people of their liberty in the long run. Until recent times no one could lay claim to being a liberal unless he strongly believed in this guiding principle.

Political liberty and economic freedom are intertwined—they cannot be separated. Any system which deprives the individual of his economic freedom—by controlling his job, or how much he can earn, or what he should buy, or how he should live—takes away his basic freedom. And it is important to remember that throughout history, whenever bureaucrats controlled people's economic lives, they soon came to control their political freedom as well. It is essential for the survival of democratic government that economic power be separated from political power. This is the *sine qua non* of democracy. It is the reason why the preservation of private capitalism is essential for the maintenance of a free society.

As an instance, take the vital matter of free press and free speech. No democracy can survive for long if these do not exist. But if the state owned all property how could any dissident hire a hall or attack government policy? If the state owned the paper mills and printing plants, how could any minority group even distribute a leaflet explaining its point of view? Today newspapers, magazines, radio, television—all present a kaleidoscopic view of economic and political opinion in our free society because they are privately owned and their owners and their managers represent different viewpoints. Can you imagine a state-owned or controlled radio or television station, newspaper or magazine, encouraging dissent on a really vital matter? Of course the government might maintain a sham tolerance on unimportant issues. But once the chips were down government officials would undoubtedly control everything ruthlessly.

Take still another instance—a man's job. If the government guarantees it, then the government will set the conditions of work, wages, and other conditions. And it will even insist upon the "mobility" of labor—that is, if there is no job for carpenters in New York they will have to move to Chicago, or some other city.

So it becomes plain that human rights are bound up with property rights. Some honestly confused people, as well as demagogues, elaborate on the conflict between human rights and property rights. There is no such conflict. If an individual cannot retain the fruits of his labor—his property—then he has been deprived of his human rights. Our own Constitution in the Bill of Rights recognizes the identify of human and property rights when it says that no person may, without due process of law, be deprived of "life, liberty, or property."

THE MOST EFFICIENT ECONOMIC SYSTEM

The second objective is to establish the most efficient economic system. What we want is the highest possible *real* income (clothing, food, conveniences, and necessities) for everyone. Competitive private enterprise and the free market are the basis of the most efficient system because they most expertly resolve the countless economic conflicts which take place all the time. No individual or group is smart enough to decide the right relationship between millions of factors which are changing every week and even every day.

Only the free market can accomplish this by permitting the laws of supply and demand to operate through free pricing. How many electric dynamos shall we make, how many pairs of shoes, how many radios, how much cleaning service, how many hotels? These and countless other questions are decided every day in the give and take of the market. It is the only democratic way of deciding these things, for the only other method is for some autocrat to try to do this job arbitrarily, with the backing of the police power of the state. The remarkable record of economic progress in this country where the real income of all working people is doubled just about every thirty years is proof of our efficiency. The shortages, the famines, the snafus, the pathetic quality of construction and the persistently depressed standard of living prevailing in Communist countries is proof of their inefficiency.

In the following chapters these statements will be amply documented. At this point I would like to make it clear that the ability of an iron-fisted Communist autocracy to direct workers in manufacturing specific items is unquestioned. They can force the production of machines, tanks, sputniks, and many other things in ample quantities. But nowhere on earth has such a hierarchy ever shown the ability to create a *high standard of living for all the people* although they are notably successful in creating luxury for themselves. One excuse usually given for the low standard of living of the Russian people is that the Communists started from scratch. This is palpably false. Russia, before the revolution, had one of

system is that i
ty for self-expres-
ism, and therefore
in this regard. The
the western world
ntrasted with the
in these fields ir

the fact that life
spiritual and aes-
le can practice his
t and he can pro-
. Furthermore, he
cannot stop him
is vital advantages
ll-out Communist
as a system want
of more collectiv-
nizing and direct-
of a "mixed econ-
s step after step to
er industries and
voluntary activity.
nd ultimately de-
not lose its free-
itil the takeover is

ird to imagine the
we need only re-
wer of Huey Long
demagogue used
ther personal con-
he southwest and

was mentioned as a presidential possibility. Long became a dictator, and in his hands vast, accumulated government power could have been used with frightful effect. And it is clear that there can be other Huey Longs.

The danger of a drift towards collectivism is enhanced by the rapid extension of welfare state measures which lead us step by step in this direction. Those who call themselves liberals today often become uneasy when they realize the conflict that arises between safeguarding human freedom and extending the power of the central government. But in practically all such cases the liberal of today is willing to close his eyes to the threat to freedom in favor of the benefits he thinks will come from the extension of government-managed "welfare" measures. Preservation of human freedom is no longer the first principle of those who today call themselves liberals. It is merely one desirable objective—together with others.

The *traditional* liberal, on the other hand (often today called a conservative), is guided by the concepts of those who built the foundations of liberalism—ranging from John Locke in the seventeenth century on through to John Stuart Mill, author of the classic *On Liberty*, to Woodrow Wilson in our own time.

John Locke inspired the framers of the American Constitution to establish a government of checks and balances with limited power for the federal government. The first ten amendments to the Constitution, known as the Bill of Rights, are replete with the phrase "Congress shall pass no law" concerning this or that. Another guiding statement of traditional liberal philosophy is Lord Acton's famous dictum, "All power tends to corrupt; absolute power corrupts absolutely." And the traditional liberal understands the wisdom of de Tocqueville who, visiting the United States early in the nineteenth century, made some astute observations about American life. He pointed out, for instance, that over here people solve many major problems for themselves which in Europe were increasingly loaded onto the state. It was the independence, virility, and individualism of Americans that impressed de Tocqueville in those times, and other traditional liberals since.

Very important, too, among traditional liberal concepts, is the rule that economic and social problems must be solved by the individual, the family, the local community—in that order. Only in case of crisis or provable necessity should the federal government enter the scene. By contrast the new-day liberal tends to think of almost every problem—from juvenile delinquency to the

259

health of each individual—as one which must be solved by the federal government. This is a dangerous road for a freedom-loving people.

It is important to note that the coercive power of the state is dangerous whether it is applied directly with full force or indirectly in subtle fashion. Take the case of agriculture. Some people think that government price support for crops is harmless. The farmers themselves vote to restrict their crops, do they not? Of course they do, because the alternative offered to them is a harsh one when applied suddenly. In effect the government says, "You can get 20 cents or 50 cents a bushel more for your corn or wheat if you sell it to government warehouses." Few farmers can resist this inducement.

Professor Friedrich Hayek, author of the monumental study of freedom entitled *The Constitution of Liberty*, explains the danger of the coercive power of the state in this fashion: "Coercion occurs when one man's actions are made to serve another man's (or the State's) will, not for his own but for the other's purpose. Coercion implies . . . that I still choose, but that my mind is made someone else's tool, because *the alternatives before me have been so manipulated that the conduct that the coercer wants me to choose becomes for me the least painful one.*"

In other words, government can corrupt large segments of the population by offering them a choice which is heavily loaded in favor of the government's plan. The same kind of coercion is offered to a worker when the government says, You have a choice of joining a specific union or not earning your living at your trade. This kind of indirectly exercised government coercion can in the long run destroy individual freedom just as completely as direct coercion and outright government domination.

NOTES ON
AUTHORS

ADAM SMITH (1723-1790), the Scottish economist and philosopher, is best known as the author of *The Wealth of Nations* (1776), the first work to establish economics as a separate science. It was the product of many years of study, during which Smith was encouraged by his friend, the more famous philosopher David Hume. The work became an immediate success, and has since been translated into almost every language. It soon became, and still is, required reading for every serious economist. As providing the theoretical justification for free-market capitalism, it has become a classic economic treatise.

The central thesis of *The Wealth of Nations*, supported by detailed arguments and examples, simply asserts that if individuals are left to pursue their own economic interests, without constraint, the whole community of man will benefit. In Smith's own words, "Man's self-interest is God's providence."

FREDERIC BASTIAT (1801-1850) devoted his life and considerable literary talent to the criticism of every form of market restriction. He was one of the first journalists to recognize the threat to both private property and individual liberty that Communism posed, and in 1848 he matched *The Communist Manifesto* of Marx and Engels with his own equally brief and direct proclamation, *The Law*. He was not an academic economist, but like Lawrence Fertig

263

a contributor to this present volume, Bastiat was an intelligent and articulate critic of socialism and a proponent of capitalism. In sum, Bastiat's writings are not contained in extensive and technical economic studies, but are generally short, readable, and trenchant criticisms of socialism—with two of the more important texts being his *Economic Sophisms* of 1846, and his *Protectionism and Communism* of 1849.

EUGEN VON BOEHM-BAWERK (1851-1914), the Austrian economist, was first a professor, and then—like Milton Friedman in our own time—entered into government service for some years, as the Austrian Finance Minister (1895-1904). He, along with Carl Menger and Friedrich von Wieser, founded the influential Austrian School of economics, whose later representatives, such as Wilhelm Roepke and Ludwig von Mises, have affected American economic thought. Bawerk's central work, *Capital and Capitalism* (1884-89), is concerned with demonstrating the practical efficiency of capitalism against contending economic approaches. In Bawerk's view, capitalism—an economic view that accepts both the free-market and private investment—is the necessary condition for efficient production, and although investment in productive forces is not immediately reflected in the fact of production, it is, in the long run, the most productive of all techniques. Capital investment is the rationally disciplined development of productive forces for the insurance of future economic efficiency.

As the chief economic advisor to the Adenauer government, WILHELM ROEPKE (1899-1966) exercised a deep influence upon the development of a liberal German economic policy. He was, along with Ludwig Erhard, the theorist of the postwar German economic "miracle."

Nevertheless, he was principally a writer and teacher. In attitude and manner similar to Ludwig von Mises and Friedrich Hayek, his interests expanded beyond the limits of technical economics into the realms of political and social philosophy. The titles of most of his major works reflect his constant concern with the delicate relation between the economic and spiritual needs of human life. Some of these works are: *Civitas Humana* (1948), *The Social Crisis of Our Time* (1950), and *Economics of the Free Society* (1963). But his most well-known work is *A Humane Economy* (1960). The *Wall Street Journal* has called it "a seminar on integral freedom, conducted by a professor of uncommon brilliance."

264

Born and educated in Austria, and long a professor at the University of Vienna, LUDWIG VON MISES (1881-1973) has been generally considered as the leading figure of the Austrian School of libertarian economics.

Just before the outbreak of war, in 1940, he left Austria for the United States and accepted an appointment at New York University.

His interests, like those of his fellow countrymen, Friedrich Hayek and Wilhelm Roepke, extended beyond the limits of economics into the fields of philosophy and political theory. Of his many works, two of the more important are *Human Action* (1949), which placed the science of economics into its full social context, and *Socialism* (1951), an analysis of the reasons given for the establishment of a politically regulated economy, together with the dangers of such a regime. His most popular work is *The Anti-Capitalist Mentality* (1956), which criticizes the critics of capitalism. A study of von Mises' works would be a necessary requirement for anyone seeking a full understanding of contemporary capitalist theory.

Of all of the contributors to this collection of essays, none is so well known as AYN RAND, whose popular novels, studies in psychology and economics, and Objectivist philosophy have exercised a continuing influence upon millions of readers and countless audiences.

Born in Russia, Ms. Rand came to America in 1926. She began her literary career as a screen writer, soon moving on to the more independent role of novelist and lecturer. She was quickly recognized—in the words of the critic Lorine Pruette—as a "writer of great power" whose early novel, *The Fountainhead* (1943), gave clear evidence that she possessed "a subtle and ingenious mind and the capacity of writing brilliantly, beautifully, bitterly . . . Good novels of ideas are rare at any time. This is the only novel of ideas written by an American woman that I can recall."

The full range and depth of her thought can only be appreciated by reading her works, but in a summary manner it can be said that she is a champion of philosophical realism, which finds its authentic expression in free-market capitalism.

JOHN CHAMBERLAIN began his long journalistic career in 1926 as a reporter for *The New York Times*. Since then he has been editor of *Fortune*, the *New York Times Book Review*, *Life*, *Barron's*, and other influential publications. He has written a number of books, among them *Farewell to Reform* (1932), *The American Stakes* (1940), *The Roots of Capitalism* (1959), and *The Enterprising Americans* (1963). He is presently a columnist for King Features.

Chamberlain is not a technically trained economist, but his lucid defense of capitalism sets him among those who have continued Bastiat's arguments in favor of the free market.

FRIEDRICH A. HAYEK is an influential member of the so-called Austrian School of political economists, which draws its inspiration from the theories of Boehm-Bawerk. He has composed a number of technical economic treatises, but is perhaps best known for his controversial work *The Road to Serfdom* (1944), which was written during his long tenure (1931-1950) as professor of economics at London University. In 1950, he accepted a professorship in economics at the University of Chicago. He is now retired, and has returned to his home in Austria.

Hayek's interests extend beyond the science of economics into psychology and philosophy, as witnessed in his 1967 work, *Studies in Philosophy, Politics, and Economics*. This, and other works, such as *Individualism and Economic Order* and *The Constitution of Liberty*, express his concern with the conflict between individual values and collective economic controls. He won the Nobel Prize for economics in 1974.

Since before World War II, the academic life of MILTON FRIEDMAN has been associated with the University of Chicago; as a professor of economics there, he became the leading figure of the so-called Chicago School, whose roots can be traced back to Boehm-Bawerk's Austrian School. Both of these economic schools have stressed the compatibility of social and market freedoms. Again, like Boehm-Bawerk, Friedman has often participated in governmental decision-making, and his theory is reflected in a number of governmental economic policies.

Friedman has written a large number of technical treatises and has contributed regularly to a number of well-known journals and magazines. His most popular work, however, is *Capitalism and Freedom* (1962), which clearly expresses his humanitarian interests.

In 1976 he received the Nobel Prize for economics, and as his friend and rival, the economist Paul A. Samuelson, has observed, "The Nobel Prize . . . is fitting recognition of his scientific contributions and his scholarly leadership."

266

Louis O. Kelso is a practicing lawyer who has, for many years, headed a large San Francisco law firm. He has also proven to be an incisive writer and accomplished theorist regarding the nature and practice of capitalism. The most important of his writings on the nature and practice of capitalism are *The Capitalist Manifesto* (1958) and *The New Capitalists* (1961), the first written with Mortimer J. Adler and the second with Patricia Hetter. He is perhaps best known for his controversial "Kelso Plan," which would, in essence, have corporations set up funds from which their own employees could borrow in order to purchase stock in the corporation. This plan is set forth in *The Economics of Reality* (1968).

Mortimer J. Adler has, for many years, been an advocate of both a liberal education and a liberal economic policy. He is best known for initiating and guiding the Great Books Program, designed to introduce the general public to major thinkers of the past. The Program has gained wide recognition and participation.

With Walter Farrell, he published in *The Thomist* between 1941 and 1944 a series of articles on the theory of Democracy that are directly relevant to the thesis of *The Capitalist Manifesto*.

Gustav Stolper (1888-1947) received his doctorate in law and economics from the University of Vienna in 1911. For many years he was editor of the influential *Austrian Economist*, but by reason of his outspoken opposition to the rise of Hitler, he was forced to emigrate to the United States in 1933. His works on the German economy, particularly *German Realities* (1943), traced the development of well-meaning demands for economic reforms into state totalitarianism. This theme is also evidenced in his more popular work, *This Age of Fable* (1942).

Although he taught economics for a time, Stolper was principally a writer, a governmental advisor, and consulting economist. His personal experiences gave him a clear view of the close relation between personal freedom and economic policy.

Professor Roy Pierce, in his work, *Contemporary French Political Thought* (1966), notes that all of Bertrand de Jouvenel's political writings "are inspired by one overriding consideration: that politics is dangerous, because if it is not rightly conducted it can produce disastrous consequences for the citizens. Whether de Jouvenel writes historically, speculatively, or analytically, this notion is fundamental to his thinking." In this, de Jouvenel follows in a tradition established by another French intellectual, Frederic Bastiat.

De Jouvenel's major works, among them *Power* (1947), *Sovereignty* (1955), and *The Pure Theory of Politics* (1963), exemplify his concern over the threatening role of government in a liberal society. In examining the troubled relation between the theory of the intellectuals and the reality of capitalism, he shares a common interest with Ludwig von Mises.

LAWRENCE FERTIG's column on economic affairs was syndicated in newspapers throughout the country. For several decades it appeared in the *New York World-Telegram and Sun* and other Scripps-Howard newspapers. He is the author of *Prosperity through Freedom,* a book that was characterized by Ludwig von Mises as "a brilliant expose of the statist philosophy."

For eighteen years Lawrence Fertig was a member of the board of trustees of New York University. In 1970 he resigned as a protest against the University's taking public positions on economic, political, and social matters.

He is a member of the international Mont Pelerin Society. He served as chairman of the board of the Foundation for Economic Education (1968-70) and has continued as a member of the board.

He has followed in the tradition of Frederic Bastiat: a public advocate of the free market, an open opponent of government economic control.

SELECT
BIBLIOGRAPHY

Anderson, Martin, *The Federal Bulldozer* (New York: McGraw-Hill).

Bastiat, Frederic, *Economic Sophisms* (Irvington-on-Hudson, N.Y.: Foundation for Economic Education).

———, *Selected Essays on Political Economy* (Irvington-on-Hudson, N.Y.: Foundation for Economic Education).

———, *The Law* (Irvington-on-Hudson, N.Y.: Foundation for Economic Education).

Boehm-Bawerk, Eugen von, *Capital and Interest* (South Holland, Ill.: Libertarian Press).

———, *The Exploitation Theory*, (South Holland, Ill.: Libertarian Press).

Chamberlain, John, *The Enterprising Americans* (New York: Harper and Row).

———, *The Roots of Capitalism* (Indianapolis: Liberty Fund).

Dietze, Gottfried, *In Defense of Property* (Baltimore: Johns Hopkins Press).

———, *The Federalist* (Baltimore: Johns Hopkins Press).

Fertig, Lawrence, *Prosperity through Freedom* (Irvington-on-Hudson, N.Y.: Foundation for Economic Education).

Friedman, Milton, *Capitalism and Freedom* (Chicago: University of Chicago Press).

Hayek, F.A., *The Constitution of Liberty* (Chicago: University of Chicago Press).

———, *The Road to Serfdom* (Chicago: University of Chicago Press).

———, *Capitalism and the Historians* (Chicago: University of Chicago Press).

Hazlitt, Henry, *The Conquest of Poverty* (New Rochelle, N.Y.: Arlington House).

————, *The Failure of the "New Economics"* (New Rochelle, N.Y.: Arlington House).

————, *The Foundations of Morality* (New York: Sheed and Ward).

————, *What You Should Know about Inflation* (New York: Funk and Wagnalls).

Kelso, Louis O. and Adler, Mortimer J., *The Capitalist Manifesto* (New York: Random House).

Mises, Ludwig von, *The Anti-Capitalist Mentality* (South Holland, Ill.: Libertarian Press).

————, *Bureaucracy* (New Rochelle, N.Y.: Arlington House).

————, *Human Action* (Chicago: Henry Regnery Co.).

————, *Omnipotent Government* (New Rochelle, N.Y.: Arlington House).

————, *Planning for Freedom* (South Holland, Ill.: Libertarian Press).

————, *Socialism: An Economic and Sociological Analysis* (London: Jonathan Cape).

Rand, Ayn, *Capitalism: The Unknown Ideal* (New York: Signet Books).

Roepke, Wilhelm, *Economics of the Free Society* (Chicago: Henry Regnery Co.).

————, *A Humane Economy* (Chicago: Henry Regnery Co.).

————, *International Economic Disintegration* (Glasgow: William Hodge Co.).

Rothbard, Murray N., *America's Great Depression* (New York: Sheed and Ward).

————, *Man, Economy and State* (New York: Sheed and Ward).

————, *What Has Government Done to Our Money?* (South Holland, Ill.: Libertarian Press).

Smith, Adam, *The Wealth Of Nations* (Baltimore: Penguin Books).

Spencer, Herbert, *Man versus the State* (New York: Reywel and Hitchcock).

Stolper, Gustav, *This Age of Fable* (New York: Harcourt Brace Jovanovich).

Weaver, Henry Grady, *The Mainspring of Human Progress* (Detroit: Talbot Books).